DATE DUE

DE 4 '03			
FE 1			
AG 14 08			
FE 11 '10			

DEMCO 38-296

100 STATISTICAL TESTS

100 STATISTICAL TESTS

New Edition

Gopal K. Kanji

SAGE Publications
London • Thousand Oaks • New Delhi

© Gopal K. Kanji 1999

First edition published 1993, reprinted 1993
Reprinted with corrections 1994
Reprinted 1995, 1997
New edition published 1999

may be reproduced, stored in a
y form or by any means,
ng or otherwise, without

SAGE Publications Inc
2455 Teller Road
Thousand Oaks, California 91320

SAGE Publications India Pvt Ltd
32, M-Block Market
Greater Kailash – I
New Delhi 110 048

British Library Cataloguing in Publication Data

A catalogue record for this book is available from the British Library

ISBN 0 7619 6152 6
ISBN 0 7619 6151 8 (Pbk)

Library of Congress catalog card number 98-61738

Typeset by the Alden Group, Oxford.
Printed in Great Britain by The Cromwell Press Ltd, Trowbridge, Wiltshire.

CONTENTS

ACKNOWLEDGEMENTS

The author and publishers wish to thank the following for permission to use copyright material:

The American Statistical Association for Table 16 adapted from Massey, F.J. Jr (1951) 'The Kolmogorov–Smirnov test for goodness of fit', *Journal of the American Statistical Association*, 4(6). Copyright © 1951 by the American Statistical Association; the Biometrika Trustees for Table 33 from Durbin, J. and Watson, G.S. (1951) 'Testing for serial correlation in least squares regression II', *Biometrika*, 38, pp. 173–5; for Table 36 from Stephens, M.A. (1964) 'The distribution of the goodness of fit statistic, U_n^2 II', *Biometrika*, 51, pp. 393–7; for Table 3 from Pearson, E.S. and Hartley, H.O. (1970) *Biometrika Tables for Statisticians*, Vol. I, Cambridge University Press; for Table 12 from Merrington, M. and Thompson, C.M. (1946) 'Tables for testing the homogeneity of a set of estimated variances', *Biometrika*, 33, pp. 296–304; and for Table 7 from Geary, R.E. and Pearson, E.S. (n.d.) 'Tests of normality'; Harcourt Brace Jovanovich Ltd for Tables 38 and 39 from Mardia, K.V. (1972) *Statistics of Directional Data*, Academic Press; and Tables 35, 36 and 37 from Batschelet, E. (1981) *Circular Statistics in Biology*, Academic Press; the Institute of Mathematical Statistics for Table 28 from Hart, B.I. (1942) 'Significance levels for the ratio of the mean square successive difference to the variance', *Annals of Mathematical Statistics*, 13, pp. 445–7; and for Table 29 from Anderson, R.L. (1942) 'Distribution of the serial correlation coefficient', *Annals of Mathematical Statistics*, 13, pp. 1–13; Longman Group UK Ltd on behalf of the Literary Executor of the late Sir Ronald A. Fisher, FRS and Dr Frank Yates FRS for Table 2 from *Statistical Tables for Biological, Agricultural and Medical Research* (6th edition, 1974) Table IV; McGraw-Hill, Inc. for Tables 8, 15, 18 and 31 from Dixon, W.J. and Massey, F.J. Jr (1957) *Introduction to Statistical Analysis*; Macmillan Publishing Company for Table 1(a) from Walpole, R.E. and Myers, R.H. (1989) *Probability and Statistics for Engineers and Scientists*, 4th edition, Table A.3. Copyright © 1989 by Macmillan Publishing Company; Routledge for Tables 4 and 22 from Neave, H.R. (1978) *Statistical Tables*, Allen & Unwin; Springer-Verlag GmbH & Co. KG for Tables 9, 10, 14, 19, 23, 26 and 32 from Sachs, L. (1972) *Statistiche Auswertungsmethoden*, 3rd edition; TNO Institute of Preventive Health Care, Leiden, for Tables 6, 11, 13, 25, 27 and 30 from De Jonge, H. (1963–4) *Inleiding tot de Medische Statistiek*, 2 vols, 3rd edition, TNO Health Research.

Every effort has been made to trace all the copyright holders, but if any have been inadvertently overlooked the publishers will be pleased to make the necessary arrangement at the first opportunity.

PREFACE

Some twenty years ago, it was only necessary to know about a dozen statistical tests in order to be a practising statistician, and these were all available in the few statistical textbooks that existed at that time. In recent years the number of tests has grown tremendously and, while modern books carry the more common tests, it is often quite difficult for a practising statistician quickly to turn up a reference to some of the less used but none the less important tests which are now in the literature. Accordingly, we have attempted to collect together information on most commonly used tests which are currently available and present it, together with a guide to further reading, to make a useful reference book for both the applied statistician and the everyday user of statistics. Naturally, any such compilation must omit some tests through oversight, and the author would be very pleased to hear from any reader about tests which they feel ought to have been included.

The work is divided into several sections. In the first we define a number of terms used in carrying out statistical tests, we define the thinking behind statistical testing and indicate how some of the tests can be linked together in an investigation. In the second section we give examples of test procedures and in the third we provide a list of all the 100 statistical tests. The fourth section classifies the tests under a variety of headings. This became necessary when we tried to arrange the tests in some logical sequence. Many such logical sequences are available and, to meet the possible needs of the reader, these cross-reference lists have been provided. The main part of the work describes most commonly used tests currently available to the working statistician. No attempts at proof are given, but an elementary knowledge of statistics should be sufficient to allow the reader to carry out the test. In every case the appropriate formulae are given and where possible we have used schematic diagrams to preclude any ambiguities in notation. Where there has been a conflict of notation between existing textbooks, we have endeavoured to use the most commonly accepted symbols. The next section provides a list of the statistical tables required for the tests followed by the tables themselves, and the last section provides references for further information.

Because we have brought together material which is spread over a large number of sources, we feel that this work will provide a handy reference source, not only for practising statisticians but also for teachers and students of statistics. We feel that no one can remember details of all the tests described here. We have tried to provide not only a memory jogger but also a first reference point for anyone coming across a particular test with which he or she is unfamiliar.

Lucidity of style and simplicity of expression have been our twin objectives, and every effort has been made to avoid errors. Constructive criticism and suggestions will help us in improving the book.

COMMON SYMBOLS

Each test or method may have its own terminology and symbols but the following are commonly used by all statisticians.

n number of observations (sample size)
K number of samples (each having n elements)

α level of significance
ν degrees of freedom
σ standard deviation (population)
s standard deviation (sample)

μ population mean
$\bar{x}$ sample mean
ρ population correlation coefficient
r sample correlation coefficient

Z standard normal deviate

INTRODUCTION TO STATISTICAL TESTING

Having collected together a number of tests, it is necessary to consider what can be tested, and we include here some very general remarks about the general problem of hypothesis testing. Students regard this topic as one full of pitfalls for the unwary, and even teachers and experienced statisticians have been known to misinterpret the conclusions of their analysis.

Broadly speaking there are two basic concepts to grasp before commencing. First, the tests are designed neither to prove nor to disprove hypotheses. We never set out to prove anything; our aim is to show that an idea is untenable as it leads to an unsatisfactorily small probability. Secondly, the hypothesis we are trying to disprove is always chosen to be the one in which there is no change; for example, there is no difference between the two population means, between the two samples, etc. This is why it is usually referred to as the null hypothesis, H_0. If these concepts were firmly held in mind, we believe that the subject of hypothesis testing would lose a lot of its mystique. (However, it is only fair to point out that some hypotheses are not concerned with such matters.)

To describe the process of hypothesis testing we feel that we cannot do better than follow the five-step method introduced by Neave (1976a):

Step 1 Formulate the practical problem in terms of hypotheses. This can be difficult in some cases. We should first concentrate on what is called the alternative hypothesis, H_1, since this is the more important from the practical point of view. This should express the range of situations that we wish the test to be able to diagnose. In this sense, a positive test can indicate that we should take action of some kind. In fact, a better name for the alternative hypothesis would be the action hypothesis. Once this is fixed it should be obvious whether we carry out a one- or two-tailed test.

The null hypothesis needs to be very simple and represents the status quo, i.e. there is no difference between the processes being tested. It is basically a standard or control with which the evidence pointing to the alternative can be compared.

Step 2 Calculate a statistic (T), a function purely of the data. All good test statistics should have two properties: (a) they should tend to behave differently when H_0 is true from when H_1 is true; and (b) their probability distribution should be calculable under the assumption that H_0 is true. It is also desirable that tables of this probability distribution should exist.

Step 3 Choose a critical region. We must be able to decide on the kind of values of T which will most strongly point to H_1 being true rather than H_0 being true. Critical regions can be of three types: right-sided, so that we reject H_0 if the test statistic is greater than or equal to some (right) critical value; left-sided, so that we reject H_0 if the test statistic is less than or equal to some (left) critical value; both-sided, so that we reject H_0 if the test statistic is *either* greater than or equal to the right critical value *or* less than or equal to the left critical value. A value of T lying in a suitably defined critical region will lead us to reject H_0 in favour of H_1; if T lies outside the critical region we do not reject H_0. We should never conclude by accepting H_0.

Step 4   Decide the size of the critical region. This involves specifying how great a risk we are prepared to run of coming to an incorrect conclusion. We define the significance level or size of the test, which we denote by α, as the risk we are prepared to take in rejecting H_0 when it is in fact true. We refer to this as an error of the first type or a Type I error. We usually set α to between 1 and 10 per cent, depending on the severity of the consequences of making such an error.

We also have to contend with the possibility of not rejecting H_0 when it is in fact false and H_1 is true. This is an error of the second type or Type II error, and the probability of this occurring is denoted by β.

Thus in testing any statistical hypothesis, there are four possible situations which determine whether our decision is correct or in error. These situations are illustrated as follows:

		Situation	
		H_0 is true	H_0 is false
Conclusion	H_0 is not rejected	Correct decision	Type II error
	H_0 is rejected	Type I error	Correct decision

Step 5   Many textbooks stop after step 4, but it is instructive to consider just where in the critical region the calculated value of T lies. If it lies close to the boundary of the critical region we may say that there is some evidence that H_0 should be rejected, whereas if it is at the other end of the region we would conclude there was considerable evidence. In other words, the actual significance level of T can provide useful information beyond the fact that T lies in the critical region.

In general, the statistical test provides information from which we can judge the significance of the increase (or decrease) in any result. If our conclusion shows that the increase is not significant then it will be necessary to confirm that the experiment had a fair chance of establishing an increase had there been one present to establish.

In order to do this we generally turn to the power function of the test, which is usually computed before the experiment is performed, so that if it is insufficiently powerful then the design can be changed. The power function is the probability of detecting a genuine increase underlying the observed increase in the result, plotted as a function of the genuine increase, and therefore the experimental design must be chosen so that the probability of detecting the increase is high. Also the choice among several possible designs should be made in favour of the experiment with the highest power. For a given experiment testing a specific hypothesis, the power of the test is given by $1 - \beta$.

Having discussed the importance of the power function in statistical tests we would now like to introduce the concept of robustness. The term 'robust' was first introduced in 1953 to denote a statistical procedure which is insensitive to departures from the assumptions underlying the model on which it is based. Such procedures are in common use, and several studies of robustness have been carried out in the field of 'analysis of variance'. The assumptions usually associated with analysis of variance are that the errors in the measurements (a) are normally distributed, (b) are statistically independent and (c) have equal variances.

Most of the parametric tests considered in this book have made the assumption that the populations involved have normal distributions. Therefore a test should only be carried out when the normality assumption is not violated. It is also a necessary part of the test to check the effect of applying these tests when the assumption of normality is violated.

In parametric tests the probability distribution of the test statistic under the null hypothesis can only be calculated by an additional assumption on the frequency distribution of the population. If this assumption is not true then the test loses its validity. However, in some cases the deviation of the assumption has only a minor influence on the statistical test, indicating a robust procedure. A parametric test also offers greater discrimination than the corresponding distribution-free test.

For the non-parametric test no assumption has to be made regarding the frequency distribution and therefore one can use estimates for the probability that any observation is greater than a predetermined value.

Neave (1976b) points out that it was the second constraint in step 2, namely that the probability distribution of the test statistic should be calculable, which led to the growth of the number of non-parametric tests. An inappropriate assumption of normality had often to be built into the tests. In fact, when comparing two samples, we need only look at the relative ranking of the sample members. In this way under H_0 all the rank sequences are equally likely to occur, and so it became possible to generate any required significance level comparatively easily.

Two simple tests based on this procedure are the Wald–Wolfowitz number of runs test and the median test proposed by Mood, but these are both low in power. The Kolmogorov–Smirnov test has higher power but is more difficult to execute. A test which is extremely powerful and yet still comparatively easy to use is the Wilcoxon–Mann–Whitney test. Many others are described in later pages of this book.

EXAMPLES OF TEST PROCEDURES

Test 1   Z-test for a population mean (variance known)

Hypotheses and alternatives

1. H_0: $\mu = \mu_0$
   H_1: $\mu \neq \mu_0$
2. H_0: $\mu = \mu_0$
   H_1: $\mu > \mu_0$

Test statistics

$$Z = \frac{\bar{x} - \mu_0}{\sigma/\sqrt{n}}$$

n is sample size
$\bar{x}$ is sample mean
σ is population standard deviation

When used

When the population variance σ^2 is known and the population distribution is normal.

Critical region

Using $\alpha = 0.05$ [see Table 1]

1.

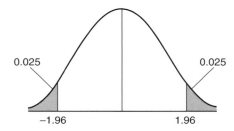

0.025   0.025

−1.96   1.96

2.

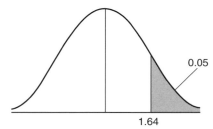

0.05

1.64

Data

H_0: $\mu_0 = 4.0$
$n = 9, \bar{x} = 4.6$
$\sigma = 1.0$
$\therefore Z = 1.8$

Conclusion

1. Do not reject H_0 [see Table 1].
2. Reject H_0.

Test 3   *Z*-test for two population means (variances known and unequal)

Hypotheses and alternatives

1. $H_0: \mu_1 - \mu_2 = \mu_0$
    $H_1: \mu_1 - \mu_2 \neq \mu_0$
2. $H_0: \mu_1 - \mu_2 = \mu_0$
    $H_1: \mu_1 - \mu_2 > \mu_0$

Test statistics

$$Z = \frac{(\bar{x}_1 - \bar{x}_2) - \mu_0}{\left(\dfrac{\sigma_1^2}{n_1} + \dfrac{\sigma_2^2}{n_2}\right)^{\frac{1}{2}}}$$

When used

When the variances of both populations, σ_1^2 and σ_2^2, are known. Populations are normally distributed.

Critical region

Using $\alpha = 0.05$ [see Table 1]

1.

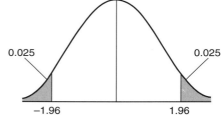

2.

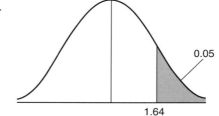

Data

$H_0: \mu_1 - \mu_2 = 0$
$n_1 = 9, n_2 = 16$
$\bar{x}_1 = 1.2, \bar{x}_2 = 1.7$
$\sigma_1^2 = 1, \sigma_2^2 = 4$
$\therefore Z = -0.832$

Conclusion

1. Do not reject H_0.
2. Do not reject H_0.

Test 7 t-test for a population mean (variance unknown)

Hypotheses and alternatives

1. $H_0: \mu = \mu_0$
    $H_1: \mu \neq \mu_0$
2. $H_0: \mu = \mu_0$
    $H_1: \mu > \mu_0$

Test statistics

$$t = \frac{\bar{x} - \mu_0}{s/\sqrt{n}}$$

where

$$s^2 = \frac{\sum (x - \bar{x})^2}{n - 1}.$$

When used

If σ^2 is not known and the estimate s^2 of σ^2 is based on a small sample (i.e. $n < 20$) and a normal population.

Critical region and degrees of freedom

1.

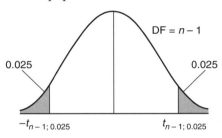

2.

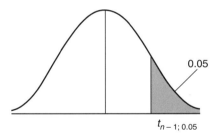

Data

$H_0: \mu_0 = 4.0$
$n = 9, \bar{x} = 3.1$
$s = 1.0$
$\therefore t = -2.7$

Conclusion

1. $t_{8;0.025} = \pm 2.306$ [see Table 2].
    Reject H_0.
2. $t_{8;0.05} = -1.860$ (left-hand side) [see Table 2].
    Reject H_0.

Test 8 *t*-test for two population means (variance unknown but equal)

Hypotheses and alternatives

1. $H_0: \mu_1 - \mu_2 = \mu_0$
    $H_1: \mu_1 - \mu_2 \neq \mu_0$
2. $H_0: \mu_1 - \mu_2 = \mu_0$
    $H_1: \mu_1 - \mu_2 > \mu_0$

Test statistics

$$t = \frac{(\bar{x}_1 - \bar{x}_2) - (\mu_1 - \mu_2)}{s\left(\dfrac{1}{n_1} + \dfrac{1}{n_2}\right)^{\frac{1}{2}}}$$

where

$$s^2 = \frac{(n_1 - 1)s_1^2 + (n_2 - 1)s_2^2}{n_1 + n_2 - 2}.$$

When used

Given two samples from normal populations with equal variances σ^2.

Critical region and degrees of freedom

1.
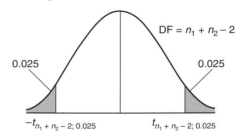
$$DF = n_1 + n_2 - 2$$
0.025   0.025
$-t_{n_1 + n_2 - 2;\, 0.025}$ $t_{n_1 + n_2 - 2;\, 0.025}$

2.
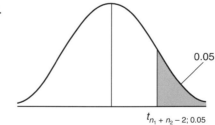
0.05
$t_{n_1 + n_2 - 2;\, 0.05}$

Data

$H_0: \mu_1 - \mu_2 = 0$
$n_1 = 16, n_2 = 16$
$\bar{x}_1 = 5.0, \bar{x}_2 = 4$
$s = 2.0$
$\therefore t = 1.414$

Conclusion

1. $t_{30;\, 0.025} = \pm 2.042$ [see Table 2].
    Do not reject H_0.
2. $t_{30;\, 0.05} = 1.697$ [see Table 2].
    Do not reject H_0.

Test 10 Method of paired comparisons

Hypotheses and alternatives

1. $H_0: \mu_d = 0$
   $H_1: \mu_d \neq 0$
2. $H_0: \mu_d = 0$
   $H_1: \mu_d > 0$

Test statistics

$$t = \frac{\bar{d} - \mu_d}{s/\sqrt{n}}$$

where $d_i = x_i - y_i$, the difference in the n paired observations.

When used

When an experiment is arranged so that each observation in one sample can be 'paired' with a value from the second sample and the populations are normally distributed.

Critical region and degrees of freedom

1.

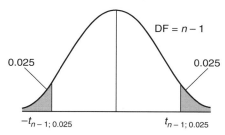

2.

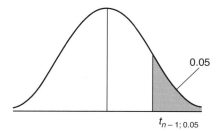

Data

$n = 16, \bar{d} = 1.0$
$s = 1.0$
$\therefore t = 4.0$

Conclusion

1. $t_{15; 0.025} = \pm 2.131$ [see Table 2].
   Reject H_0.
2. $t_{15; 0.05} = 1.753$ [see Table 2].
   Reject H_0.

Test 15　χ^2-test for a population variance

Hypothesis and alternatives	1.　$H_0: \sigma^2 = \sigma_0^2$ $H_1: \sigma^2 \neq \sigma_0^2$ 2.　$H_0: \sigma^2 = \sigma_0^2$ $H_1: \sigma^2 > \sigma_0^2$

Test statistics

$$\chi^2 = \frac{(n-1)s^2}{\sigma_0^2}$$

When used　　Given a sample from a normal population with unknown variance.

Critical region and degrees of freedom

1.

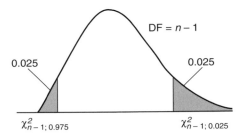

DF = $n - 1$

0.025　　　　　0.025

$\chi^2_{n-1;\,0.975}$　　　$\chi^2_{n-1;\,0.025}$

2.

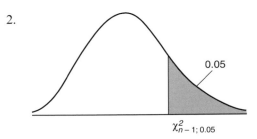

0.05

$\chi^2_{n-1;\,0.05}$

Data

$H_0: \sigma^2 = 4.0$
$n = 17,\ s^2 = 7.0$
$\therefore \chi^2 = 28.0$

Conclusion

1.　$\chi^2_{16;\,0.025} = 28.85$ [see Table 5].
　　$\therefore$ Do not reject H_0.
2.　$\chi^2_{16;\,0.05} = 26.30$ [see Table 5].
　　$\therefore$ Reject H_0.

Test 16   *F*-test for two population variances

Hypotheses and
alternatives

1. $H_0: \sigma_1^2 = \sigma_2^2$
    $H_1: \sigma_1^2 \neq \sigma_2^2$
2. $H_0: \sigma_1^2 = \sigma_2^2$
    $H_1: \sigma_1^2 > \sigma_2^2$

Test statistics

$$F = \frac{s_1^2}{s_2^2}, \quad (s_1^2 > s_2^2)$$

where s_1^2 and s_2^2 are sample variances.
(If, in 2, $s_1^2 < s_2^2$, do not reject H_0.)

When used

Given two samples with unknown variances σ_1^2
and σ_2^2 and normal populations.

Critical region and
degrees of freedom

1.

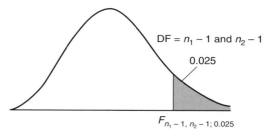

DF = $n_1 - 1$ and $n_2 - 1$

0.025

$F_{n_1 - 1, \, n_2 - 1; \, 0.025}$

2.

0.05

$F_{n_1 - 1, \, n_2 - 1; \, 0.05}$

Data

$H_0: \sigma_1^2 = \sigma_2^2$
$n_1 = 11, n_2 = 16$
$s_1^2 = 6.0, s_2^2 = 3.0$
$\therefore F = 2.0$

Conclusion

1. $F_{10, \, 15; \, 0.025} = 3.06$.
    Do not reject H_0.
2. $F_{10, \, 15; \, 0.05} = 2.54$ [see Table 3].
    Do not reject H_0.

Test 37 χ^2-test for goodness of fit

Hypotheses and alternatives

Goodness of fit for Poisson distribution with known mean λ

Test statistics

$$\chi^2 = \sum \frac{(O_i - E_i)^2}{E_i}$$

O_i is the ith observed frequency, $i = 1$ to k;
E_i is expected frequency,
where E_i must be >5.

When used

To compare observed frequencies against those obtained under assumptions about the parent populations.

Critical region and degrees of freedom

Using $\alpha = 0.05$ [see Table 5]
DF: variable, normally one less than the number of frequency comparisons (k) in the summation in the test statistic.

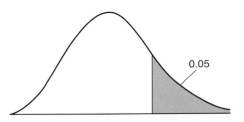

0.05

Data

H_0: Distribution.
Poisson with $\lambda = 2$.

x_i	O_i	E_i
0	10	13.5
1	27	27.0
2	30	27.0
3	19	18.0
4	8	9.0
$\geqslant 5$	6	5.5

$\therefore \chi^2 = 1.45$

Conclusion

$\nu = 5$.
$\chi^2_{5;0.05} = 11.07$ [see Table 5].
Do not reject H_0.

Test 44 χ^2-test for independence

Hypotheses and alternatives

Contingency table

Test statistics

$$\chi^2 = \sum \frac{(O_i - E_i)^2}{E_i} \text{ [see Table 5]}$$

When used

Given a bivariate frequency table for attributes with m and n levels.

Critical region and degrees of freedom

Using $\alpha = 0.05$ [see Table 5]

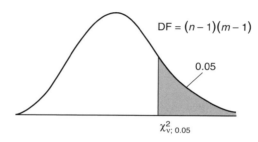

DF = $(n-1)(m-1)$

0.05

$\chi^2_{\text{v}; 0.05}$

Data

	Machine				
	I		II		
Grade	O_i	E_i	O_i	E_i	Total
A	3	4	7	6	10
B	9	8	11	12	20
C	8	8	12	12	20
Total	20	20	30	30	50

$\chi^2 = 0.625$

Conclusion

$\chi^2_{2; 0.05} = 5.99$ [see Table 5].
Do not reject H_0. The grades are independent of the machine.

LIST OF TESTS

CLASSIFICATION OF TESTS

For linear data	Test numbers		
	1 sample	2 samples	K samples
Parametric classical tests			
for central tendency	1, 7, 19	2, 3, 8, 9, 10, 18	22, 26, 27, 28, 29, 30, 77, 78, 79, 80, 87
for proportion	4	5, 6, 25	–
for variability	15, 21, 24, 34	16, 17	31, 32, 86
for distribution functions	20, 33, 75, 88, 89, 94	–	76
for association	11, 12, 13, 81, 82	14, 23, 84, 92	85
for probability	83	–	–
Parametric tests			
for distribution function	35, 37	36, 39, 40	38, 41, 42, 43, 44
Distribution-free tests			
for central tendency	45, 47	46, 48, 50, 52, 93	51, 54, 55, 56, 57
for variability	–	53	–
for distribution functions	–	49	–
for association	58, 59	–	72, 73, 74
for randomness	63, 64, 65, 66, 67, 69, 70, 71	68	–
Sequential tests			
central tendency	60, 90	–	–
variability	61	–	–
for proportion	62	–	–
for ratio	91	–	–

For circular data	Test numbers		
	1 sample	2 samples	K samples
Parametric tests			
for randomness	95	–	–
for distribution function	96	–	–
for central tendency	–	97, 98	–
for variability	–	99	100

THE TESTS

Test 1   Z-test for a population mean (variance known)

Object

To investigate the significance of the difference between an assumed population mean μ_0 and a sample mean $\bar{x}$.

Limitations

1. It is necessary that the population variance σ^2 is known. (If σ^2 is not known, see the t-test for a population mean (Test 7).)
2. The test is accurate if the population is normally distributed. If the population is not normal, the test will still give an approximate guide.

Method

From a population with assumed mean μ_0 and known variance σ^2, a random sample of size n is taken and the sample mean $\bar{x}$ calculated. The test statistic

$$Z = \frac{\bar{x} - \mu_0}{\sigma/\sqrt{n}}$$

may be compared with the standard normal distribution using either a one-tailed or two-tailed test, with critical region of size α.

Example data

$\mu_0 = 4.0$, $n = 9$, $\bar{x} = 4.6$, $\sigma = 1.0$

$Z = 1.8$

Critical value $Z_{0.05} = 1.96$ [Table 1].

H_0: $\mu = \mu_0$, H_1: $\mu \neq \mu_0$. (Do not reject the null hypothesis H_0.)

H_0: $\mu = \mu_0$, H_1: $\mu > \mu_0$. (Reject H_0.)

Test 2   Z-test for two population means (variances known and equal)

Object

To investigate the significance of the difference between the means of two populations.

Limitations

1. Both populations must have equal variances and this variance σ^2 must be known. (If σ^2 is not known, see the t-test for two population means (Test 8).)
2. The test is accurate if the populations are normally distributed. If not normal, the test may be regarded as approximate.

Method

Consider two populations with means μ_1 and μ_2. Independent random samples of size n_1 and n_2 are taken which give sample means $\bar{x}_1$ and $\bar{x}_2$. The test statistic

$$Z = \frac{(\bar{x}_1 - \bar{x}_2) - (\mu_1 - \mu_2)}{\sigma \left(\dfrac{1}{n_1} + \dfrac{1}{n_2} \right)^{\frac{1}{2}}}$$

may be compared with the standard normal distribution using either a one-tailed or two-tailed test.

Example data

$n_1 = 9, n_2 = 16, \bar{x}_1 = 1.2, \bar{x}_2 = 1.7, \sigma = 1.4405, \sigma^2 = 2.0750$

$Z = -0.833$

Critical value $Z_{0.05} = 1.96$ [Table 1].

$H_0\colon \mu_1 - \mu_2 = 0, H_1\colon \mu_1 - \mu_2 \neq 0.$ (Do not reject H_0.)

$H_1\colon \mu_1 - \mu_2 = 0, H_1\colon \mu_1 - \mu_2 > \mu_0.$ (Do not reject H_0.)

Test 3 *Z*-test for two population means (variances known and unequal)

Object

To investigate the significance of the difference between the means of two populations.

Limitations

1. It is necessary that the two population variances be known. (If they are not known, see the *t*-test for two population means (Test 9).)
2. The test is accurate if the populations are normally distributed. If not normal, the test may be regarded as approximate.

Method

Consider two populations with means μ_1 and μ_2 and variances σ_1^2 and σ_2^2. Independent random samples of size n_1 and n_2 are taken and sample means $\bar{x}_1$ and $\bar{x}_2$ are calculated. The test statistic

$$Z = \frac{(\bar{x}_1 - \bar{x}_2) - (\mu_1 - \mu_2)}{\left(\dfrac{\sigma_1^2}{n_1} + \dfrac{\sigma_2^2}{n_2}\right)^{\frac{1}{2}}}$$

may be compared with the standard normal distribution using either a one-tailed or two-tailed test.

Example data

$n_1 = 13$, $n_2 = 8$, $\bar{x}_1 = 80.02$, $\bar{x}_2 = 79.98$, $\sigma_1^2 = 0.000576$, $\sigma_2^2 = 0.001089$

$Z = 2.98$

Critical value $Z_{0.05} = 1.96$ [Table 1].

Reject the null hypothesis of no difference between means.

Test 4   Z-test for a proportion (binomial distribution)

Object

To investigate the significance of the difference between an assumed proportion p_0 and an observed proportion p.

Limitations

The test is approximate and assumes that the number of observations in the sample is sufficiently large (i.e. $n \geqslant 30$) to justify the normal approximation to the binomial.

Method

A random sample of n elements is taken from a population in which it is assumed that a proportion p_0 belongs to a specified class. The proportion p of elements in the sample belonging to this class is calculated. The test statistic is

$$Z = \frac{|p - p_0| - 1/2n}{\left\{ \dfrac{p_0(1 - p_0)}{n} \right\}^{\frac{1}{2}}}.$$

This may be compared with a standard normal distribution using either a one-tailed or two-tailed test.

Example data

$n = 100$, $p = 0.4$, $p_0 = 0.5$

$Z = -2.0$

Critical value $Z_{0.05} = \pm 1.96$ [Table 1].

Reject the null hypothesis of no difference in proportions.

Test 5 Z-test for the equality of two proportions (binomial distribution)

Object

To investigate the assumption that the proportions π_1 and π_2 of elements from two populations are equal, based on two samples, one from each population.

Limitations

The test is approximate and assumes that the number of observations in the two samples is sufficiently large (i.e. $n_1, n_2 \geqslant 30$) to justify the normal approximation to the binomial.

Method

It is assumed that the populations have proportions π_1 and π_2 with the same characteristic. Random samples of size n_1 and n_2 are taken and respective proportions p_1 and p_2 calculated. The test statistic is

$$Z = \frac{(p_1 - p_2)}{\left\{ P(1 - P)\left(\frac{1}{n_1} + \frac{1}{n_2} \right) \right\}^{\frac{1}{2}}}$$

where

$$P = \frac{p_1 n_1 + p_2 n_2}{n_1 + n_2}.$$

Under the null hypothesis that $\pi_1 = \pi_2$, Z is approximately distributed as a standard normal deviate and the resulting test may be either one-tailed or two-tailed.

Example data

$n_1 = 952$, $n_2 = 1168$, $p_1 = 0.00325$, $p_2 = 0.0573$

$Z = -6.93$

Critical value $Z_{0.05} = \pm 1.96$ [Table 1].

Reject the null hypothesis.

Test 6   Z-test for comparing two counts (Poisson distribution)

Object

To investigate the significance of the difference between two counts.

Limitations

The test is approximate and assumes that the counts are large enough for the normal approximation to the Poisson to apply.

Method

Let n_1 and n_2 be the two counts taken over times t_1 and t_2, respectively. Then the two average frequencies are $R_1 = n_1/t_1$ and $R_2 = n_2/t_2$. To test the assumption of equal average frequencies we use the test statistic

$$Z = \frac{R_1 - R_2}{\left(\dfrac{R_1}{t_1} + \dfrac{R_2}{t_2}\right)^{\frac{1}{2}}}.$$

This may be compared with a standard normal distribution using either a one-tailed or two-tailed test.

Example data

$$n_1 = 952, \; n_2 = 1168, \; R_1 = \frac{n_1}{t_1} = 43.27, \; R_2 = \frac{n_2}{t_2} = 38.93$$

$$t_1 = 22, \; t_2 = 30$$

$$Z = \frac{R_1 - R_2}{\left(\dfrac{R_1}{t_1} + \dfrac{R_2}{t_2}\right)^{\frac{1}{2}}} = \frac{4.34}{(3.26)^{\frac{1}{2}}} = \frac{4.34}{1.81} = 2.40$$

Critical value $Z_{0.05} = 1.96$ [Table 1].

Reject the null hypothesis of no difference between the counts.

Test 7 t-test for a population mean (variance unknown)

Object

To investigate the significance of the difference between an assumed population mean μ_0 and a sample mean $\bar{x}$.

Limitations

1. If the variance of the population σ^2 is known, a more powerful test is available: the Z-test for a population mean (Test 1).
2. The test is accurate if the population is normally distributed. If the population is not normal, the test will give an approximate guide.

Method

From a population with assumed mean μ_0 and unknown variance, a random sample of size n is taken and the sample mean $\bar{x}$ calculated as well as the sample standard deviation using the formula

$$s = \left\{ \frac{\sum_{i=1}^{n} (x_i - \bar{x})^2}{n-1} \right\}^{\frac{1}{2}}.$$

The test statistic is

$$t = \frac{\bar{x} - \mu_0}{s/\sqrt{n}}$$

which may be compared with Student's t-distribution with $n - 1$ degrees of freedom. The test may be either one-tailed or two-tailed.

Example data

$\mu_0 = 4$, $n = 9$, $\bar{x} = 3.1$, $s = 1.0$, $\nu = n - 1$

$t = -2.7$

Critical value $t_{8;0.025} = \pm 2.3$ [Table 2].

H_0: $\mu = \mu_0$, H_1: $\mu \neq \mu_0$. (Reject H_0.)

Test 8 t-test for two population means (variances unknown but equal)

Object

To investigate the significance of the difference between the means of two populations.

Limitations

1. If the variance of the populations is known, a more powerful test is available: the Z-test for two population means (Test 2).
2. The test is accurate if the populations are normally distributed. If the populations are not normal, the test will give an approximate guide.

Method

Consider two populations with means μ_1 and μ_2. Independent random samples of size n_1 and n_2 are taken from which sample means $\bar{x}_1$ and $\bar{x}_2$, together with sums of squares

$$s_1^2 = \sum_{i=1}^{n_1} (x_i - \bar{x}_1)^2$$

and

$$s_2^2 = \sum_{i=1}^{n_2} (x_i - \bar{x}_2)^2$$

are calculated. The best estimate of the population variance is found as $s^2 = [(n_1 - 1)s_1^2 + (n_2 - 1)s_2^2]/(n_1 + n_2 - 2)$. The test statistic is

$$t = \frac{(\bar{x}_1 - \bar{x}_2) - (\mu_1 - \mu_2)}{s\left(\dfrac{1}{n_1} + \dfrac{1}{n_2}\right)^{\frac{1}{2}}}$$

which may be compared with Student's t-distribution with $n_1 + n_2 - 2$ degrees of freedom. The test may be either one-tailed or two-tailed.

Example data

$n_1 = 12$, $n_2 = 12$, $\bar{x}_1 = 31.75$, $\bar{x}_2 = 28.67$, $\nu = n_1 + n_2 - 2$
$s_1^2 = 112.25$, $s_2^2 = 66.64$
$s^2 = 89.445$
$t = 0.798$, $\nu = 12 + 12 - 2 = 22$

Critical value $t_{22; 0.025} = 2.07$ [Table 2].

Reject the alternative hypothesis.

Test 9   t-test for two population means (variances unknown and unequal)

Object

To investigate the significance of the difference between the means of two populations.

Limitations

1. If the variances of the populations are known, a more powerful test is available: the Z-test for two population means (Test 3).
2. The test is approximate if the populations are normally distributed or if the sample sizes are sufficiently large.
3. The test should only be used to test the hypothesis $\mu_1 = \mu_2$.

Method

Consider two populations with means μ_1 and μ_2. Independent random samples of size n_1 and n_2 are taken from which sample means $\bar{x}_1$ and $\bar{x}_2$ and variances

$$s_1^2 = \frac{\sum_{i=1}^{n_1} (x_i - \bar{x}_1)^2}{n_1 - 1} \quad \text{and} \quad s_2^2 = \frac{\sum_{i=1}^{n_2} (x_i - \bar{x}_2)^2}{n_2 - 1}$$

are calculated. The test statistic is

$$t = \frac{(\bar{x}_1 - \bar{x}_2) - (\mu_1 - \mu_2)}{\left(\dfrac{s_1^2}{n_1} + \dfrac{s_2^2}{n_2}\right)^{\frac{1}{2}}}$$

which may be compared with Student's t-distribution with degrees of freedom given by

$$\nu = \left\{ \frac{\left\{\dfrac{s_1^2}{n_1} + \dfrac{s_2^2}{n_2}\right\}^2}{\dfrac{s_1^4}{n_1^2(n_1 - 1)} + \dfrac{s_2^4}{n_2^2(n_2 - 1)}} \right\}.$$

Example data

$n_1 = 4$, $n_2 = 9$, $\bar{x}_1 = 3166.0$, $\bar{x}_2 = 2240.4$, $s_1^2 = 6328.67$, $s_2^2 = 221\,661.3$

$t = 5.72$, $\nu = 9$ (rounded)

Critical value $t_{9;0.025} = 2.26$ [Table 2].

Reject the null hypothesis.

Test 10   *t*-test for two population means (method of paired comparisons)

Object

To investigate the significance of the difference between two population means, μ_1 and μ_2. No assumption is made about the population variances.

Limitations

1. The observations for the two samples must be obtained in pairs. Apart from population differences, the observations in each pair should be carrried out under identical, or almost identical, conditions.
2. The test is accurate if the populations are normally distributed. If not normal, the test may be regarded as approximate.

Method

The differences d_i are formed for each pair of observations. If there are n such pairs of observations, we can calculate the variance of the differences by

$$s^2 = \sum_{i=1}^{n} \frac{(d_i - \bar{d})^2}{n - 1}.$$

Let the means of the samples from the two populations be denoted by $\bar{x}_1$ and $\bar{x}_2$. Then the test statistic becomes

$$t = \frac{(\bar{x}_1 - \bar{x}_2) - 0}{s/n^{\frac{1}{2}}}$$

which follows Student's *t*-distribution with $n - 1$ degrees of freedom. The test may be either one-tailed or two-tailed.

Example data

$\bar{d} = \bar{x}_1 - \bar{x}_2 = -0.1, n = 10, \nu = n - 1, s = 2.9$

$t = -0.11, \nu = 9$

Critical value $t_{9;0.025} = 2.26$ [Table 2].

Do not reject the null hypothesis of no difference between means.

Test 11   *t*-test of a regression coefficient

Object

To investigate the significance of the regression coefficient of y on x.

Limitations

The usual assumptions for regression should apply, namely:
1. the variable y follows a normal distribution for each value of x;
2. the variance among the y values remains constant for any given values of x.

Method

In order to estimate a linear regression of the form $y = A + B(x - \bar{x})$, a sample of n pairs of points (x_i, y_i) is required. B is called the regression coefficient, and to test the null hypothesis that this is equal to zero we first calculate the sample estimate

$$b = \frac{\sum x_i y_i - \frac{1}{n} \sum x_i \sum y_i}{\sum x_i^2 - \frac{1}{n} \left(\sum x_i \right)^2}.$$

The variance of the xs and the variance of the ys about the regression line are calculated as follows:

$$s_x^2 = \frac{\sum (x_i - \bar{x})^2}{n - 1} \quad \text{and} \quad s_{y \cdot x}^2 = \frac{\sum \{y_i - \bar{y} - b(x_i - \bar{x})\}^2}{n - 2}$$

where $\bar{x}$ and $\bar{y}$ are the means of the xs and ys, respectively. The test statistic becomes

$$t = \frac{b s_x}{s_{y \cdot x}} (n - 1)^{-\frac{1}{2}}$$

which follows Student's t-distribution with $n - 2$ degrees of freedom. The test must be two-tailed since b may be positive or negative. However, the test may be one-tailed if the alternative hypothesis is directional.

Example data

$$\sum x_i = 766, \ \sum y_i = 1700, \ \sum x_i^2 = 49\,068,$$

$$\sum y_i^2 = 246\,100, \ \sum x_i y_i = 109\,380$$

$n = 12$, $\bar{x} = 68.83$, $\bar{y} = 141.67$, $\nu = n - 2$

$s_x^2 = 15.61, s_y^2 = 478.8, b = 5.029$
$s_{y \cdot x}^2 = 92.4$
$t = 6.86, \nu = 10$
Critical value $t_{10;\,0.025} = \pm 2.23$ [Table 2].
Reject the null hypothesis.

Test 12 *t*-test of a correlation coefficient

Object

To investigate whether the difference between the sample correlation coefficient and zero is statistically significant.

Limitations

It is assumed that the x and y values originate from a bivariate normal distribution, and that the relationship is linear. To test an assumed value of the population coefficient other than zero, refer to the Z-test for a correlation coefficient (Test 13).

Method

Given a sample of n points (x_i, y_i) the correlation coefficient r is calculated from the formula

$$r = \frac{\sum (x_i - \bar{x})(y_i - \bar{y})}{\left[\sum (x_i - \bar{x})^2 \sum (y_i - \bar{y})^2 \right]^{\frac{1}{2}}}.$$

To test the null hypothesis that the population value of r is zero, the test statistic

$$t = \frac{r}{\sqrt{1 - r^2}} \cdot \sqrt{n - 2}$$

is calculated and this follows Student's t-distribution with $n - 2$ degrees of freedom. The test will normally be two-tailed but in certain cases could be one-tailed.

Example data

$n = 18, r = 0.32, \nu = n - 2$

$$t = \frac{r\sqrt{n - 2}}{\sqrt{1 - r^2}} = \frac{0.32\sqrt{16}}{\sqrt{1 - (0.32)^2}} = 1.35$$

Critical value $t_{16;0.05} = 1.75$ [Table 2].

Do not reject the null hypothesis. *NB*: In this case the x and y variables are independent.

Test 13   *Z*-test of a correlation coefficient

Object

To investigate the significance of the difference between a correlation coefficient and a specified value ρ_0.

Limitations

1. The x and y values originate from normal distributions.
2. The variance in the y values is independent of the x values.
3. The relationship is linear.

When these conditions cannot be met, the user should turn to the Kendall rank correlation test (Test 59).

Method

With r as defined in the t-test of a correlation coefficient (Test 12), using the Fisher Z-transformation we have

$$Z_1 = \tfrac{1}{2} \log_e \left(\frac{1+r}{1-r} \right) = 1.1513 \log_{10} \left(\frac{1+r}{1-r} \right).$$

The distribution of Z_1 is approximately normal with mean μ_{Z_1} and standard deviation σ_{Z_1} where

$$\mu_{Z_1} = \tfrac{1}{2} \log_e \left(\frac{1+\rho_0}{1-\rho_0} \right) = 1.1513 \log_{10} \left(\frac{1+r}{1-r} \right)$$

$$\sigma_{Z_1} = \frac{1}{\sqrt{n-3}}.$$

The test statistic is now

$$Z = \frac{Z_1 - \mu_{Z_1}}{\sigma_{Z_1}}.$$

Example data

$r = 0.75$, $\rho_0 = 0.50$, $n = 24$

$$\mu_{Z_1} = 1.1513 \log_{10} 3 = 0.5493, \quad Z_1 = 1.1513 \log_{10} \left(\frac{1+0.75}{1-0.75} \right) = 0.9730$$

[Table 4]

$\sigma_{Z_1} = 0.2182$

$$Z = \frac{Z_1 - \mu_{Z_1}}{\sigma_{Z_1}} = 1.94$$

The critical value at $\alpha = 0.10$ is 1.64 [Table 1].
The calculated value is greater than the critical value.
Reject the null hypothesis of no difference.

Test 14 *Z*-test for two correlation coefficients

Object

To investigate the significance of the difference between the correlation coefficients for a pair of variables occurring from two different samples and the difference between two specified values ρ_1 and ρ_2.

Limitations

1. The x and y values originate from normal distributions.
2. The variance in the y values is independent of the x values.
3. The relationships are linear.

Method

Using the notation of the Z-test of a correlation coefficient, we form for the first sample

$$Z_1 = \tfrac{1}{2} \log_e \left(\frac{1 + r_1}{1 - r_1} \right) = 1.1513 \log_{10} \left(\frac{1 + r_1}{1 - r_1} \right)$$

which has mean $\mu_{Z_1} = \tfrac{1}{2} \log_e[(1 + \rho_1)/(1 - \rho_1)]$ and variance $\sigma_{Z_1} = 1/\sqrt{n_1 - 3}$, where n_1 is the size of the first sample; Z_2 is determined in a similar manner. The test statistic is now

$$Z = \frac{(Z_1 - Z_2) - (\mu_{Z_1} - \mu_{Z_2})}{\sigma}$$

where $\sigma = (\sigma_{Z_1}^2 + \sigma_{Z_2}^2)^{\frac{1}{2}}$. Z is normally distributed with mean 0 and with variance 1.

Example data

$n_1 = 28$, $n_2 = 35$, $r_1 = 0.50$, $r_2 = 0.30$, $\alpha = 0.05$

$$Z_1 = 1.1513 \log_{10} \left(\frac{1 + r_1}{1 - r_1} \right) = 0.5493 \text{ [Table 4]}$$

$$Z_2 = 1.1513 \log_{10} \left(\frac{1 + r_2}{1 - r_2} \right) = 0.3095 \text{ [Table 4]}$$

$$\sigma = \left(\frac{1}{n_1 - 3} + \frac{1}{n_2 - 3} \right)^{\frac{1}{2}} = 0.2669$$

$$Z = \frac{0.5493 - 0.3095}{0.2669} = 0.8985$$

The critical value at $\alpha = 0.05$ is 1.96 [Table 1].

Do not reject the null hypothesis.

Test 15 χ^2-test for a population variance

Object

To investigate the difference between a sample variance s^2 and an assumed population variance σ_0^2.

Limitations

It is assumed that the population from which the sample is drawn follows a normal distribution.

Method

Given a sample of n values $x_1, x_2, \ldots, x_n$, the values of

$$\bar{x} = \frac{\sum x_i}{n} \quad \text{and} \quad s^2 = \frac{\sum (x_i - \bar{x})^2}{n - 1}$$

are calculated. To test the null hypothesis that the population variance is equal to σ_0^2, the test statistic $(n - 1)s^2/\sigma_0^2$ will follow a χ^2-distribution with $n - 1$ degrees of freedom. The test may be either one-tailed or two-tailed.

Example data

$\bar{x} = 70$, $\sigma_0^2 = 9$, $n = 25$, $s^2 = 12$, $\nu = 24$

$$\chi^2 = (n - 1)s^2/\sigma_0^2 = \frac{24 \times 12}{9} = 32.0$$

Critical value $\chi^2_{24;0.05} = 36.42$ [Table 5].

Do not reject the null hypothesis. The difference between the variances is not significant.

Test 16 *F*-test for two population variances (variance ratio test)

Object

To investigate the significance of the difference between two population variances.

Limitations

The two populations should both follow normal distributions. (It is not necessary that they should have the same means.)

Method

Given samples of size n_1 with values $x_1, x_2, \ldots, x_{n_1}$ and size n_2 with values $y_1, y_2, \ldots, y_{n_2}$ from the two populations, the values of

$$\bar{x} = \frac{\sum x_i}{n_1}, \qquad \bar{y} = \frac{\sum y_i}{n_2}$$

and

$$s_1^2 = \frac{\sum (x_i - \bar{x})^2}{n_1 - 1}, \qquad s_2^2 = \frac{\sum (y_i - \bar{y})^2}{n_2 - 1}$$

can be calculated. Under the null hypothesis that the variances of the two populations are equal the test statistic $F = s_1^2/s_2^2$ follows the *F*-distribution with $(n_1 - 1, n_2 - 1)$ degrees of freedom. The test may be either one-tailed or two-tailed.

Example data

$n_1 = 4$, $n_2 = 6$, $\sum x = 0.4$, $\sum x^2 = 0.30$, $s_1^2 = 0.087$

$\sum y = 0.06$, $\sum y^2 = 1.78$, $s_2^2 = 0.36$

$$F_{3,5} = \frac{0.36}{0.087} = 4.14$$

Critical value $F_{3,5;0.05} = 5.41$ [Table 3].

Do not reject the null hypothesis. The two population variances are not significantly different from each other.

Test 17   F-test for two population variances (with correlated observations)

Object

To investigate the difference between two population variances when there is correlation between the pairs of observations.

Limitations

It is assumed that the observations have been performed in pairs and that correlation exists between the paired observations. The populations are normally distributed.

Method

A random sample of size n yields the following pairs of observations $(x_1, y_1), (x_2, y_2), \ldots, (x_n, y_n)$. The variance ratio F is calculated as in Test 16. Also the sample correlation r is found from

$$r = \frac{\sum (x_i - \bar{x})(y_i - \bar{y})}{\left[\sum (x_i - \bar{x})^2 \sum (y_i - \bar{y})^2 \right]^{\frac{1}{2}}}.$$

The quotient

$$\gamma_F = \frac{F - 1}{[(F + 1)^2 - 4r^2 F]^{\frac{1}{2}}}$$

provides a test statistic with degrees of freedom $\nu = n - 2$. The critical values for this test can be found in Table 6. Here the null hypothesis is $\sigma_1^2 = \sigma_2^2$, when the population correlation is not zero. Here F is greater than 1.

Example data

$$n_1 = n_2 = 6, \; \sum x = 0.4, \; \sum x^2 = 0.30, \; s_1^2 = 0.087$$

$$\sum y = 0.06, \; \sum y^2 = 1.78, \; s_2^2 = 0.36, \; F = \frac{s_2^2}{s_1^2} = 4.14, \; r = 0.811$$

$$\gamma_F = \frac{F - 1}{[(F + 1)^2 - 4r^2 F]^{\frac{1}{2}}} = \frac{4.14 - 1}{[(5.14)^2 - 4r^2 \cdot 4.14]^{\frac{1}{2}}}$$

$$= \frac{3.14}{[26.42 - 20.56 \times 0.658]^{\frac{1}{2}}} = 0.874$$

$\alpha = 0.05, \; \nu = n - 2 = 4, \; r = 0.811$ [Table 6].

Hence do not reject the hypothesis of no difference between variances.

Test 18 Hotelling's T^2-test for two series of population means

Object

To compare the results of two experiments, each of which yields a multivariate result. In other words, we wish to know if the mean pattern obtained from the first experiment agrees with the mean pattern obtained for the second.

Limitations

All the variables can be assumed to be independent of each other and all variables follow a multivariate normal distribution. (The variables are usually correlated.)

Method

Denote the results of the two experiments by subscripts A and B. For ease of description we shall limit the number of variables to three and we shall call these x, y and z. The number of observations is denoted by n_A and n_B for the two experiments. It is necessary to solve the following three equations to find the statistics a, b and c:

$$a[(xx)_A + (xx)_B] + b[(xy)_A + (xy)_B] + c[(xz)_A + (xz)_B]$$
$$= (n_A + n_B - 2)(\bar{x}_A - \bar{x}_B)$$
$$a[(xy)_A + (xy)_B] + b[(yy)_A + (yy)_B] + c[(yz)_A + (yz)_B]$$
$$= (n_A + n_B - 2)(\bar{y}_A - \bar{y}_B)$$
$$a[(xz)_A + (xz)_B] + b[(yz)_A + (yz)_B] + c[(zz)_A + (zz)_B]$$
$$= (n_A + n_B - 2)(\bar{z}_A - \bar{z}_B)$$

where $(xx)_A = \sum (x_A - \bar{x}_A)^2$, $(xy)_A = \sum (x_A - \bar{x}_A)(y_A - \bar{y}_A)$, and similar definitions exist for other terms.

Hotelling's T^2 is defined as

$$T^2 = \frac{n_A n_B}{n_A + n_B} \cdot \{a(\bar{x}_A - \bar{x}_B) + b(\bar{y}_A - \bar{y}_B) + c(\bar{z}_A - \bar{z}_B)\}$$

and the test statistic is

$$F = \frac{n_A + n_B - p - 1}{p(n_A + n_B - 2)} T^2$$

which follows an F-distribution with $(p, n_A + n_B - p - 1)$ degrees of freedom. Here p is the number of variables.

Example data

$n_A = 6$, $n_B = 4$, $\mathrm{DF} = \nu = 6 + 4 - 4 = 6$, $\alpha = 0.05$
$(xx) = (xx)_A + (xx)_B = 19$, $(yy) = 30$, $(zz) = 18$, $(xy) = -6$, $\nu_1 = p = 3$
$(xz) = 1$, $(yz) = -7$, $\bar{x}_A = 7$, $\bar{x}_B = 4.5$, $\bar{y}_A = 8$, $\bar{y}_B = 6$, $\bar{z}_A = 6$, $\bar{z}_B = 5$

The equations

$$19a - 6b + c = 20$$
$$-6a + 30b - 7c = 16$$
$$a - 7b + 18c = 8$$

are satisfied by $a = 1.320$, $b = 0.972$, $c = 0.749$. Thus

$$T^2 = \frac{6 \times 4}{10} \cdot (1.320 \times 2.5 + 0.972 \times 2 + 0.749 \times 1) = 14.38$$

$$F = \frac{6}{3 \times 8} \times 14.38 = 3.60$$

Critical value $F_{3, 6; 0.05} = 4.76$ [Table 3].

Do not reject the null hypothesis.

Test 19   Discriminant test for the origin of a *p*-fold sample

Object

To investigate the origin of one series of values for p random variates, when one of two markedly different populations may have produced that particular series.

Limitations

This test provides a decision rule which is closely related to Hotelling's T^2-test (Test 18), hence is subject to the same limitations.

Method

Using the notation of Hotelling's T^2-test, we may take samples from the two populations and obtain two quantities

$$D_A = a\bar{x}_A + b\bar{y}_A + c\bar{z}_A$$
$$D_B = a\bar{x}_B + b\bar{y}_B + c\bar{z}_B$$

for the two populations. From the series for which the origin has to be traced we can obtain a third quantity

$$D_S = a\bar{x}_S + b\bar{y}_S + c\bar{z}_S.$$

If $D_A - D_S < D_B - D_S$ we say that the series belongs to population A, but if $D_A - D_S > D_B - D_S$ we conclude that population B produced the series under consideration.

Example data

$a = 1.320, b = 0.972, c = 0.749$

$\bar{x}_A = 7, \bar{y}_A = 8, \bar{z}_A = 6, \bar{x}_B = 4.5, \bar{y}_B = 6, \bar{z}_B = 5$

$D_A = 1.320 \times 7 + 0.972 \times 8 + 0.749 \times 6 = 21.510$

$D_B = 1.320 \times 4.5 + 0.972 \times 6 + 0.749 \times 5 = 15.517$

If $\bar{x}_S = 6, \bar{y}_S = 6$ and $\bar{z}_S = 7$, then

$D_S = 1.320 \times 6 + 0.972 \times 6 + 0.749 \times 7 = 18.995$

$D_A - D_S = 21.510 - 18.995 = 2.515$

$D_B - D_S = 15.517 - 18.995 = -3.478$

D_S lies closer to D_A. D_S belongs to population A.

Test 20   Fisher's cumulant test for normality of a population

Object

To investigate the significance of the difference between a frequency distribution based on a given sample and a normal frequency distribution with the same mean and the same variance.

Limitations

The sample size should be large, say $n > 50$. If the two distributions do not have the same mean and the same variance then the w/s-test (Test 33) can be used.

Method

Sample moments can be calculated by

$$M_r = \sum_{i=1}^{n} x_i^r \qquad \text{or} \qquad M_r = \sum_{i=1}^{n} x_i^n f_i$$

where the x_i are the interval midpoints in the case of grouped data and f_i is the frequency. The first four sample cumulants (Fisher's K-statistics) are

$$K_1 = \frac{M_1}{n}$$

$$K_2 = \frac{nM_2 - M_1^2}{n(n-1)}$$

$$K_3 = \frac{n^2 M_3 - 3nM_2 M_1 + 2M_1^3}{n(n-1)(n-2)}$$

$$K_4 = \frac{(n^3 + n^2)M_4 - 4(n^2 + n)M_3 M_1 - 3(n^2 - n)M_2^2 + 12M_2 M_1^2 - 6M_1^4}{n(n-1)(n-2)(n-3)}$$

To test for skewness the test statistic is

$$u_1 = \frac{K_3}{(K_2)^{\frac{3}{2}}} \times \left(\frac{n}{6}\right)^{\frac{1}{2}}$$

which should follow a standard normal distribution.
To test for kurtosis the test statistic is

$$u_2 = \frac{K_4}{(K_2)^2} \times \left(\frac{n}{24}\right)^{\frac{1}{2}}$$

which should follow a standard normal distribution.

A combined test can be obtained using the test statistic

$$\chi^2 = \left[\frac{K_3}{(K_2)^{\frac{3}{2}}} \times \left(\frac{n}{6}\right)^{\frac{1}{2}}\right]^2 + \left[\frac{K_4}{(K_2)^2} \times \left(\frac{n}{24}\right)^{\frac{1}{2}}\right]^2$$

which will approximately follow a χ^2-distribution with two degrees of freedom.

Example data

Example A

$$\sum f = n = 190, \quad \sum fx = 151, \quad \sum fx^2 = 805,$$

$$\sum fx^3 = 1837, \quad \sum fx^4 = 10\,753$$

i.e. $M_1 = 151, M_2 = 805, M_3 = 1837, M_4 = 10\,753$

$$K_2 = \frac{(190 \times 805) - (151)^2}{190 \times 189} = 3.624310$$

$$K_3 = \frac{(190)^2 \times 1837 - 3 \times 190 \times 805 \times 151 + 2(151)^3}{190 \times 189 \times 188} = 0.5799445$$

$$K_4 = \frac{2\,795\,421\,924}{190 \times 189 \times 188 \times 187} = 2.214280$$

Test for skewness

$$u_1 = \frac{0.579945}{3.624310\sqrt{3.624310}} \times 5.6273 = 0.08405 \times 5.6273 = 0.473$$

The critical value at $\alpha = 0.05$ is 1.96.
Do not reject the null hypothesis [Table 1].

Test for kurtosis

$$u_2 = \frac{2.214279}{(3.62431)^2} \times \left(\frac{190}{24}\right)^{\frac{1}{2}} = 0.1686 \times 2.813657 = 0.474$$

The critical value at $\alpha = 0.05$ is 1.96.
Do not reject the null hypothesis [Table 1].

Combined test

$$\chi^2 = (0.473)^2 + (0.474)^2 = 0.2237 + 0.2250 = 0.449$$

which is smaller than the critical value 5.99 [Table 5].

Example B

Let skewness $= g_1 = \dfrac{K_3}{K_2\sqrt{K_2}} = \dfrac{0.579945}{3.624310\sqrt{3.624310}}$

$\qquad\qquad = 0.084052$

kurtosis $= g_2 = \dfrac{K_4}{K_2^2} = \dfrac{2.214279}{(3.624310)^2} = 0.168570$

standard deviation $\sigma(g_1) = \sqrt{\dfrac{6n(n-1)}{(n-2)(n+1)(n+3)}}$

$\qquad\qquad = \sqrt{\dfrac{6 \times 190 \times 189}{188 \times 191 \times 193}} = \sqrt{0.0310898} = 0.176323$

standard deviation $\sigma(g_2) = \sqrt{\dfrac{24n(n-1)^2}{(n-3)(n-2)(n+3)(n+5)}}$

$\qquad\qquad = \sqrt{\dfrac{24 \times 190 \times 189^2}{187 \times 188 \times 193 \times 195}} = 0.350872$

Here $u_1 = \dfrac{0.084052}{0.176323} = 0.477$, $u_2 = \dfrac{0.168570}{0.350872} = 0.480$.

Critical values for g_1 lie between 0.282 (for 200) and 0.301 (for 175) [Table 7].
The right-side critical value for g_2 lies between 0.62 and 0.66 [Table 7].
Hence the null hypothesis should not be rejected.

Test 21   Dixon's test for outliers

Object

To investigate the significance of the difference between a suspicious extreme value and other values in the sample.

Limitations

1. The sample size should be greater than 3.
2. The population which is being sampled is assumed normal.

Method

Consider a sample of size n, where the sample is arranged with the suspect value in front, its nearest neighbour next and then the following values arranged in ascending (or descending) order. The order is determined by whether the suspect value is the largest or the smallest. Denoting the ordered series by $x_1, x_2, \ldots, x_n$, the test statistic r where

$$r = (x_2 - x_1)/(x_n - x_1) \qquad \text{if } 3 < n \leqslant 7,$$
$$r = (x_2 - x_1)/(x_{n-1} - x_1) \qquad \text{if } 8 \leqslant n \leqslant 10,$$
$$r = (x_3 - x_1)/(x_{n-1} - x_1) \qquad \text{if } 11 \leqslant n \leqslant 13,$$
$$r = (x_3 - x_1)/(x_{n-2} - x_1) \qquad \text{if } 14 \leqslant n \leqslant 25.$$

Critical values for r can be obtained from Table 8. The null hypothesis that the outlier belongs to the sample is rejected if the observed value of r exceeds the critical value.

Example data

$x_1 = 326$, $x_2 = 177$, $x_3 = 176$, $x_4 = 157$, $n = 4$

Here $r = \dfrac{x_2 - x_1}{x_n - x_1} = \dfrac{177 - 326}{157 - 326} = 0.882$.

The critical value at $\alpha = 0.05$ is 0.765 [Table 8].

The calculated value exceeds the critical value.

Hence reject the null hypothesis that the value x_1 comes from the same population.

Test 22　F-test for K population means (analysis of variance)

Object

To test the null hypothesis that K samples are from K populations with the same mean.

Limitations

It is assumed that the populations are normally distributed and have equal variances. It is also assumed that the samples are independent of each other.

Method

Let the jth sample contain n_j elements ($j = 1, \ldots, K$). Then the total number of elements is

$$N = \sum_{j=1}^{K} n_j$$

The ith element of the jth sample can be denoted by x_{ij} ($i = 1, \ldots, n_j$), and the mean of the jth sample becomes

$$x_{\cdot j} = \sum_{i=1}^{n} x_{ij}/n_j$$

The variance of the observations with respect to their own sample means becomes

$$s_1^2 = \frac{\displaystyle\sum_j \sum_i (x_{ij} - x_{\cdot j})^2}{N - K}$$

or equivalently, denoting the total sum of squares of all the observations as s_T^2,

$$(s_T^2 - s_2^2)/(N - K)$$

with $N - K$ degrees of freedom. Similarly, the variance of the sample means with respect to the grand mean becomes

$$s_2^2 = \frac{\displaystyle\sum_j n_j(x_{\cdot j} - x_{\cdot\cdot})^2}{K - 1}$$

where

$$x_{\cdot\cdot} = \frac{1}{K} \sum_i \sum_j x_{ij}$$

and s_2^2 has $K - 1$ degrees of freedom.

The test statistic is $F = s_2^2/s_1^2$, which follows the F-distribution with $(K - 1,$ $N - K)$ degrees of freedom. A one-tailed test is carried out as it is necessary to ascertain whether s_2^2 is larger than s_1^2.

Example data

$K = 3$, $N = 12$, $n_1 = 3$, $n_2 = 5$, $n_3 = 4$, $\alpha = 0.05$

$$\sum_{i=1}^{n_1} x_{i1} = 53.5, \ \sum_{i=1}^{n_2} x_{i2} = 102.5, \ \sum_{i=1}^{n_3} x_{i3} = 64.4$$

$T = 53.5 + 102.5 + 64.4 = 220.4$

$x_{.1} = 17.83$, $x_{.2} = 20.50$, $x_{.3} = 16.10$, $x_{..} = T/N = 18.37$

$T^2/N = 4048.01$

$$s_T^2 = \left[\left(\sum_{i=1}^{n_1} x_{i1}^2 + \sum_{i=1}^{n_2} x_{i2}^2 + \sum_{i=1}^{n_3} x_{i3}^2 \right) - \frac{T^2}{N} \right]$$

$$= 4097.54 - 4048.01$$

$$= 49.53$$

$s_2^2 = 44.17$

$$F_{2,9} = \frac{s_2^2/(K - 1)}{s_1^2/(N - K)} = \frac{s_2^2/(K - 1)}{(s_T^2 - s_2^2)/(N - K)}$$

$$= \frac{44.17/2}{(49.53 - 44.17)/9} \simeq 37$$

Critical value $F_{2,9;0.05} = 4.26$ [Table 3].

The calculated value is greater than the critical value.

The variance between the samples is significantly larger than the variance within the samples.

Test 23   The Z-test for correlated proportions

Object

To investigate the significance of the difference between two correlated proportions in opinion surveys. It can also be used for more general applications.

Limitations

1. The same people are questioned both times on a yes–no basis.
2. The sample size must be quite large.

Method

N people respond to a yes–no question both before and after a certain stimulus. The following two-way table can then be built up:

		First poll Yes	First poll No
Second poll	Yes	a	b
	No	c	d
			N

To decide whether the stimulus has produced a significant change in the proportion answering 'yes', we calculate the test statistic

$$Z = \frac{b - c}{N\sigma}$$

where

$$\sigma = \sqrt{\frac{(b + c) - (b - c)^2 / N}{N(N - 1)}}.$$

Example data

$a = 30, b = 15, c = 9, d = 51, N = 105$

The null hypothesis is that there is no apparent change due to the stimulus. The difference in proportion is

$$\frac{b - c}{N} = \frac{15}{105} - \frac{9}{105} = \frac{6}{105} = 0.0571$$

$$\sigma = \sqrt{\frac{(9+15) - (9-15)^2/105}{105 \times 104}} = 0.465$$

$$Z = \frac{0.0571}{0.0465} = 1.23$$

The critical value at $\alpha = 0.05$ is 1.96 [Table 1].
The calculated value is less than the critical value.
Do not reject the null hypothesis.

Test 24 χ^2-test for an assumed population variance

Object

To investigate the significance of the difference between a population variance σ^2 and an assumed value σ_0^2.

Limitations

It is assumed that the sample is taken from a normal population.

Method

The sample variance

$$s^2 = \frac{\sum_{i=1}^{n}(x_i - \bar{x})^2}{n-1}$$

is calculated. The test statistic is then

$$\chi^2 = \frac{s^2}{\sigma_0^2}(n-1)$$

which follows a χ^2-distribution with $n-1$ degrees of freedom.

Example data

$n = 25, \bar{x} = 71, s^2 = 12, \sigma_0^2 = 9$

$H_0: \sigma^2 = \sigma_0^2, H_1: \sigma^2 \neq \sigma_0^2$

$$\chi^2 = 24 \times \frac{12}{9} = 32$$

Critical value $\chi^2_{24;0.05} = 36.4$ [Table 5].

Do not reject the null hypothesis. The difference between the variances is not significant.

Test 25   *F*-test for two counts (Poisson distribution)

Object

To investigate the significance of the difference between two counted results (based on a Poisson distribution).

Limitations

It is assumed that the counts satisfy a Poisson distribution and that the two samples were obtained under similar conditions.

Method

Let μ_1 and μ_2 denote the means of the two populations and N_1 and N_2 the two counts. To test the hypothesis $\mu_1 = \mu_2$ we calculate the test statistic

$$F = \frac{N_1}{N_2 + 1}$$

which follows the *F*-distribution with $(2(N_2 + 1), 2N_1)$ degrees of freedom. When the counts are obtained over different periods of time t_1 and t_2, it is necessary to compare the counting rates N_1/t_1 and N_2/t_2. Hence the appropriate test statistic is

$$F = \frac{\dfrac{1}{t_1}(N_1 + 0.5)}{\dfrac{1}{t_2}(N_2 + 0.5)}$$

which follows the *F*-distribution with $(2N_1 + 1, 2N_2 + 1)$ degrees of freedom.

Example data

$N_1 = 13, N_2 = 3, t_1 = t_2$

$f_1 = 2(N_2 + 1) = 2(3 + 1) = 8, f_2 = 2N_1 = 2 \times 13 = 26$

$$F = \frac{N_1}{N_2 + 1} = \frac{13}{3 + 1} = 3.25$$

Critical value $F_{8, 26; 0.05} = 2.32$ [Table 3].

The calculated value exceeds the table value.

Hence reject the null hypothesis.

Test 26   F-test for the overall mean of K subpopulations (analysis of variance)

Object

To investigate the significance of the difference between the overall mean of K subpopulations and an assumed value μ_0 for the population mean. Two different null hypotheses are tested; the first being that the K subpopulations have the same mean ($\mu_1 = \mu_2 = \cdots = \mu_K$) and the second that the overall mean is equal to the assumed value ($\mu = \mu_0$).

Limitations

The K samples from the subpopulations are independent of each other. The subpopulations should also be normally distributed and have the same variance.

Methods

Method A

To test $H_0: \mu_1 = \mu_2 = \cdots = \mu_K$, we calculate the test statistic

$$F = \frac{s_1^2/(K-1)}{s_2^2/(N-K)}$$

where N is the total number of observations in the K samples, n_j is the number of observations in the jth sample,

$$\left.\begin{array}{l} s_1^2 = \displaystyle\sum_j n_j(x_{.j} - x_{..})^2 \\[2mm] s_2^2 = \displaystyle\sum_i \sum_j (x_{ij} - x_{.j})^2 \end{array}\right\} \quad i = 1, \ldots, n_j, \quad j = 1, \ldots, K,$$

and x_{ij} is the ith observation in the jth sample

$$x_{.j} = \frac{1}{n_j}\sum_i x_{ij}$$

$$x_{..} = \frac{1}{N}\sum_i \sum_j x_{ij}$$

The value of F should follow the F-distribution with $(K-1, N-K)$ degrees of freedom.

Method B

To test $H_0: \mu = \mu_0$, we calculate the test statistic

$$F = \frac{N(x_{..} - \mu_0)^2}{s_1^2/(K-1)}$$

which should follow the F-distribution with $(1, K-1)$ degrees of freedom.

Example data

$n_1 = n_2 = n_3 = n_4 = n_5 = n_6 = 5, K = 6, N = 30, \mu_0 = 1500$

$x_{.1} = 1505, x_{.2} = 1528, x_{.3} = 1564, x_{.4} = 1498, x_{.5} = 1600, x_{.6} = 1470$

$\bar{x}_{..} = 9165/6 = 1527.5$

$s_1^2/5 = 11\,272, s_2^2/24 = 2451, s_T^2 = 3972$

$N(x_{..} - \mu_0)^2 = 22\,687.5$

(a) $F = 11\,272/2451 = 4.60$.
 Critical value $F_{5, 24; 0.05} = 2.62$ [Table 3].
 Reject the null hypothesis.
(b) $F = 22\,687.5/11\,272 = 2.01$.
 Critical value $F_{1, 5; 0.05} = 6.61$ [Table 3].
 Do not reject the null hypothesis.

Test 27   *F*-test for multiple comparison of contrasts between *K* population means

Object

This test is an extension of the preceding one, to investigate which particular set of mean values or linear combination of mean values shows differences with the other mean values.

Limitations

As for the preceding test, with the addition that the comparisons to be examined should be decided on at or before the start of the analysis.

Method

With the notation as before, we must define a contrast as a linear function of the means

$$\lambda = \sum_{j=1}^{K} a_j \mu_j$$

under the condition that $\sum_{j=1}^{K} a_j = 0$.

The test statistic becomes

$$F = \frac{1}{s^2} \frac{\left(\sum_{j=1}^{K} a_j x_{.j} \right)^2}{\sum_{j=1}^{K} a_j^2 / n_j}$$

(see Test 26) which should follow the *F*-distribution with $(1, N - K)$ degrees of freedom. Here,

$$s^2 = \frac{\sum_{j=1}^{K} \sum_{i=1}^{n_j} (x_{ij})^2 - \sum_{j=1}^{K} n_j \bar{x}_j^2}{N - K}.$$

For simple differences of the type $\bar{x}_{.i} - \bar{x}_{.j}$ the test statistic becomes

$$F = \frac{(x_{.i} - \bar{x}_{.j}) / \left(\frac{1}{n_i} + \frac{1}{n_j} \right)}{s^2}$$

Example data

$n_1 = 6, n_2 = 4, n_3 = 2, N = 12, K = 3, \nu_1 = 1, \nu_2 = 9$

$$\bar{x}_{.1} = 2.070, \ \bar{x}_{.2} = 2.015, \ \bar{x}_{.3} = 2.595, \ \bar{x} = 2.139$$

$$\sum_i \sum_j x_{ij}^2 = 55.5195, \qquad \sum n_j \bar{x}_j^2 = 55.41835$$

$$\lambda_1 = \mu_1 - \mu_2, \ \lambda_2 = \mu_1 - \mu_3, \ \lambda_3 = \mu_2 - \mu_3 \text{ (contrasts)}$$

$$\bar{x}_{.1} - \bar{x}_{.2} = 0.055$$

$$\bar{x}_{.1} - \bar{x}_{.3} = -0.525$$

$$\bar{x}_{.2} - \bar{x}_{.3} = -0.580$$

$$\frac{(x_{.1} - x_{.2})^2}{\left(\dfrac{1}{n_1} + \dfrac{1}{n_2}\right)} = \frac{(0.055)^2}{\left(\dfrac{1}{6} + \dfrac{1}{4}\right)} = 0.00726$$

$$\frac{(x_{.1} - x_{.3})^2}{\left(\dfrac{1}{n_1} + \dfrac{1}{n_3}\right)} = \frac{(-0.525)^2}{\left(\dfrac{1}{6} + \dfrac{1}{2}\right)} = 0.4134$$

$$\frac{(x_{.2} - x_{.3})^2}{\left(\dfrac{1}{n_2} + \dfrac{1}{n_3}\right)} = \frac{(0.580)^2}{\left(\dfrac{1}{4} + \dfrac{1}{2}\right)} = 0.4485$$

$$s^2 = \frac{55.5195 - 55.41835}{9} = \frac{0.10115}{9} = 0.01124$$

$$F_1 = \frac{0.00726}{0.01124} = 0.646, \ F_2 = \frac{0.4134}{0.01124} = 36.78, \ F_3 = \frac{0.4485}{0.01124} = 39.90$$

Critical value $F_{1, 9; 0.05} = 5.12$ [Table 3]. Both F_2 and F_3 are larger than 5.12. There is no significant difference between the means for group 1 and group 2, but there is a significant difference between group 3 and groups 1 and 2.

Test 28   Tukey test for multiple comparison of K population means (unequal sample sizes)

Object

To investigate the significance of all possible differences between K population means.

Limitations

The K populations are normally distributed with equal variances.

Method

Consider samples of size $n_1, n_2, \ldots, n_K$ from the K populations. From Table 9 the critical values of q can be found using as degrees of freedom

$$\nu = \left(\sum_{j=1}^{K} n_j \right) - K.$$

The total variance of the samples is now calculated from

$$s^2 = \frac{\sum_{j=1}^{K} (n_j - 1) \cdot s_j^2}{N - K}$$

where s_j^2 is the variance of the jth sample and N is the total sample size. Finally, a limit W is calculated

$$W = \frac{qs}{n^{\frac{1}{2}}}$$

where $q \, (= w/s)$ is the Studentized range and

$$n = \frac{K}{\left(\dfrac{1}{n_1} + \dfrac{1}{n_2} + \cdots + \dfrac{1}{n_K} \right)}.$$

If this limit W is exceeded by the absolute difference between any two sample means, then the corresponding population means differ significantly.

Example data

$n_1 = n_2 = n_3 = n_4 = n_5 = 5$, $K = 5$, $N = 25$

$s_1^2 = 406.0$, $s_2^2 = 574.8$, $s_3^2 = 636.8$, $s_4^2 = 159.3$, $s_5^2 = 943.2$

$\bar{x}_1 = 534.0$, $\bar{x}_2 = 536.4$, $\bar{x}_3 = 562.6$, $\bar{x}_4 = 549.4$, $\bar{x}_5 = 526.8$

$s^2 = \dfrac{2720.1}{5} = 544.02$, $s = 23.32$, $\nu = 25 - 5 = 20$

Critical value for q for $K = 5$, and $\nu = 20$ at $\alpha = 0.05$ is 5.29 [Table 9].

$$W = \frac{5.29 \times 23.32}{\sqrt{5}} = 55.3$$

The largest difference between the sample means is $562.6 - 526.8 = 35.8$ which is less than 55.3. Hence the population means do not differ significantly.

Test 29   The Link–Wallace test for multiple comparison of K population means (equal sample sizes)

Object

To investigate the significance of all possible differences between K population means.

Limitations

1. The K populations are normally distributed with equal variances.
2. The K samples each contain n observations.

Method

The test statistic is

$$K_L = \frac{nw(\bar{x})}{\sum_{i=1}^{k} w_i(x)}$$

where $w_i(x)$ is the range of the x values for the ith sample
$w(\bar{x})$ is the range of the sample means
n is the sample size.

The null hypothesis $\mu_1 = \mu_2 = \cdots = \mu_K$ is rejected if the observed value of K_L is larger than the critical value obtained from Table 10.

Example data

$n = 8$, $w_1(x) = 7$, $w_2(x) = 6$, $w_3(x) = 4$, $K = 3$
$w_1(\bar{x}) = 4.750$, $w_2(\bar{x}) = 4.625$, $w_3(\bar{x}) = 7.750$

$$K_L = \frac{nw(\bar{x})}{\sum_{i=1}^{k} w_i(x)} = \frac{8(7.750 - 4.625)}{7 + 6 + 4} = 1.47$$

Critical value $K_{8,3;0.05} = 1.18$ [Table 10].

Reject the null hypothesis of equal means.
    Using $K_{8,3;0.05} = 1.18$, the critical value for the sample mean differences is

$$D = \frac{1.18 \sum w_i(x)}{n} = \frac{1.18 \times 17}{8} = 2.51$$

Since $w_1(\bar{x}) - w_2(\bar{x}) = 0.125$ (less than D)

$\qquad w_3(\bar{w}) - w_2(\bar{x}) = 3.125$ (greater than D)

$\qquad w_3(\bar{x}) - w_1(\bar{x}) = 3.00$ (greater than D)

reject the null hypothesis $\mu_1 = \mu_3$ and $\mu_2 = \mu_3$.

Test 30 Dunnett's test for comparing K treatments with a control

Object

To investigate the significance of the differences, when several treatments are compared with a control.

Limitations

1. The $K + 1$ samples, consisting of K treatments and one control, all have the same size n.
2. The samples are drawn independently from normally distributed populations with equal variances.

Method

The variance within the $K + 1$ groups is calculated from

$$S_W^2 = \frac{S_0^2 + S_1^2 + \cdots + S_K^2}{(K-1)(n-1)}$$

where S_0^2 is the sum of squares of deviations from the group mean for the control group and S_j^2 is a similar expression for the jth treatment group. The standard deviation of the differences between treatment means and control means is then

$$S(\bar{d}) = \sqrt{2S_W^2/n}.$$

The quotients

$$D_j = \frac{\bar{x}_j - \bar{x}_0}{S(\bar{d})} \qquad (j = 1, 2, \ldots, K)$$

are found and compared with the critical values of $|D_j|$ found from Table 11. If an observed value is larger than the tabulated value, one may conclude that the corresponding difference in means between treatment j and the control is significant.

Example data

$K = 4, n = 10, \bar{x}_0 = 14.5, \bar{x}_1 = 25.0, \bar{x}_2 = 15.7, \bar{x}_3 = 18.1, \bar{x}_4 = 21.9$
$S_0^2 = 261.0, S_1^2 = 586.0, S_2^2 = 292.6, S_3^2 = 320.4, S_4^2 = 556.4$

$$S_W^2 = \frac{261 + 586 + 292.6 + 320.4 + 556.4}{(4-1)(10-1)} = 74.681$$

$$S(\bar{d}) = \sqrt{2S_W^2/n} = \left(\frac{2 \times 44.8089}{10}\right)^{\frac{1}{2}} = 3.865$$

Critical value $D_{4, 45; 0.05} = 2.23$ [Table 11].

$D_1 = 2.72, D_2 = 0.31, D_3 = 0.93, D_4 = 1.91$

The value of D_1 is larger than the critical value. Hence D_1 is significantly different from the control value.

Test 31   Bartlett's test for equality of K variances

Object

To investigate the significance of the differences between the variances of K normally distributed populations.

Limitations

It is assumed that all the populations follow a normal distribution.

Method

Samples are drawn from each of the populations. Let s_j^2 denote the variance of a sample of n_j items from the jth population ($j = 1, \ldots, K$). The overall variance is defined by

$$s^2 = \frac{\sum\limits_{j=1}^{K}(n_j - 1) \cdot s_j^2}{\sum\limits_{j=1}^{K}(n_j - 1)}.$$

The test statistic is

$$B = \frac{2.30259}{C}\left\{\sum(n_j - 1)\log s^2 - \sum(n_j - 1)\log s_j^2\right\}$$

where

$$C = 1 + \frac{1}{3(K + 1)}\left\{\sum\frac{1}{(n_j - 1)} - \frac{1}{\sum(n_j - 1)}\right\}$$

and $\log_e 10 = 2.30259$.

Case A $(n_j > 6)$

B will approximate to a χ^2-distribution with $K - 1$ degrees of freedom. The null hypothesis of equal variances is rejected if B is larger than the critical value.

Case B $(n_j \leqslant 6)$

The test statistic becomes $BC = M$ and this should be referred to Table 12. When the value of M exceeds the tabulated value, the null hypothesis can be rejected.

Example data

Example A

$n_1 = 31, n_2 = 15, n_3 = 20, n_4 = 42, K = 4$

$s_1^2 = 5.47, s_2^2 = 4.64, s_3^2 = 11.47, s_4^2 = 11.29$

$$s^2 = \frac{910}{104} = 8.75, \ \log s^2 = 0.94201, \ C = 1.02$$

$$\sum(n_j - 1)\log s^2 = 97.9690, \ \sum(n_j - 1)s_j^2 = 94.7647$$

$$B = \frac{1}{1.02}[2.3026(97.9690 - 94.7647)] = \frac{7.38}{1.02} = 7.24$$

Critical value $\chi_{3;0.05}^2 = 7.81$ [Table 5].

Hence the null hypothesis is not rejected.

Example B

$n_1 = 3, \ n_2 = 3, \ n_3 = 3, \ n_4 = 4$

$s_1^2 = 6.33, \ s_2^2 = 1.33, \ s_3^2 = 4.33, \ s_4^2 = 4.33$

Pooled variance $s^2 = \dfrac{(12.66 + 2.66 + 8.66 + 12.99)}{2 + 2 + 2 + 3} = 4.11$

Further

$$M = 2.30259\{9\log 4.11 - 2\log 6.33 - 2\log 1.33 - 2\log 4.33 - 3\log 4.33\}$$

$$= 2.30259\{9 \times 0.6138 - 2 \times 0.8014 - 2 \times 0.1239 - 2 \times 0.6365$$

$$- 3 \times 0.6365\}$$

$$C = \{\tfrac{1}{2} + \tfrac{1}{2} + \tfrac{1}{2} + \tfrac{1}{3} - \tfrac{1}{9}\} = 1.7222$$

The critical value of M for $\alpha = 0.05$, $K = 4$ is 9.21 [Table 12]; even for $C = 2.0$. Do not reject the null hypothesis.

Test 32   Hartley's test for equality of K variances

Object

To investigate the significance of the differences between the variances of K normally distributed populations.

Limitations

1. The populations should be normally distributed.
2. The sizes of the K samples should be (approximately) equal.

Method

Samples are drawn from each of the populations. The test statistic is $F_{max} = s_{max}^2 / s_{min}^2$ where s_{max}^2 is the largest of the K sample variances and s_{min}^2 is the smallest of the K sample variances.

Critical values of F_{max} can be obtained from Table 13. If the observed ratio exceeds this critical value, the null hypothesis of equal variances should be rejected.

Example data

$n_1 = n_2 = n_3 = n_4 = 30, K = 4$

$s_1^2 = 16.72, s_2^2 = 36.27, s_3^2 = 14.0, s_4^2 = 15.91$

$$F = \frac{36.27}{14.0} = 2.59$$

The critical value of F_{max}, at a 5 per cent level of significance, for $n = 30$, $K = 4$ is 2.61 [Table 13].

Hence do not reject the null hypothesis.

Test 33   The w/s-test for normality of a population

Object

To investigate the significance of the difference between a frequency distribution based on a given sample and a normal frequency distribution.

Limitations

This test is applicable if the sample is taken from a population with continuous distribution.

Method

This is a much simpler test than Fisher's cumulant test (Test 20). The sample standard deviation (s) and the range (w) are first determined. Then the Studentized range $q = w/s$ is found.

The test statistic is q and critical values are available for q from Table 14. If the observed value of q lies outside the two critical values, the sample distribution cannot be considered as a normal distribution.

Example data

$n_1 = 4$, $n_2 = 9$, $\bar{x}_1 = 3166$, $\bar{x}_2 = 2240.4$, $\alpha = 0.025$

$s_1^2 = 6328.67$, $s_2^2 = 221\,661.3$, $s_1 = 79.6$, $s_2 = 471$

$w_1 = 171$, $w_2 = 1333$

$\dfrac{w_1}{s_1} = 2.15$, $\dfrac{w_2}{s_2} = 2.83$

Critical values for this test are:

for $n_1 = 4$, 1.93 and 2.44 [Table 14];

for $n_2 = 9$, 2.51 and 3.63 [Table 14].

Hence the null hypothesis cannot be rejected.

Test 34   Cochran's test for variance outliers

Object

To investigate the significance of the difference between one rather large variance and $K - 1$ other variances.

Limitations

1. It is assumed that the K samples are taken from normally distributed populations.
2. Each sample is of equal size.

Method

The test statistic is

$$C = \frac{\text{largest of the } s_i^2}{\text{sum of all } s_i^2}$$

where s_i^2 denotes the variance of the ith sample. Critical values of C are available from Table 15. The null hypothesis that the large variance does not differ significantly from the others is rejected if the observed value of C exceeds the critical value.

Example data

$s_1^2 = 26, s_2^2 = 51, s_3^2 = 40, s_4^2 = 24, s_5^2 = 28$

$n_1 = n_2 = n_3 = n_4 = n_5 = 10, K = 5, \nu = n - 1 = 9$

$$C = \frac{51}{26 + 51 + 40 + 24 + 28} = 0.302$$

Critical value $C_{9;0.05} = 0.4241$ [Table 15].

The calculated value is less than the critical value.

Do not reject the null hypothesis.

Test 35 The Kolmogorov–Smirnov test for goodness of fit

Object

To investigate the significance of the difference between an observed distribution and a specified population distribution.

Limitations

This test is applicable when the population distribution function is continuous.

Method

From the sample, the cumulative distribution $S_n(x)$ is determined and plotted as a step function. The cumulative distribution $F(x)$ of the assumed population is also plotted on the same diagram.

The maximum difference between these two distributions

$$D = |F - S_n|$$

provides the test statistic and this is compared with the value $D(\alpha)$ obtained from Table 16.

If $D > D_\alpha$ the null hypothesis that the sample came from the assumed population is rejected.

Example data

To test the hypothesis that the data constitute a random sample from a Poisson population with mean 7.6.

$$F(x) = \frac{e^{-\lambda}\lambda^x}{x!}, \ \lambda = 7.6, \ n = 3366$$

$$S_n(x_i) = \frac{cu(x_i)}{3366}, \ F(x_i) = \frac{e^{-7.6}7.6^6}{6!} = 0.3646 \text{ etc.}$$

No.	1	2	3	4	5	6	7	8	9	10	11	12	13	14
x_i	5	14	24	57	111	197	278	378	418	461	433	413	358	219
$cu(x_i)$	5	19	43	100	211	408	686	1064	1482	1943	2376	2789	3147	3366
$S_n(x_i)$	0.001	0.005	0.012	0.029	0.062	0.121	0.204	0.316	0.440	0.577	0.705	0.828	0.935	1.0
$F(x_i)$	0.004	0.009	0.055	0.125	0.231	0.365	0.510	0.648	0.765	0.854	0.915	0.954	0.976	0.989
D	0.003	0.014	0.043	0.096	0.169	0.244	0.306	0.332	0.325	0.277	0.210	0.126	0.041	0.011

$$\max D = 0.332, \ D_{14;0.01} = \frac{1.63}{\sqrt{3366}} = \frac{1.63}{58.01} = 0.028 \text{ where } D > D_\alpha \text{ [Table 16].}$$

The hypothesis may be rejected.

Test 36   The Kolmogorov–Smirnov test for comparing two populations

Object

To investigate the significance of the difference between two population distributions, based on two sample distributions.

Limitations

The best results are obtained when the samples are sufficiently large – say, 15 or over.

Method

Given samples of size n_1 and n_2 from the two populations, the cumulative distribution functions $S_{n_1}(x)$ and $S_{n_2}(y)$ can be determined and plotted. Hence the maximum value of the difference between the plots can be found and compared with a critical value obtained from Table 16. If the observed value exceeds the critical value the null hypothesis that the two population distributions are identical is rejected.

Example data

$n_1 = n_2 = n = 10$

Sample x	0.6	1.2	1.6	1.7	1.7	2.1	2.8	2.9	3.0	3.2
cu(x)	0.6	1.8	3.4	5.1	6.8	8.9	11.7	14.6	17.6	20.8
Sample y	2.1	2.3	3.0	3.1	3.2	3.2	3.5	3.8	4.6	7.2
cu(y)	2.1	4.4	7.4	10.5	13.7	16.9	20.4	24.2	28.8	36.0
$S_{n_1}(x)$	0.029	0.086	0.163	0.245	0.327	0.428	0.562	0.702	0.846	1.0
$S_{n_2}(y)$	0.058	0.122	0.205	0.291	0.380	0.469	0.566	0.672	0.800	1.00
Difference D	0.029	0.036	0.042	0.046	0.053	0.041	0.004	0.03	0.046	0

max $D = 0.053$

Critical value $D_{20;0.01} = 0.356$ [Table 16].

Do not reject the hypothesis. Both samples come from the same population.

Test 37 The χ^2-test for goodness of fit

Object

To investigate the significance of the differences between observed data arranged in K classes, and the theoretically expected frequencies in the K classes.

Limitations

1. The observed and theoretical distributions should contain the same number of elements.
2. The division into classes must be the same for both distributions.
3. The expected frequency in each class should be at least 5.
4. The observed frequencies are assumed to be obtained by random sampling.

Method

The test statistic is

$$\chi^2 = \sum_{i=1}^{K} \frac{(O_i - E_i)^2}{E_i}$$

where O_i and E_i represent the observed and theoretical frequencies respectively for each of the K classes. This statistic is compared with a value obtained from χ^2 tables with ν degrees of freedom. In general, $\nu = K - 1$. However, if the theoretical distribution contains m parameters to be estimated from the observed data, then ν becomes $K - 1 - m$. For example, to fit data to a normal distribution may require the estimation of the mean and variance from the observed data. In this case ν would become $K - 1 - 2$.

If χ^2 is greater than the critical value we reject the null hypothesis that the observed and theoretical distributions agree.

Example data

A die is thrown 120 times. Denote the observed number of occurrences of i by O_i, $i = 1, \ldots, 6$. Can we consider the die to be fair at the 5 per cent level of significance?

$K = 6$, $\nu = 6 - 1$

$O_i = 25$, $O_2 = 17$, $O_3 = 15$, $O_4 = 23$, $O_5 = 24$, $O_6 = 16$

$E_1 = 20$, $E_2 = 20$, $E_3 = 20$, $E_4 = 20$, $E_5 = 20$, $E_6 = 20$

$$\chi^2 = \frac{25}{20} + \frac{9}{20} + \frac{25}{20} + \frac{9}{20} + \frac{16}{20} + \frac{16}{20} = 5.0$$

Critical value $\chi^2_{5;0.05} = 11.1$ [Table 5].

The calculated value is less than the critical value.

Hence there are no indications that the die is not fair.

Test 38   The χ^2-test for compatibility of K counts

Object

To investigate the significance of the differences between K counts.

Limitations

The counts must be obtained under comparable conditions.

Method

Method (a)   Times for counts are all equal

Let the ith count be denoted by N_i. Then the null hypothesis is that $N_i = \text{constant}$, for $i = 1, \ldots, K$. The test statistic is

$$\chi^2 = \sum_{i=1}^{K} \frac{(N_i - \bar{N})^2}{\bar{N}}$$

where $\bar{N}$ is the mean of the K counts $\sum_{i=1}^{K} N_i/K$. This is compared with a value obtained from χ^2 tables with $K - 1$ degrees of freedom. If χ^2 exceeds this value the null hypothesis is rejected.

Method (b)   Times for counts are not all equal

Let the time to obtain the ith count be t_i. The test statistic becomes

$$\chi^2 = \sum_{i=1}^{K} \frac{(N_i - t_i \bar{R})^2}{t_i \bar{R}}$$

where $\bar{R} = \sum N_i / \sum t_i$. This is compared with Table 5 as above.

Example data

$N_1 = 5$, $N_2 = 12$, $N_3 = 18$, $N_4 = 19$, $\bar{N} = 11$, $\nu = K - 1 = 4 - 1 = 3$

Using method (a), $\chi^2 = 13.6$.

The critical value $\chi^2_{3;0.05} = 7.81$ [Table 5].

Hence reject the null hypothesis. The four counts are not consistent with each other.

Test 39   Fisher's exact test for consistency in a 2 × 2 table

Object

To investigate the significance of the differences between observed frequencies for two dichotomous distributions.

Limitations

This test is applicable if the classification is dichotomous and the elements originate from two sources. It is usually applied when the number of elements is small or the expected frequencies are less than 5.

Method

A 2 × 2 contingency table is built up as follows:

	Class 1	Class 2	Total
Sample 1	a	b	$a + b$
Sample 2	c	d	$c + d$
Total	$a + c$	$b + d$	$n = a + b + c + d$

The test statistic is

$$\sum p = \frac{(a+b)!(c+d)!(a+c)!(b+d)!}{n!} \sum_i \frac{1}{a_i! b_i! c_i! d_i!}$$

where the summation is over all possible 2 × 2 schemes with a cell frequency equal to or smaller than the smallest experimental frequency (keeping the row and column totals fixed as above).

If $\sum p$ is less than the significance level chosen, we may reject the null hypothesis of independence between samples and classes, i.e. that the two samples have been drawn from one common population.

Example data

class 1 = accepted, class 2 = rejected, significance level $\alpha = 0.05$

$a = 9, b = 2, c = 7, d = 6, a + b = 11, c + d = 13, a + c = 16, b + d = 8$

Two possible sets of data which deviate more from the null hypothesis are $a = 10, b = 1, c = 6, d = 7$ and $a = 11, b = 0, c = 5, d = 8$.

We add the three probabilities of the three schemes according to hyper-geometric distributions. This gives

$$\sum p = \frac{11!\, 13!\, 16!\, 8!}{24!} \left\{ \frac{1}{2!\, 6!\, 7!\, 9!} + \frac{1}{1!\, 6!\, 7!\, 10!} + \frac{1}{0!\, 5!\, 8!\, 11!} \right\} = 0.156.$$

This is greater than 0.05. Do not reject the null hypothesis.

Test 40   The χ^2-test for consistency in a 2 × 2 table

Object

To investigate the significance of the differences between observed frequencies for two dichotomous distributions.

Limitations

It is necessary that the two sample sizes are large enough. This condition is assumed to be satisfied if the total frequency is $n > 20$ and if all the cell frequencies are greater than 3. When continuous distributions are applied to discrete values one has to apply Yates' correction for small sample sizes.

Method

When two samples are each divided into two classes the following 2 × 2 table can be built up:

	Class 1	Class 2	Total
Sample 1	a	b	$a+b$
Sample 2	c	d	$c+d$
Total	$a+c$	$b+d$	$n = a+b+c+d$

The test statistic is

$$\chi^2 = \frac{(n-1)(ad-bc)^2}{(a+b)(a+c)(b+d)(c+d)}.$$

This is compared with a value obtained from χ^2 tables with 1 degree of freedom. If χ^2 exceeds the critical value the null hypothesis of independence between samples and classes is rejected. In other words, the two samples were not drawn from one common population.

Example data

$a = 15, b = 85, c = 4, d = 77$

$a + b = 100, c + d = 81, a + c = 19, b + d = 162$

$\alpha = 0.10, \nu = 1, \chi^2_{1;0.10} = 2.7, n = 181$ [Table 5]

$$\chi^2 = \frac{180(15 \times 77 - 4 \times 85)^2}{100 \times 81 \times 19 \times 162} = 4.79$$

Hence do not reject the null hypothesis.

Test 41 The χ^2-test for consistency in a $K \times 2$ table

Object

To investigate the significance of the differences between K observed frequency distributions with a dichotomous classification.

Limitations

It is necessary that the K sample sizes are large enough. This is usually assumed to be satisfied if the cell frequencies are equal to 5.

Method

When the observations in K samples are divided into two classes the following $K \times 2$ table can be built up:

	Class 1	Class 2	Total
Sample 1	x_1	$n_1 - x_1$	n_1
$\vdots$	$\vdots$	$\vdots$	$\vdots$
Sample i	x_i	$n_i - x_i$	n_i
$\vdots$	$\vdots$	$\vdots$	$\vdots$
Sample K	x_K	$n_K - x_K$	n_K
Total	$x = \sum_{i=1}^{K} x_i$	$n - x$	$n = \sum_{i=1}^{K} n_i$

The test statistic is

$$\chi^2 = \frac{n^2}{x(n-x)} \left\{ \sum_{i=1}^{K} \frac{x_i^2}{n_i} - \frac{x^2}{n} \right\}.$$

This is compared with a value obtained from χ^2 tables with $K - 1$ degrees of freedom. The null hypothesis of independence between samples and classes is rejected if χ^2 exceeds the critical value.

Example data

$x_{11} = 14, x_{12} = 22, x_{21} = 18, x_{22} = 16, x_{31} = 8, x_{32} = 2$
(Here $x_{i_1} = x_1$ and $x_{i_2} = n_1 - x_1$.)
$n_1 = 36, n_2 = 34, n_3 = 10, n = \sum n_i = 80$
$\alpha = 0.05, \nu = 2, \chi^2_{2;0.05} = 5.99, n = 80, x = 40$ [Table 5]

$$\chi^2 = \frac{80^2}{40 \times 40} \left[\frac{14^2}{36} + \frac{18^2}{34} + \frac{8^2}{10} \right] - \frac{40^2}{80} = 65.495$$

Hence reject the null hypothesis.

Test 42   The Cochran test for consistency in an $n \times K$ table of dichotomous data

Object

To investigate the significance of the differences between K treatments on the same n elements with a binomial distribution.

Limitations

1. It is assumed that there are K series of observations on the same n elements.
2. The observations are dichotomous and the observations in the two classes are represented by 0 or 1.
3. The number of elements must be sufficiently large – say, greater than 10.

Method

From the $n \times K$ table, let R_i denote the row totals $(i = 1, \ldots, n)$ and C_j denote the column totals $(j = 1, \ldots, K)$. Let S denote the total score, i.e. $S = \sum_i R_i = \sum_j C_j$. The test statistic is

$$Q = \frac{K(K-1) \sum_j (C_j - \bar{C})^2}{KS - \sum_i R_i^2} \qquad \text{where } \bar{C} = \frac{\sum_j C_j}{K}.$$

This approximately follows a χ^2-distribution with $K - 1$ degrees of freedom.

The null hypothesis that the K samples come from one common dichotomous distribution is rejected if Q is larger than the tabulated value.

Example data

$K = 4$, $C_1 = 12$, $C_2 = 8$, $C_3 = 6$, $C_4 = 3$, $\sum C_i^2 = 253$

$\sum R_i = 29$, $\bar{C} = 7.25$, $\sum R_i^2 = 75$

$\alpha = 0.05$, $\nu = 3$, $\chi^2_{3;0.05} = 7.81$ [Table 5]

$$Q = \frac{3(4 \times 253 - 29^2)}{4 \times 29 - 75} = \frac{513}{41} = 12.51$$

Hence reject the null hypothesis.

Test 43   The χ^2-test for consistency in a $2 \times K$ table

Object

To investigate the significance of the differences between two distributions based on two samples spread over K classes.

Limitations

1. The two samples are sufficiently large.
2. The K classes when put together form a complete series.

Method

The $2 \times K$ table can be described symbolically by the following table:

	Class						
	1	2	$\cdots$	j	$\cdots$	K	Total
Sample 1	n_{11}	n_{12}	$\cdots$	n_{1j}	$\cdots$	n_{1K}	N_1
Sample 2	n_{21}	n_{22}	$\cdots$	n_{2j}	$\cdots$	n_{2K}	N_2
Total	$n_{.1}$	$n_{.2}$	$\cdots$	$n_{.j}$	$\cdots$	$n_{.K}$	$N_1 + N_2$

where n_{ij} represents the frequency of individuals in the ith sample in the jth class ($i = 1, 2$ and $j = 1, \ldots, K$). Another table of expected frequencies is now calculated where the value in the ith row and jth column is

$$e_{ij} = \frac{N_i n_{.j}}{N_1 + N_2}.$$

The test statistic is

$$\chi^2 = \sum_{j=1}^{K} \frac{(n_{1j} - e_{1j})^2}{e_{1j}} + \sum_{j=1}^{K} \frac{(n_{2j} - e_{2j})^2}{e_{2j}}.$$

This is compared with the value obtained from a χ^2 table with $K - 1$ degrees of freedom. If χ^2 exceeds this critical value, the null hypothesis that the two samples originate from two populations with the same distribution is rejected.

Example data

$n_{11} = 50$, $n_{12} = 47$, $n_{13} = 56$, $n_{21} = 5$, $n_{22} = 14$, $n_{23} = 8$

$n_{.1} = 55$, $n_{.2} = 61$, $n_{.3} = 64$, $N_1 = 153$, $N_2 = 27$, $N = 180$

$e_{11} = 46.75$, $e_{12} = 51.85$, $e_{13} = 54.40$, $e_{21} = 8.25$, $e_{22} = 9.15$, $e_{23} = 9.60$

$\alpha = 0.05$, $\nu = (3 - 1)(2 - 1) = 2$, $\chi^2_{2;0.05} = 5.99$ [Table 5]

$$\chi^2 = \frac{3.25^2}{46.75} + \frac{(-4.85)^2}{51.85} + \frac{1.6^2}{54.40} + \frac{(-3.25)^2}{8.25} + \frac{4.85^2}{9.15} + \frac{(-1.6)^2}{9.60}$$

$$= 4.84$$

Do not reject the null hypothesis.

Test 44   The χ^2-test for independence in a $p \times q$ table

Object

To investigate the difference in frequency when classified by one attribute after classification by a second attribute.

Limitations

The sample should be sufficiently large. This condition will be satisfied if each cell frequency is greater than 5.

Method

The sample, of size N, can be categorized into p classes by the first attribute and into q classes by the second. The frequencies of individuals in each classification can be shown symbolically by the table:

		First attribute						
		1	2	$\cdots$	i	$\cdots$	p	Total
	1	n_{11}	n_{21}	$\cdots$	n_{i1}	$\cdots$	n_{p1}	$n_{.1}$
	2	n_{12}	n_{22}	$\cdots$	n_{i2}	$\cdots$	n_{p2}	$n_{.2}$
	.	.	.		.		.	.
Second attribute	j	n_{1j}	n_{2j}	$\cdots$	n_{ij}	$\cdots$	n_{pj}	$n_{.j}$
	.	.	.		.		.	.
	q	n_{1q}	n_{2q}	$\cdots$	n_{iq}	$\cdots$	n_{pq}	$n_{.q}$
	Total	$n_{1.}$	$n_{2.}$	$\cdots$	$n_{i.}$	$\cdots$	$n_{p.}$	N

The test statistic is

$$\chi^2 = \sum_{i=1}^{p} \sum_{j=1}^{q} \frac{(n_{ij} - n_{i.}n_{.j}/N)^2}{n_{i.}n_{.j}/N}$$

which follows a χ^2 distribution with $(p-1)(q-1)$ degrees of freedom. If χ^2 exceeds the critical value then the null hypothesis that the two attributes are independent of each other is rejected.

Example data

$n_{11} = 32,\ n_{21} = 12,\ n_{12} = 14,\ n_{22} = 22,\ n_{13} = 6,\ n_{23} = 9$

$n_{1.} = 52,\ n_{2.} = 43,\ n_{.1} = 44,\ n_{.2} = 36,\ n_{.3} = 15,\ N = 95$

$\alpha = 0.05,\ \nu = (3-1)(2-1) = 2,\ \chi^2_{2;0.05} = 5.99$ [Table 5]

$$\chi^2 = \frac{7.9^2}{24.1} + \frac{(-7.9)^2}{19.9} + \frac{(-5.7)^2}{19.7} + \frac{5.7^2}{16.3} + \frac{(-2.2)^2}{8.2} + \frac{2.2^2}{6.2} = 10.74$$

Hence reject the null hypothesis.

Test 45   The sign test for a median

Object

To investigate the significance of the difference between a population median and a specified value M_0.

Limitations

It is assumed that the observations in the sample are independent of each other. Any sample values equal to M_0 should be discarded from the sample.

Method

A count is made of the number n_1 of sample values exceeding M_0, and also of the number n_2 below M_0. The null hypothesis is that the population median equals M_0. If the alternative hypothesis is that the population median does not equal M_0 then the test statistic, T, is the smaller of n_1 and n_2 with n taken as the sum of n_1 and n_2.

If the alternative hypothesis is that the population median is less than M_0, then $T = n_1$. If the alternative hypothesis is that the population median is greater than M_0, then $T = n_2$. The null hypothesis is rejected if T is less than the critical value obtained from Table 17.

Example data

Sample values $x_1 = 0.28$, $x_2 = 0.18$, $x_3 = 0.24$, $x_4 = 0.30$, $x_5 = 0.40$
$x_6 = 0.36$, $x_7 = 0.15$, $x_8 = 0.42$, $x_9 = 0.23$, $x_{10} = 0.48$
Null hypothesis: $H_0 = 0.28$
$n_1 = 5$, $n_2 = 4$, $T = 4$, $n = 5 + 4 = 9$
The critical value at $\alpha = 0.05$ is 7 [Table 17].
Hence do not reject the null hypothesis.

Test 46 The sign test for two medians (paired observations)

Object

To investigate the significance of the difference between the medians of two distributions.

Limitations

The observations in the two samples should be taken in pairs, one from each distribution. Each one of a pair of observations should be taken under the same conditions, but it is not necessary that different pairs should be taken under similar conditions.

It is not necessary to take readings provided the sign of the difference between two observations of a pair can be determined.

Method

The signs of the differences between each pair of observations are recorded. The test statistic, r, is the number of times that the least frequent sign occurs. If this is less than the critical value obtained from Table 18 the null hypothesis that the two population medians are equal is rejected.

Example data

x_i	0.19	0.22	0.18	0.17	1.20	0.14	0.09	0.13	0.26	0.66
y_i	0.21	0.27	0.15	0.18	0.40	0.08	0.14	0.28	0.30	0.68
Sign	−	−	+	−	+	+	−	−	−	−

There are 3 plus signs, 7 minus signs, $r = 3$

$n = 10$, $r_{10;0.10} = 1$ [Table 18].

Reject the null hypothesis.

Test 47   The signed rank test for a mean

Object

To investigate the significance of the difference between a population mean and a specified value μ_0.

Limitations

This is a distribution-free test and requires a symmetrical population. The observations must be obtained randomly and independently from a continuous distribution.

Method

From the sample values x_i, determine the differences $x_i - \mu_0$ and arrange them in ascending order irrespective of sign. Sample values equal to $x_i - \mu_0 = 0$ are not included in the analysis.

Rank numbers are now assigned to the differences. Where ties occur among differences, the ranks are averaged among them. Then each rank number is given the sign of the corresponding difference $x_i - \mu_0$.

The sum of the ranks with a positive sign and the sum of the ranks with a negative sign are calculated. The test statistic T is the smaller of these two sums. Critical values of this statistic can be found from Table 17. When the value of T falls in the critical region, the null hypothesis that the population mean is equal to μ_0 is rejected.

Example data

$\mu_0 = 0.28$, $n = 10$, $\alpha = 0.05$, $T_{9;\alpha} = 7$

Here $n = 10 - 1 = 9$ (one zero).

x_i	0.28	0.18	0.24	0.30	0.40	0.36	0.15	0.42	0.23	0.48
$x_i - \mu_0$	0	−0.10	−0.04	+0.02	+0.12	+0.08	−0.13	+0.14	−0.05	+0.20
Signed rank	–	−5	−2	+1	+6	+4	−7	+8	−3	+9

Sum of plus ranks $= 28$, sum of minus ranks $= 17$, $T = 17$

$T > T_{9;\alpha}$ [Table 17].

Hence do not reject the null hypothesis.

Test 48   The signed rank test for two means (paired observations)

Object

To investigate the significance of the difference between the means of two similarly shaped distributions.

Limitations

The observations in the two samples should be taken in pairs, one from each distribution. Each one of a pair of observations should be taken under the same conditions, but it is not necessary that different pairs should be taken under similar conditions. Any pair of observations giving equal values will be ignored in the analysis.

Method

The differences between pairs of observations are formed and these are ranked, irrespective of sign. Where ties occur, the average of the corresponding ranks is used. Then each rank is allocated the sign from the corresponding difference.

The sum of the ranks with a positive sign and the sum of the ranks with a negative sign are calculated. The test statistic T is the smaller of these two sums. Critical values of this statistic can be found from Table 19. When the value of T is less than the critical value, the null hypothesis of equal population means is rejected.

Example data

x_i	1.38	9.69	0.39	1.42	0.54	5.94	0.59	2.67	2.44	0.56	0.69	0.71	0.95	0.50
y_i	1.42	10.37	0.39	1.46	0.55	6.15	0.61	2.69	2.68	0.53	0.72	0.72	0.93	0.53
$x_i - y_i$	−0.04	−0.68	0	−0.04	−0.01	−0.21	−0.02	−0.02	−0.24	+0.03	−0.03	−0.01	+0.02	−0.03
Rank	−9.5	−13	0	−9.5	−1.5	−11	−4	−4	−12	+7	−7	−1.5	+4	−7

Minus signs = 11, plus signs = 2, rank for plus sign = 4 + 7 = 11

$T_{13;0.05} = 17$ [Table 19]

Reject the null hypothesis.

Test 49   The Wilcoxon inversion test (*U*-test)

Object

To test if two random samples could have come from two populations with the same frequency distribution.

Limitations

It is assumed that the two frequency distributions are continuous and that the two samples are random and independent.

Method

Samples of size n_1 and n_2 are taken from the two populations. When the two samples are merged and arranged in ascending order, there will be a number of jumps (or inversions) from one series to the other. The smaller of the number of inversions and the number of non-inversions forms the test statistic, U. The null hypothesis of the same frequency distribution is rejected if U exceeds the critical value obtained from Table 20.

Example data

$n_1 = 5, n_2 = 5, \alpha = 0.05$

x_i	11.79	11.21	13.20	12.66	13.37
y_i	10.34	11.40	10.19	12.10	11.46

Rearrangement gives the following series

10.19, 10.34, <u>11.21</u> , 11.40, 11.46, <u>11.79</u> , 12.10, <u>12.66</u> , <u>13.20</u> , <u>13.37</u>
                  (2)   (4)   (5)   (5)   (5)

where underlined values come from the first row (x_i). Below these underlines, the corresponding number of inversions, i.e. the number of times a y-value comes after an x-value, is given in parentheses.

The number of inversions is $2 + 4 + 5 + 5 + 5 = 21$.

The number of non-inversions is $n_1 n_2 - 21 = 25 - 21 = 4$.

The critical value at $\alpha = 0.05$ is 4 [Table 20].

The sample value of U is equal to the critical value.

The null hypothesis may be rejected; alternatively, the experiment could be repeated by collecting a second set of data.

Test 50   The median test of two populations

Object

To test if two random samples could have come from two populations with the same frequency distribution.

Limitations

The two samples are assumed to be reasonably large.

Method

The median of the combined sample of $n_1 + n_2$ elements is found. Then, for each series in turn, the number of elements above and below this median can be found and entered in a 2×2 table of the form:

	Sample 1	Sample 2	Total
Left of median	a	b	$a+b$
Right of median	c	d	$c+d$
Total	$n_1 = a+c$	$n_2 = b+d$	$N = n_1 + n_2$

The test statistic is

$$\chi^2 = \frac{\{|ad - bc| - \frac{1}{2}N\}^2 N}{(a+b)(a+c)(b+d)(c+d)}.$$

If this value exceeds the critical value obtained from χ^2 tables with one degree of freedom, the null hypothesis of the same frequency distribution is rejected.

Example data

$a = 9, b = 6, c = 6, d = 9$

$a + b = a + c = b + d = c + d = 15$

$n_1 = 15, n_2 = 15, N = 30$

$$\chi^2 = \frac{\{|9^2 - 6^2| - 15\}^2 \times 30}{15 \times 15 \times 15 \times 15} = \frac{8}{15} = 0.53$$

$\chi^2_{1;0.05} = 3.84$ [Table 5]

Do not reject the null hypothesis.

Test 51　The median test of K populations

Object

To test if K random samples could have come from K populations with the same frequency distribution.

Limitations

The K samples are assumed to be reasonably large – say, greater than 5.

Method

The K samples are first amalgamated and treated as a single grand sample, of which the median is found. Then, for each of the K samples, the number of elements above and below this median can be found. These can be arranged in the form of a $2 \times K$ table and then a χ^2-test can be carried out.

| | \multicolumn{5}{c}{Sample} | |
	1	2	$\ldots$	j	$\ldots$	K	Total
Above median	a_{11}	a_{12}	$\ldots$	a_{1j}	$\ldots$	a_{1K}	A
Below median	a_{21}	a_{22}	$\ldots$	a_{2j}	$\ldots$	a_{2K}	B
Total	a_1	a_2	$\ldots$	a_j	$\ldots$	a_K	N

In this table, a_{1j} represents the number of elements above the median and a_{2j} the number of elements below the median in the jth sample ($j = 1, 2, \ldots, K$). Expected frequencies are calculated from

$$e_{1j} = \frac{Aa_j}{N} \qquad \text{and} \qquad e_{2j} = \frac{Ba_j}{N}.$$

The test statistic is

$$\chi^2 = \sum_{j=1}^{K} \frac{(a_{1j} - e_{1j})^2}{e_{1j}} + \sum_{j=1}^{K} \frac{(a_{2j} - e_{2j})^2}{e_{2j}}.$$

This is compared with a critical value from Table 5 with $K - 1$ degrees of freedom. The null hypothesis that the K populations have the same frequency distribution is rejected if χ^2 exceeds the critical value.

Example data

| | \multicolumn{5}{c}{Sample} | |
	1	2	3	4	5	Total
Above median	20	30	25	40	30	145
Below median	25	35	30	45	32	167
Total	45	65	55	85	62	312

$$e_{11} = \frac{145 \times 45}{312} = 20.91 \qquad e_{21} = \frac{167 \times 45}{312} = 24.08$$

$$e_{12} = 30.21 \qquad\qquad e_{22} = 34.79$$

$$e_{13} = 25.56 \qquad\qquad e_{23} = 29.44$$

$$e_{14} = 39.50 \qquad\qquad e_{24} = 45.50$$

$$e_{15} = 28.81 \qquad\qquad e_{25} = 33.19$$

$$\chi^2 = 0.0399 + 0.0014 + 0.0123 + 0.0062 + 0.0488$$
$$+ 0.0346 + 0.0012 + 0.0107 + 0.0054 + 0.0424$$
$$= 0.2029$$

$\chi^2_{4;0.05} = 9.49$ [Table 5]

Hence do not reject the null hypothesis.

Test 52   The Wilcoxon–Mann–Whitney rank sum test of two populations

Object

To test if two random samples could have come from two populations with the same mean.

Limitations

It is assumed that the two populations have continuous frequency distributions with the same shape and spread.

Method

The results of the two samples x and y are combined and arranged in order of increasing size and given a rank number. In cases where equal results occur the mean of the available rank numbers is assigned. The rank sum R of the smaller sample is now found. Let N denote the size of the combined samples and n denote the size of the smaller sample.

A second quantity

$$R^1 = n(N + 1) - R$$

is now calculated. The values R and R^1 are compared with critical values obtained from Table 21. If either R or R^1 is less than the critical value the null hypothesis of equal means would be rejected.

Note   If the samples are of equal size, then the rank sum R is taken as the smaller of the two rank sums which occur.

Example data

											Total
x	50.5	37.5	49.8	56.0	42.0	56.0	50.0	54.0	48.0			
Rank	9	1	7	15.5	2	15.5	8	13	6			77
y	57.0	52.0	51.0	44.2	55.0	62.0	59.0	45.2	53.5	44.4		
Rank	17	11	10	3	14	19	18	5	12	4		113

$R = 77$, $n_1 = 9$, $n_2 = 10$, $N = 19$, $R^1 = 9 \times 20 - 77 = 103$

The critical value at $\alpha = 0.05$ is 69 [Table 21].

Hence there is no difference between the two means.

Test 53   The Siegel–Tukey rank sum dispersion test of two variances

Object

To test if two random samples could have come from two populations with the same variance.

Limitations

It is assumed that the two populations have continuous frequency distributions and that the sample sizes are not too small, e.g. $n_1 + n_2 > 20$.

Method

The results of the two samples are combined and arranged in order of increasing size. Ranks are allocated according to the following scheme:

- The lowest value is ranked 1.
- The highest two values are ranked 2 and 3 (the largest value is given the value 2).
- The lowest two unranked values are ranked 4 and 5 (the smallest value is given the value 4).
- The highest two unranked values are ranked 6 and 7 (the largest value is given the value 6).

This procedure continues, working from the ends towards the centre, until no more than one unranked value remains. That is to say, if the number of values is odd, the middle value has no rank assigned to it.

Let n_1 and n_2 denote the sizes of the two samples and let $n_1 \leqslant n_2$. Let R_1 be the rank sum of the series of size n_1. The test statistic is

$$Z = \frac{R_1 - n_1(n_1 + n_2 + 1)/2 + \frac{1}{2}}{\sqrt{n_1 n_2 (n_1 + n_2 + 1)/12}}.$$

This will approximately follow a standard normal distribution. The null hypothesis of equal variance is rejected if Z falls in the critical region.

Example data

Combined rank assignment of two sample data x, y:

Sample	x	y	y	y	y	y	x	x	y	x
Value	2.4	2.9	3.3	3.6	4.2	4.9	6.1	7.3	7.3	8.5
Rank	1	4	5	8	9	12	13	16	17	20

Sample	x	x	x	x	x	y	x	y	y	y
Value	8.8	9.4	9.8	10.1	10.1	11.7	12.6	13.1	15.3	16.5
Rank	19	18	15	14	11	10	7	6	3	2

$n_1 = n_2 = 10$

$R_x = 1 + 13 + 16 + 20 + 19 + 18 + 15 + 14 + 11 + 7 = 134$

$R_y = 4 + 5 + 8 + 9 + 12 + 17 + 10 + 6 + 3 + 2 = 76$

Hence $R_1 = 76$

$$Z = \frac{76 - 10(10 + 10 + 1)/2 + \frac{1}{2}}{\sqrt{10.10(10 + 10 + 1)/12}} = \frac{-28.5}{\sqrt{175}} = \frac{-28.5}{13.23} = -2.154$$

The critical values at $\alpha = 0.05$ are -1.96 and $+1.96$ [Table 1]. Hence reject the null hypothesis.

Test 54 The Kruskall–Wallis rank sum test of K populations (H-test)

Object

To test if K random samples could have come from K populations with the same mean.

Limitations

Each sample size should be at least 5 in order for χ^2 to be used, though sample sizes need not be equal. The K frequency distributions should be continuous.

Method

The K samples are combined and arranged in order of increasing size and given a rank number. Where ties occur the mean of the available rank numbers is used. The rank sum for each of the K samples is calculated.

Let R_j be the rank sum of the jth sample, n_j be the size of the jth sample, and N be the size of the combined sample. The test statistic is

$$H = \left\{ \frac{12}{N(N+1)} \sum_{j=1}^{K} \frac{R_j^2}{n_j} \right\} - 3(N+1).$$

This follows a χ^2-distribution with $K - 1$ degrees of freedom. The null hypothesis of equal means is rejected when H exceeds the critical value. Critical values for H for small sample sizes and $K = 3$, 4, 5 are given in Table 22.

Example data

Combined rank assignment of three sample data x_1, x_2, x_3:

Sample	x_1	x_1	x_1	x_1	x_1	x_1	x_1	x_1	x_1	x_2
Value	1.7	1.9	6.1	12.5	16.5	25.1	30.5	42.1	82.5	13.6
Rank	1	2	3	4	7	10.5	14	15	20	6

Sample	x_2	x_2	x_2	x_2	x_2	x_3	x_3	x_3	x_3	x_3
Value	19.8	25.2	46.2	46.2	61.1	13.4	20.9	25.1	29.7	46.9
Rank	8	12	16.5	16.5	19	5	9	10.5	13	18

$R_1 = 76.5$, $R_2 = 78.0$, $R_3 = 55.5$

$H = \dfrac{12}{420} (2280.30) - 63 = 2.15$, $\chi^2_{2;0.10} = 4.61$ [Table 5].

Do not reject the hypothesis.

Test 55   The rank sum difference test for the multiple comparison of K population means

Object

To test if K random samples came from populations with the same mean.

Limitations

The K samples must have the same size, and the frequency distributions of the population are assumed continuous.

Method

The K samples are combined and arranged in order of increasing size and then given a rank number. The highest raw value is assigned rank 1. For each sample the rank sum is determined.

To compare two population means the rank sums of the corresponding samples, R_i and R_j, are taken and the test statistic is $R_i - R_j$. Critical values of this test statistic can be obtained from Table 23. When $R_i - R_j$ exceeds the critical value the null hypothesis of equal means is rejected.

Example data

		Sample	
1	2	3	4
70 (16)	12 (2)	10 (1)	29 (6)
52 (14)	18 (3)	43 (11)	31 (7)
51 (13)	35 (8)	28 (5)	41 (10)
67 (15)	36 (9)	26 (4)	44 (12)
$R_1 = 58$	$R_2 = 22$	$R_3 = 21$	$R_4 = 35$

$n = 4, K = 4$

The values in the brackets are the assigned rank numbers.

Here
$$R_1 - R_2 = 58 - 22 = 36 \qquad R_2 - R_3 = 22 - 21 = 1$$
$$R_1 - R_3 = 58 - 21 = 37 \qquad R_2 - R_4 = 22 - 35 = -13$$
$$R_1 - R_4 = 58 - 35 = 23 \qquad R_3 - R_4 = 21 - 35 = -14$$

The critical value at $\alpha = 0.05$ is 34.6 [Table 23].

Hence samples 1 and 2 and samples 1 and 3 are significantly different.

Test 56 The rank sum maximum test for the largest K population means

Object

To investigate the difference between the largest mean and the $K - 1$ other population means.

Limitations

It is assumed that the populations have continuous frequency distributions and that the K samples are of equal size n.

Method

The K samples are merged together and rank numbers allocated to the Kn observations. The sum of the rank numbers of the observations belonging to a particular sample is formed. This is repeated for each sample and the test statistic is the largest of these rank sums. When the test statistic exceeds the critical value obtained from Table 24 the mean of the population generating the maximum rank sum is said to be significantly large.

Example data

Combined rank assignment of four samples, i.e. $K = 4$, $n = 4$.

Sample	x_1	x_1	x_1	x_1	x_2	x_2	x_2	x_2	x_3	x_3	x_3	x_3	x_4	x_4	x_4	x_4
Value	70	52	51	67	12	18	35	36	10	43	28	26	29	31	41	44
Rank	16	14	13	15	2	3	8	9	1	11	5	4	6	7	10	12

$R_1 = 58$, $R_2 = 22$, $R_3 = 21$, $R_4 = 35$

The critical value at $\alpha = 0.05$ is 52 [Table 24].

The calculated value of R_1 is greater than the critical value.

Hence the sample 1 is statistically significantly greater than the others.

Test 57   The Steel test for comparing K treatments with a control

Object

To test the null hypothesis that all treatments have the same effect as the control treatment.

Limitations

The $K + 1$ samples, one from each treatment and one from the control, should all be of the same size.

Method

Each of the treatment samples is compared with the control sample in turn. To test the jth sample, it is merged with the control sample and rank numbers are allocated to the $2n$ observations. This provides two rank sums and the smallest of these is used as the test statistic if a two-tailed test is desired. To test the alternative hypothesis that treatment j has a smaller effect than the control treatment, the rank sum for the jth sample forms the test statistic. In both cases, the null hypothesis that there is no difference between the jth treatment and the control is rejected if the test statistic is less than the critical value obtained from Table 25.

Example data

$n = 10$, $K = 24$

Rank assignment and rank sums are as follows:

											Total
Control 1	1.5	1.5	3	4	6	7	8	11	13	14.5	69.5
Treatment 1	5	9	10	12	14.5	16	17	18	19	20	140.5
Control 2	2.5	2.5	5	7	8	9	12	15	18	19	98
Treatment 2	1	4	6	10.5	10.5	13	15	15	17	20	112
Control 3	1.5	1.5	3	5	8	9	10.5	14	15	18	85.5
Treatment 3	4	6.5	6.5	10.5	12	13	16.5	16.5	19	20	124.5
Control 4	1.5	1.5	3	5	6	7	9	12	15	16	76
Treatment 4	4	8	10	12	13	14	17	18	19	20	134

The critical value at $\alpha = 0.05$ is 76 [Table 25].

Since control 1 and control 4 are less than or equal to the critical value, treatments 1 and 4 are significant.

Test 58   The Spearman rank correlation test (paired observations)

Object

To investigate the significance of the correlation between two series of observations obtained in pairs.

Limitations

It is assumed that the two population distributions are continuous and that the observations x_i and y_i have been obtained in pairs.

Method

The x_i observations are assigned the rank numbers 1, 2, ..., n in order of increasing magnitude. A similar procedure is carried out for all the y_i observations. For each pair of observations, the difference in the ranks, d_i, can be determined. The quantity $R = \sum_{i=1}^{n} d_i^2$ is now calculated.

For large samples ($n > 10$) the test statistic is

$$Z = \frac{6R - n(n^2 - 1)}{n(n+1)\sqrt{(n-1)}}$$

which may be compared with tables of the standard normal distribution. For small samples, the test statistic

$$r_S = 1 - \frac{6R}{n(n^2 - 1)}$$

must be compared with critical values obtained from Table 26. In both cases, if the experimental value lies in the critical region one has to reject the null hypothesis of no correlation between the two series.

Example data

d_i: $0, -1, -2, 0, +3, -1, -1, +2, 0, 0, 2$

Hence $R = 24$, $n = 11$

$$Z = \frac{6 \times 24 - 11(11^2 - 1)}{11 \times 12\sqrt{10}} = \frac{144 - 1320}{132 \times 3.1623} = \frac{-1176}{417.42} = -2.81$$

The critical value of Z at $\alpha = 0.05$ is 1.64 [Table 1].

Hence reject the null hypothesis.

Test 59   The Kendall rank correlation test (paired observations)

Object

To investigate the significance of the correlation between two series of observations obtained in pairs.

Limitations

It is assumed that the two population distributions are continuous and that the observations x_i and y_i have been obtained in pairs.

Method

The x_i observations are assigned the rank numbers 1, 2, ..., n in order of increasing magnitude. A similar procedure is carried out for all the y_i observations. Each of the possible pairs of rank numbers (there will be $\frac{1}{2}n(n-1)$ of these) is now examined. Each pair (x_i, y_i) will be compared successively and systematically with each other pair (x_j, y_j). When $x_i - x_j$ and $y_i - y_j$ have the same sign a score of $+1$ is obtained. When they have opposite signs a score of -1 is obtained. When there is a difference of zero, no score is obtained. These scores are summed together and this sum is denoted S. In this manner we can work with observational results without having determined the rank numbers.

For large n ($n > 10$), Z follows a normal distribution and hence the test statistic

$$Z = \frac{S}{\{n(n-1)(2n+5)/18\}^{\frac{1}{2}}}$$

may be compared with tables of the standard normal distribution. For small samples, critical values of S may be obtained from Table 27.

In both cases, if the experimental value lies in the critical region one has to reject the null hypothesis of no correlation between the two series.

Example data

Observation 1	7.1	8.3	10.7	9.4	12.6	11.1	10.3	13.1	9.6	12.4
Observation 2	62	66	74	74	82	76	72	79	68	74
Plus scores	9	8	5	3	4	3	3	2	1	0
Minus scores	0	0	0	2	1	1	1	0	0	0

Total plus scores = 38, total minus scores = 5

$S = 38 - 5 = 33$, $n = 10$

Critical value $S_{10;0.05} = 21$ [Table 27].

The calculated value is greater than the critical value.

Reject the null hypothesis.

Test 60   The sequential test for a population mean (variance known)

Object

To test the null hypothesis that the mean μ of a population with known variance has the value μ_0 rather than the value μ_1.

Limitations

1. The observations can be obtained sequentially as necessary.
2. The observations are independent and follow a normal distribution with known variance σ^2.

Method

First the Type I and Type II errors for the test must be fixed, say, α and β. The test consists of plotting a sequential analysis chart. In this case, as the observations are obtained the cumulative value $\sum_{i=1}^{m}(x_i - c)$ is plotted against the sample size to date, m. The constant c is chosen as a convenient value close to $\frac{1}{2}(\mu_0 + \mu_1)$.

On the chart are two boundary lines:

$$\sum_{i=1}^{m}(x_i - c) = \frac{\sigma^2}{\mu_1 - \mu_0}\log\left(\frac{1-\beta}{\alpha}\right) + m\left(\frac{\mu_0 + \mu_1}{2} - c\right),$$

$$\sum_{i=1}^{m}(x_i - c) = \frac{\sigma^2}{\mu_1 - \mu_0}\log\left(\frac{\beta}{1-\alpha}\right) + m\left(\frac{\mu_0 + \mu_1}{2} - c\right).$$

If the plot crosses the upper boundary the null hypothesis is rejected, and it will not be rejected if the plot crosses the lower boundary.

Example data

Successive observations: 8.34, 8.29, 8.30, 8.31, 8.30, 8.32, 8.30

$\mu_0 = 8.30$, $\mu_1 = 8.33$, $\alpha = 0.05$, $\beta = 0.05$

$\mu_1 - \mu_0 = 8.33 - 8.30 = 0.03$, $\bar{\mu} = 8.315$

Let the standard deviation be 0.02.

$$\frac{\sigma^2}{\mu_1 - \mu_0}\log\left(\frac{\beta}{1-\alpha}\right) = \frac{0.02^2}{0.03} \times \log\left(\frac{0.05}{0.95}\right) = -0.039$$

$$\frac{\sigma^2}{\mu_1 - \mu_0}\log\left(\frac{1-\beta}{\alpha}\right) = +0.039$$

Critical boundary lines are

$$\sum x_i = -0.039 + 8.315m \quad \text{or} \quad \sum x_i' = -0.039 + 0.015m$$

and

$$\sum x_i = 0.039 - 8.315m \quad \text{or} \quad \sum x_i' = 0.039 + 0.015m$$

m	1	2	3	4	5	6	7	8	9	10
x_i'	0.04	−0.01	0.00	0.01	0.00	+0.02	0.00			
cu sum	0.04	0.03	0.03	0.04	0.04	0.06	0.06			
H_0 boundary	−0.024	−0.009	0.006	0.021	0.036	0.051	0.066	0.081	0.096	0.111
H_1 boundary	0.054	0.069	0.084	0.099	0.114	0.129	0.144	0.159	0.174	0.189

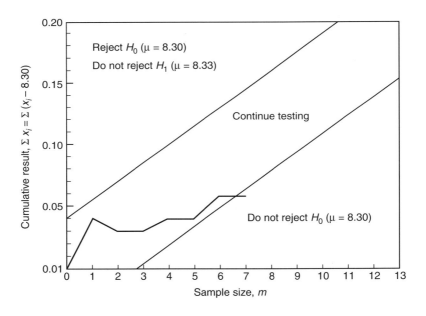

Test 61   The sequential test for a standard deviation (mean known)

Object

To test the null hypothesis that the standard deviation σ, of a population with known mean, has the value σ_0 rather than the value σ_1.

Limitations

1. The observations can be obtained sequentially as necessary.
2. The observations are independent and come from a normal distribution with known mean μ.

Method

First the Type I and Type II errors for the test must be decided upon, say, α and β. The test consists of plotting a sequential analysis chart. As the observations are obtained the cumulative value $\sum_{i=1}^{m}(x_i - \mu)^2$ is plotted against the sample size to date, m.

On the chart are two boundary lines:

$$\sum_{i=1}^{m}(x_i - \mu)^2 = \frac{2\sigma_0^2\sigma_1^2}{\sigma_1^2 - \sigma_0^2}\log\left(\frac{1-\beta}{\alpha}\right) - m\frac{2\sigma_0^2\sigma_1^2}{\sigma_1^2 - \sigma_0^2}\log\left(\frac{\sigma_0}{\sigma_1}\right),$$

$$\sum_{i=1}^{m}(x_i - \mu)^2 = \frac{2\sigma_0^2\sigma_1^2}{\sigma_1^2 - \sigma_0^2}\log\left(\frac{\beta}{1-\alpha}\right) - m\frac{2\sigma_0^2\sigma_1^2}{\sigma_1^2 - \sigma_0^2}\log\left(\frac{\sigma_0}{\sigma_1}\right).$$

If the plot crosses the upper boundary, the null hypothesis is rejected; if the plot crosses the lower boundary, the null hypothesis is not rejected.

Example data

Consider a sample from $N(2, \sigma^2)$ and
$H_0: \sigma^2 = 4$ against $H_1: \sigma^2 = 6$.
Let $\alpha = 0.15$, $\beta = 0.25$ and $m = 10$.
Then continue sampling if

$$\frac{24\left[2\log\left(\frac{0.25}{0.85}\right) + 10\log\left(\frac{16}{4}\right)\right]}{6-4}$$

$$< \sum_{i=1}^{m}(x_i - 2)^2 < \frac{24\left[2\log\left(\frac{0.75}{0.15}\right) + 10\log\left(\frac{6}{4}\right)\right]}{6-4}$$

$$\frac{24[-1.22 + 4.05]}{2} < \sum_{i=1}^{m}(x_i - 2)^2 < \frac{24[3.22 + 4.05]}{2}$$

or

$$33.96 < \sum_{i=1}^{m}(x_i - 2)^2 < 87.24$$

Hence do not reject H_0 if $\sum_{i=1}^{m}(x_i - 2)^2 \leqslant 33.96$ and reject H_0 if $\sum_{i=1}^{m}(x_i - 2)^2 \geqslant 87.24$.

Test 62   The sequential test for a dichotomous classification

Object

To test the null hypothesis that the parameter p of a population has the value p_0 rather than the value p_1.

Limitations

1. The observations can be obtained sequentially as necessary.
2. The observations are independent and follow a Bernoulli distribution.

Method

This test is typically used in quality control when we wish to determine if the proportion defective in a sample falls below p_0 (accept batch) or exceeds p_1 (reject batch). First we need to decide on the Type I and Type II errors for the test, say α and β.

The test consists of plotting a sequential analysis chart. As the observations are obtained the number of defective items r_m is plotted against the sample size to date, m. On the chart are two boundary lines:

$$r_m \left\{ \log\left(\frac{p_1}{p_0}\right) - \log\left(\frac{1-p_1}{1-p_0}\right) \right\} + m \log\left(\frac{1-p_1}{1-p_0}\right) = \log\left(\frac{\beta}{1-\alpha}\right)$$

$$r_m \left\{ \log\left(\frac{p_1}{p_0}\right) - \log\left(\frac{1-p_1}{1-p_0}\right) \right\} + m \log\left(\frac{1-p_1}{1-p_0}\right) = \log\left(\frac{1-\beta}{\alpha}\right).$$

If the plot crosses the upper boundary the null hypothesis is rejected; if the plot crosses the lower boundary the null hypothesis is not rejected.

Example data

H_0: $p = p_0 = 0.10$ and H_1: $p = p_1 = 0.20$
Let $\alpha = 0.01$ and $\beta = 0.05$, and results are:

$a, a, a, r, a, r, a, a, r, a, a, a, r, r, a, r, r, a, r$

(where a = not defective and r = defective).
Then

$$\log\left(\frac{p_1}{p_0}\right) = \log\left(\frac{0.20}{0.10}\right) = 0.693$$

$$\log\left(\frac{1-p_1}{1-p_0}\right) = \log\left(\frac{0.80}{0.90}\right) = -0.118$$

$$\log\left(\frac{\beta}{1-\alpha}\right) = \log\left(\frac{0.05}{0.99}\right) = -2.986$$

$$\log\left(\frac{1-\beta}{\alpha}\right) = \log\left(\frac{0.95}{0.01}\right) = 4.554$$

Boundary lines are:

$0.811r_m - 0.118m = -2.986$

$0.811r_m - 0.118m = 4.554.$

If $m = 0$, the two boundary lines are $r_{m_1} = -3.68$ and $r_{m_2} = 0.562$.

If $m = 30$, the two boundary lines are $r_{m_1} = 0.68$ and $r_{m_2} = 9.98$.

The first line intersects the m-axis at $m = 25.31$. The sequential analysis chart is now as follows:

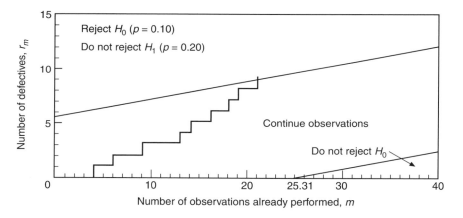

After the 21st observation we can conclude that the alternative hypothesis H_1 may not be rejected. This means that $p \geqslant 0.20$. The percentage of defective elements is too large. The whole lot has to be rejected.

Test 63   The adjacency test for randomness of fluctuations

Object

To test the null hypothesis that the fluctuations in a series are random in nature.

Limitations

It is assumed that the observations are obtained independently of each other and under similar conditions.

Method

For a series of n terms, x_i $(i = 1, \ldots, n)$, the test statistic is defined as

$$L = 1 - \frac{\sum_{i=1}^{n-1}(x_{i+1} - x_i)^2}{2\sum_{i=1}^{n}(x_i - \bar{x})^2}.$$

For $n > 25$, this approximately follows a normal distribution with mean zero and variance

$$\sqrt{\frac{(n-2)}{(n-1)(n+1)}}.$$

For $n < 25$, critical values for

$$D = \frac{\sum_{i=1}^{n-1}(x_{i+1} - x_i)^2}{\sum_{i=1}^{n}(x_i - \bar{x})^2}$$

are available in Table 28.

In both cases the null hypothesis is rejected if L exceeds the critical values.

Example data

$$\sum x_i = 2081.94, \quad \sum x_i^2 = 166\,736.9454$$

$$\sum_{i=1}^{n}(x_i - \bar{x})^2 = 26.4006, \quad \sum_{i=1}^{n-1}(x_{i+1} - x_i)^2 = 31.7348, \quad n = 25$$

$$D = \frac{\sum_{i=1}^{n-1}(x_{i+1} - x_i)^2}{\sum_{i=1}^{n}(x_i - \bar{x})^2} = \frac{31.7348}{26.4006} = 1.20$$

The critical values at $\alpha = 0.05$ are 1.37 (lower limit) and 2.63 (upper limit) [Table 28].

The calculated value is less than the lower limit.

Hence the null hypothesis is to be rejected.

Test 64 The serial correlation test for randomness of fluctuations

Object

To test the null hypothesis that the fluctuations in a series have a random nature.

Limitations

It is assumed that the observations are obtained independently of each other and under similar conditions.

Method

The first serial correlation coefficient for a series of n terms, x_i ($i = 1, \ldots, n$), is defined as

$$r_1 = \frac{n}{n-1} \left\{ \frac{\sum_{i=1}^{n-1} (x_i - \bar{x})(x_{i+1} - \bar{x})}{\sum_{i=1}^{n} (x_i - \bar{x})^2} \right\}$$

and this forms the test statistic.

For $n \leqslant 30$, critical values for r_1 can be found from Table 29. For $n > 30$, the normal distribution provides a reasonable approximation. In both cases the null hypothesis is rejected if the test statistic exceeds the critical values.

Example data

x_i: 69.76, 67.88, 68.28, 68.48, 70.15, 71.25, 69.24, 71.82, 71.27, 68.79,
    68.89, 69.24, 69.86, 68.35, 67.61, 67.64, 68.06, 68.72, 69.37, 68.18
    69.35, 69.72, 70.46, 70.94, 69.26, 70.20

$n = 26$, $\sum x_i = 1804.38$, $\bar{x} = 69.40$, $\sum (x_i - \bar{x})^2 = 34.169$

$\sum x_{i+1} \cdot x_i = 125\,242.565$, $\sum x_{i+1} \cdot x_i - (\sum x_i)^2/n = 19.981$

$$r_1 = \frac{19.981}{34.169} = 0.585$$

The critical value at $\alpha = 0.05$ is about 0.276 [Table 29].

Hence the null hypothesis is rejected; the correlation between successive observations is significant.

Test 65   The turning point test for randomness of fluctuations

Object

To test the null hypothesis that the variations in a series are independent of the order of the observations.

Limitations

It is assumed that the number of observations, n, is greater than 15, and the observations are made under similar conditions.

Method

The number of turning points, i.e. peaks and troughs, in the series is determined and this value forms the test statistic. For large n, it may be assumed to follow a normal distribution with mean $\frac{2}{3}(n-2)$ and variance $(16n - 29)/90$. If the test statistic exceeds the critical value, the null hypothesis is rejected.

Example data

p = peak, t = trough, $n = 19$, $\alpha = 0.05$

0.68;   0.34(t);   0.62;   0.73(p); 0.57;
0.32(t); 0.58(p); 0.34(t); 0.59(p); 0.56;
0.49;   0.17(t);   0.30;   0.39;   0.42(p);
0.41(t); 0.46;   0.50

Mean $= \frac{2}{3} \times 17 = 11.3$, variance $= \dfrac{16 \times 19 - 29}{90} = 3.05$,

standard deviation $= 1.75$

Test statistic $= \left| \dfrac{9 - 11.3}{1.75} \right| = 1.31$

The critical value at $\alpha = 0.05$ is 1.96 [Table 1].

Hence the departure from randomness is not significant.

Test 66   The difference sign test for randomness in a sample

Object

To test the null hypothesis that the fluctuations of a sample are independent of the order in the sequence.

Limitations

It is assumed that the number of observations is large and that they have been obtained under similar conditions.

Method

From the sequence of observations a sequence of successive differences is formed. The number of + signs, p, in this derived sequence forms the test statistic.

Let n be the initial sample size. For large n, p may be assumed to follow a normal distribution with mean $(n - 1)/2$ and variance $(n + 1)/12$. When the test statistic lies in the critical region the null hypothesis is rejected.

Example data

$n = 20$, $\alpha = 0.05$

List	S_1	S_2	S_3	S_4	S_5
p	16	11	10	9	10

$$\text{Mean} = \frac{n - 1}{2} = \frac{19}{2} = 9.5, \quad \text{variance} = \frac{20 + 1}{12} = 1.75,$$

standard deviation $= 1.32$

$$p(S_1) = \frac{16 - 9.5 - 0.5}{1.32} = 4.54$$

The critical value at $\alpha = 0.05$ is 1.64 [Table 1].

Reject the null hypothesis in this case.

However, $p(S_2) = 0.76$, $p(S_3) = 0.0$, $p(S_4) = -0.76$, $p(S_5) = 0$.

Do not reject the null hypothesis in these cases, where a positive trend is indicated.

Test 67   The run test on successive differences for randomness in a sample

Object

To test the null hypothesis that observations in a sample are independent of the order in the sequence.

Limitations

It is necessary that the observations in the sample be obtained under similar conditions.

Method

From the sequence of observations, a sequence of successive differences is formed, i.e. each observation has the preceding one subtracted from it. The number of runs of $+$ and $-$ signs in this sequence of differences, K, provides the test statistic.

Let n be the initial sample size. For $5 \leqslant n \leqslant 40$, critical values of K can be obtained from Table 30. For $n > 40$, K may be assumed to follow a normal distribution with mean $(2n - 1)/3$ and variance $(16n - 29)/90$. In both cases, when the test statistic lies in the critical region, the null hypothesis is rejected.

Example data

Lists	A	B	C	D	E
Number (K) of runs (plus and minus)	7	12	6	19	12

$n = 20$, $\alpha = 0.05$

The critical values are (left) 9 and (right) 17 [Table 30].

For cases A, C and D

$K(A) = 7$ and $K(C) = 6$, which are less than 9, and $K(D) = 19$ which is greater than 17.

Hence reject the null hypothesis.

For cases B and E

Test statistics do not lie in the critical region [Table 30].

Do not reject the null hypothesis.

Test 68   The run test for randomness of two related samples

Object

To test the null hypothesis that the two samples have been randomly selected from the same population.

Limitations

It is assumed that the two samples have been taken under similar conditions and that the observations are independent of each other.

Method

The first sample of n_1 elements are all given a $+$ sign and the second sample of n_2 elements are all given a $-$ sign. The two samples are then merged and arranged in increasing order of magnitude (the allocated signs are to differentiate between the two samples and do not affect their magnitudes). A succession of values with the same sign, i.e. from the same sample, is called a run. The number of runs (K) of the combined samples is found and is used to calculate the test statistic, Z. For n_1 and $n_2 \geqslant 10$,

$$Z = \frac{K - \mu_K + \frac{1}{2}}{\sigma_K}$$

can be compared with the standard normal distribution: here

$$\mu_K = \frac{2n_1 n_2}{n_1 + n_2} + 1 \text{ and } \sigma_K^2 = \frac{2n_1 n_2(2n_1 n_2 - n_1 - n_2)}{(n_1 + n_2)^2 \cdot (n_1 + n_2 - 1)}.$$

When the test statistic lies in the critical region, reject the null hypothesis.

Example data

$n_1 = 10$, $n_2 = 10$, $K = 11$, $\alpha = 0.05$
Sample S_1: 26.3, 28.6, 25.4, 29.2, 27.6, 25.6, 26.4, 27.7, 28.2, 29.0
Sample S_2: 28.5, 30.0, 28.8, 25.3, 28.4, 26.5, 27.2, 29.3, 26.2, 27.5
S_1 and S_2 are merged and arranged in increasing order of magnitude, and signs are allocated to obtain the number of runs K:

$$- + + - + + - - - + + + - - + - + + - -$$

$$\mu_K = \frac{2 \times 10 \times 10}{10 + 10} + 1 = \frac{200}{20} + 1 = 11$$

$$\sigma_K^2 = \frac{2 \times 10 \times 10(2 \times 10 \times 10 - 10 - 10)}{(10 + 10)^2(10 + 10 - 1)} = 4.74, \ \sigma_K = 2.18$$

$$Z = \frac{11 - 11 + \frac{1}{2}}{2.17} = 0.23. \text{ Critical value at } \alpha = 0.05 \text{ is } 1.96 \text{ [Table 1]}.$$

Hence do not reject the hypothesis.

Test 69   The run test for randomness in a sample

Object

To test the significance of the order of the observations in a sample.

Limitations

It is necessary that the observations in the sample be obtained under similar conditions.

Method

All the observations in the sample larger than the median value are given a $+$ sign and those below the median are given a $-$ sign. If there is an odd number of observations then the median observation is ignored. This ensures that the number of $+$ signs (n) is equal to the number of $-$ signs. A succession of values with the same sign is called a run and the number of runs, K, of the sample in the order of selection is found. This forms the test statistic.

For $n > 30$, this test statistic can be compared with a normal distribution with mean $n + 1$ and variance $\frac{1}{2}n(2n - 2)/(2n - 1)$. The test may be one- or two-tailed depending on whether we wish to test if K is too high, too low or possibly both.

For $n < 30$, critical values for K are provided in Table 31. In both cases the null hypothesis that the observations in the sample occurred in a random order is rejected if the test statistic lies in the critical region.

Example data

$n_1 = n_2 = 13$

Sample A

81.02, 80.08, 80.05, 79.70, 79.13, 77.09, 80.09

(+)   (−)   (−)   (−)   (−)   (−)   (−)

79.40, 80.56, 80.97, 80.17, 81.35, 79.64, 80.82, 81.26

(−)   (+)   (+)   (+)   (+)   (−)   (+)   (+)

80.75, 80.74, 81.59, 80.14, 80.75, 81.01, 79.09,

(+)   (+)   (+)   (+)   (+)   (+)   (−)

78.73, 78.45, 79.56, 79.80

(−)   (−)   (−)   (−)

Median value = 80.12 and number of runs = 6.

Sample B

69.76, 67.88, 68.28, 68.48, 70.15, 71.25, 69.94,

(+) (−) (−) (−) (+) (+) (+)

71.82, 71.27, 69.70, 68.89, 69.24, 69.86, 68.35,

(+) (+) (+) (−) (−) (+) (−)

67.61, 67.64, 68.06, 68.72, 69.37, 68.18, 69.35,

(−) (−) (−) (−) (+) (−) (−)

69.72, 70.46, 70.94, 69.26, 70.20

(+) (+) (+) (−) (+)

Median value $= 69.36$ and number of runs $= 11$.

The critical values at $\alpha = 0.10$ are (lower) 9 and (upper) 19 [Table 31].

For Sample A number of runs $K = 6$ lies in the critical region. Hence reject the null hypothesis (i.e. the fluctuation is not random).

For Sample B number of runs $K = 11$ does not lie in the critical region.

Do not reject the null hypothesis (i.e. the fluctuation may be considered to be random).

Test 70 The Wilcoxon–Mann–Whitney rank sum test for the randomness of signs

Object

To test that the occurrence of $+$ and $-$ signs in a sequence is random.

Limitations

This is a distribution-free test, applicable if the observations are random and independent and the two frequency distributions are continuous.

Method

Let n_1 be the number of $+$ or $-$ signs, whichever is the larger, n_2 be the number of opposite signs, and $N = n_1 + n_2$. From the integers describing the natural order of the signs, the rank sum R of the smallest number of signs is determined. The value $R' = n_2(N + 1) - R$ is calculated. The smaller of R and R' is used as the test statistic. If it is less than the critical value obtained from Table 21 the null hypothesis of random $+$ and $-$ signs is rejected.

Example data

Successive observations in a sequence are coded with a plus or minus sign:

1 2 3 4   5 6 7   8 9 10 11 12 13 14
+ + + − + + + + − − − + − −

$n_1 = 8$, $n_2 = 6$ (minus signs), $N = 14$

Rank sum of minus signs $= 4 + 9 + 10 + 11 + 13 + 14 = 61$
$R' = 6(14 + 1) - 61 = 29$

The critical value at $\alpha = 0.025$ is 29 [Table 21].

Reject the null hypothesis; alternatively, the experiment could be repeated.

Test 71   The rank correlation test for randomness of a sample

Object

To test that the fluctuations in a sample have a random nature. This test may be used to test the elements of a time series for the presence of a trend.

Limitations

This is a distribution-free test, applicable if the observations occur in a natural sequence and have been obtained under similar or comparable conditions. It is sensitive to the occurrence of a positive or negative trend, and relatively insensitive to the occurrence of sudden jumps.

Method

The observations are ranked in increasing order of magnitude R_i. The correlation between these rank and the integers representing the natural order of the observations is then calculated. This can be tested using the Spearman rank correlation test (Test 58) or the Kendall rank correlation test (Test 59).

Example data

Order (x_i)	1	2	3	4	5	6	7	8	9	10
Obs.	98	101	110	105	99	106	104	109	100	102
Rank (y_i)	1	4	10	7	2	8	6	9	3	5

Order (x_i)	11	12	13	14	15	16	17	18	19	20
Obs.	119	123	118	116	122	130	115	124	127	114
Rank (y_i)	15	17	14	13	16	20	12	18	19	11

$$\sum (x_i - y_i)^2 = 304 = R$$

$$r_R = 1 - \frac{6R}{n(n^2 - 1)} = 0.771$$

$$T = \frac{6R - n(n^2 - 1)}{n(n + 1)\sqrt{n - 1}} = 3.36$$

The critical value at $\alpha = 0.05$ is 1.96 [Table 1].

The calculated value is greater than the critical value.

Reject the null hypothesis.

Test 72   The Wilcoxon–Wilcox test for comparison of multiple treatments of a series of subjects

Object

To compare the significance of the difference in response for K treatments applied to n subjects.

Limitations

It is assumed that a subject's response to one treatment is not affected by the same subject's response to another treatment; and that the response distribution for each subject is continuous.

Method

The data are represented by a table of n rows and K columns. The rank numbers 1, 2, ..., K are assigned to each row and then the sum of the rank numbers for each column, R_j $(j = 1, 2, \ldots, K)$ is determined. A pair of treatments, say p and q, can now be compared by using as test statistic $|R_p - R_q|$. If this exceeds the critical value obtained from Table 32 the null hypothesis of equal effects of the p and q treatments is rejected.

Example data

			Rank sums						Rank sum differences $|R_p - R_q|$				
			Sample						D	B	C	E	F
Serial no.	A	B	C	D	E	F							
								A 8	2	15	17	19*	25*
1	1	5	3	2	4	6		D 10		13	15	17	23*
2	1	3	6	2	4	5		B 23			2	4	10
3	2	3	4	1	5	6		C 25				2	8
4	1	4	3	2	6	5		E 27					6
5	2	5	3	1	4	6							
6	1	3	6	2	4	5		*Exceeds critical value.					
Rank sum	8	23	25	10	27	33							

$K = 6$, $n = 6$, $\alpha = 0.05$, critical value $= 18.5$ [Table 32].

Test 73 Friedman's test for multiple treatment of a series of subjects

Object

To investigate the significance of the differences in response for K treatments applied to n subjects.

Limitations

It is assumed that a subject's response to one treatment is not affected by the same subject's response to another treatment; and that the response distribution for each subject is continuous.

Method

The data can be represented by a table of n rows and K columns. In each row the rank numbers $1, 2, \ldots, K$ are assigned in order of increasing value. For each of the K columns the rank sum R_j $(j = 1, 2, \ldots, K)$ is determined.

The test statistic is

$$G = \frac{12}{nK(K+1)} \sum_{j=1}^{K} R_j^2 - 3n(K+1).$$

If this exceeds the critical χ^2 value obtained from Table 5 with $K - 1$ degrees of freedom, the null hypothesis that the effects of the K treatments are all the same is rejected.

If ties occur in the ranking procedure one has to assign the average rank member for each series of equal results. In this case the test statistic becomes

$$G = \frac{12(K-1)S}{nK^3 - D}$$

where $S = \sum_{j=1}^{K} (R_j - \bar{R})^2$ and $D = \sum f_i t_i^3$.

Example data

t_i is the size of the ith group of equal observations.

$$n = 15, \ K = 4, \ \bar{R} = \frac{n(K+1)}{2}$$

Rank numbers (showing many ties)

Rows (n)	Columns (K)			
	c_1	c_2	c_3	c_4
1	3.5	3.5	1.5	1.5
2	4.0	2.0	2.0	2.0
3	1.5	3.5	2.5	2.5
4	3.5	3.5	1.5	1.5
5	3.0	3.0	3.0	1.0
6	3.0	3.0	1.0	3.0
7	3.5	1.5	3.5	1.5
8	2.5	2.5	2.5	2.5
9	3.0	3.0	1.0	3.0
10	2.5	2.5	2.5	2.5
11	3.5	1.5	3.5	1.5
12	4.0	2.0	2.0	2.0
13	2.5	2.5	2.5	2.5
14	3.0	3.0	3.0	1.0
15	4.0	2.0	3.0	1.0
R_j	47	39	35	29
$\bar{R}$	37.5	37.5	37.5	37.5
$R_j - \bar{R}$	+9.5	+1.5	−2.5	−8.5

$$S = \sum (R_j - \bar{R})^2 = 171$$

Here 1, 2, 3 and 4 are the size of the groups of equal observations and $D = \sum f_i t_i^3$.

t_i	f_i	$f_i t_i$	$f_i t_i^3$
1	7	7	7
2	10	20	80
3	7	21	189
4	3	12	192
Total		60	468

Hence $D = 468$

$$G = \frac{12 \times (4 - 1) \times 171}{15 \times 4^3 - 468} = 12.51$$

The critical value is $\chi^2_{3;\,0.05} = 7.81$ [Table 5].

Since $G > 7.81$, reject the null hypothesis.

Test 74   The rank correlation test for agreement in multiple judgements

Object

To investigate the significance of the correlation between n series of rank numbers, assigned by n members of a committee to K subjects.

Limitations

This test can be applied if the judges decide independently and if the subjects show obvious differences in the quality being judged.

Method

Let n judges give rank numbers to K subjects.

Compute $S = nK(K^2 - 1)/12$ and $S_D =$ the sum of squares of the differences between subjects' mean ranks and the overall mean rank. Let

$$D_1 = \frac{S_D}{n_1}, \qquad D_2 = S - D_1, \qquad S_1^2 = \frac{D_1}{K - 1}, \qquad S_2^2 = \frac{D_2}{K(n - 1)}.$$

The test statistic is $F = S_1^2/S_2^2$, which follows the F-distribution with $(K - 1, K(n - 1))$ degrees of freedom. If this exceeds the critical value obtained from Table 3, the null hypothesis of agreement between the judgements is rejected.

Example data

$n = 3$, $K = 10$, $\nu_1 = K - 1 = 9$, $\nu_2 = K(n - 1) = 20$

	A	B	C	D	Rank number E	F	G	H	I	J	Total
Judge 1	1	2	3	4	5	6	7	8	9	10	55
Judge 2	7	10	4	1	6	8	9	5	2	3	55
Judge 3	9	6	10	3	5	4	7	8	2	1	55
Total score	17	18	17	8	16	18	23	21	13	14	165
Mean	16.5	16.5	16.5	16.5	16.5	16.5	16.5	16.5	16.5	16.5	165
Difference	0.5	1.5	0.5	−8.5	−0.5	1.5	6.5	4.5	−3.5	−2.5	

$$S = \frac{3 \times 10(100 - 1)}{12} = 247.5, \qquad S_D = 158.50,$$

$$D_1 = \frac{158.50}{3} = 52.83, \qquad D_2 = S - D_1 = 247.50 - 52.83 = 194.67,$$

$$S_1^2 = \frac{52.83}{9} = 5.87, \qquad S_2^2 = \frac{194.67}{10 \times 2} = \frac{194.67}{20} = 9.73$$

$$F = S_1^2/S_2^2 = \frac{5.87}{9.73} = 0.60$$

Critical value $F_{9;20;0.05} = 2.39$ [Table 3].

Do not reject the null hypothesis.

Test 75   A test for the continuous distribution of a random variable

Object

To test a model for the distribution of a random variable of the continuous type.

Limitations

This test is applicable if some known continuous distribution function is being tested. A partition of the random values into different sets must be available using the closed interval $[0, 1]$.

Method

Let $F(W)$ be the distribution function of W which we want to test. The null hypothesis is

$$H_0\colon F(W) = F_0(W)$$

where $F_0(W)$ is some known continuous distribution function.

The test is based on the χ^2 statistic. In order to use this, we must partition the set of possible values of W into k (not necessarily equal) sets. Partition the interval $[0, 1]$ into k sets such that $0 = b_0 < \cdots < b_k = 1$. Let $a_i = F_0^{-1}(b_i)$, $i = 1, 2, \ldots, k-1$, $A_1 = [-\alpha, a_1]$, $A_i = [-a_{i-1}, a_i]$, for $i = 2, 3, \ldots, k-1$ and $A_k = (a_{k-1}, \alpha)$; $p_i = P(W \in A_i)$, $i = 1, 2, \ldots, k$. Let Y_i denote the number of times the observed value of W belongs to A_i, $i = 1, 2, \ldots, k$ in n independent repetitions of the experiment. Then $Y_1, Y_2, \ldots, Y_k$ have a multinomial distribution with parameters $n, p_1, p_2, \ldots, p_k$. Let $\pi_i = P(W \in A_i)$ when the distribution function of W is $F_0(W)$.

Then we test the hypothesis:

$$H_0^*\colon p_i = \pi_i, \qquad i = 1, 2, \ldots, k.$$

H_0^* is rejected if the observed value of the χ^2 statistic

$$Q_{k-1} = \sum_{i=1}^{k-1} \frac{(Y_i - n\pi_i)^2}{n\pi_i}$$

is at least as great as C, where C is selected to yield the desired significance level.

Example data

Let W denote the outcome of a random experiment. Let $F(W)$ denote the distribution function of W and let

$$F_0(W) = \begin{cases} 0, & W < -1 \\ \frac{1}{2}(W^3 + 1), & -1 \leqslant W < 1 \\ 1, & W \geqslant 1. \end{cases}$$

The interval $[-1, 1]$ can be partitioned into 10 sets of equal probability with the point $b_i = i/10$, $i = 0, 1, \ldots, 10$.

If $a_i = F^{-1}(b_i) = (2b_i - 1)^{\frac{1}{3}}$, $i = 1, 2, \ldots, 9$ then the sets $A_1 = [-1, a_1]$, $A_2 = [a_1, a_2], \ldots, A_{10} = [A_9, 1]$ will each have probability 0.1. If the random sample of size $n = 50$ is observed then $n\pi_i = 50 \times 0.1 = 5.0$. Let the summary of the 50 observed values be

$A_1 = 6$, $A_2 = 4$, $A_3 = 5$, $A_4 = 6$, $A_5 = 4$, $A_6 = 4$, $A_7 = 6$, $A_8 = 8$, $A_9 = 3$, $A_{10} = 4$.

Then the calculated value of Q_9 is

$$Q_9 = \frac{(6-5)^2}{5} + \frac{(4-5)^2}{5} + \cdots + \frac{(4-5)^2}{5} = 4.0.$$

Critical value $\chi^2_{9;0.05} = 16.92$ [Table 5].

Hence do not reject the null hypothesis.

Test 76   A test for the equality of multinomial distributions

Object

To test the equality of h independent multinomial distributions.

Limitations

If p_i is the probability of an item being assigned to the ith class, then this test is applicable if y_{ij} is the number of items occurring in the class associated with p_i.

Method

Let $p_{ij} = P(A_i)$, $i = 1, 2, \ldots, k$; $j = 1, 2, \ldots, h$. It is required to test

$$H_0: p_{i1} = p_{i2} = \cdots = p_{ih} = p_i, \qquad i = 1, 2, \ldots, k.$$

Carry out the jth experiment n_j times, making sure that the n_j instances are independent, and let $Y_{1j}, Y_{2j}, \ldots, Y_{kj}$ denote the frequencies of the respective events $A_1, A_2, \ldots, A_k$. Then

$$Q = \sum_{j=1}^{h} \sum_{i=1}^{k} \frac{(Y_{ij} - n_j p_{ij})^2}{n_j p_{ij}}$$

has an approximate χ^2-distribution with $h(k - 1)$ degrees of freedom. Under H_0, we estimate $k - 1$ probabilities from

$$\hat{p}_i = \frac{\displaystyle\sum_{j=1}^{h} Y_{ij}}{\displaystyle\sum_{j=1}^{h} n_j}, \qquad i = 1, 2, \ldots, k - 1;$$

the estimate of p_k then follows from $\hat{p}_k = 1 - \sum_{i=1}^{k-1} \hat{p}_i$. Then

$$Q = \sum_{j=1}^{h} \sum_{i=1}^{k} \frac{(Y_{ij} - n_j \hat{p}_i)^2}{n_j \hat{p}_i}$$

has an approximate χ^2-distribution with

$$h(k - 1) - (k - 1) = (h - 1)(k - 1)$$

degrees of freedom.

Example data

Group	A_1	A_2	Grade A_3	A_4	A_5	Total
1	8	13	16	10	3	50
2	4	9	14	16	7	50

$n = 50$

$$P(A_1) = \frac{8+4}{100} = 0.12, \ P(A_2) = 0.22, \ P(A_3) = 0.30$$

$$P(A_4) = 0.26, \ P(A_5) = 0.10$$

Thus we have estimates of $n_1 P_{i1} = 6$, $n_2 P_{i2} = 11$, $n_3 P_{i3} = 15$, $n_4 P_{i4} = 13$ and $n_5 P_{i5} = 5$, respectively.

Hence the computed value of Q is:

$$Q = \frac{(8-6)^2}{6} + \frac{(13-11)^2}{11} + \frac{(16-15)^2}{15} + \frac{(10-13)^2}{13} + \frac{(3-5)^2}{5}$$
$$+ \frac{(4-6)^2}{6} + \frac{(9-11)^2}{11} + \frac{(14-15)^2}{13} + \frac{(16-13)^2}{13} + \frac{(7-5)^2}{5}$$
$$= 5.19.$$

The critical value is $\chi^2_{4;0.05} = 9.488$ [Table 5].

The calculated value is less than the critical value. Do not reject the null hypothesis.

Test 77   *F*-test for non-additivity

Object

To test for non-additivity in a two-way classification.

Limitations

This test is applicable if the observations are independently and normally distributed with constant variance.

Method

In the two-way classification with one observation per cell (fixed effects model), we assume additivity (absence of interaction effects). In the case of any doubt about this additivity, Tukey proposed a test under the following set-up:

$$Y_{ij} = \mu + \alpha_i + \beta_j + \lambda\alpha_i\beta_j + e_{ij}$$

subject to the conditions that

$$\sum_i \alpha_i = \sum_j \beta_j = 0$$

and that the e_{ij} are independently $N(0, \sigma^2)$. Under this set-up, the interaction effect is represented by $\lambda\alpha_i\beta_j$, where

$$\sum_{\substack{i \\ \text{all } j}} \lambda\alpha_i\beta_j = \sum_{\substack{j \\ \text{all } i}} \lambda\alpha_i\beta_j = 0.$$

A test for non-additivity is obtained by a test for H_0: $\lambda = 0$ or equivalently by a test H_0: $E(Y_{ij}) = \mu + \alpha_i + \beta_j$ under this set-up. But this set-up does not conform to the Gauss–Markov model for $E(Y_{ij})$ which are not linear in the parameter μ, α_i, β_j and λ. A set of unbiased estimators for μ, α_i and β_j are:

$$\mu^* = Y_{00}, \qquad \alpha_i^* = Y_{i0} - Y_{00}, \qquad \beta_j^* = Y_{0j} - Y_{00}.$$

The least squares (unbiased) estimator of λ is obtained by minimizing

$$s_E^2 = \sum_i \sum_j (Y_{ij} - \mu - \alpha_i - \beta_j - \lambda\alpha_i\beta_j)^2$$

with respect to λ under the assumption that α_i and β_j are known. Thus

$$\lambda^* = \frac{\displaystyle\sum_i \sum_j \alpha_i\beta_j Y_{ij}}{\displaystyle\sum_i \alpha_i^2 \sum_j \beta_j^2}.$$

Then the sum of squares due to interaction, i.e. due to λ^*, is given by

$$s_{\lambda^*}^2 = \frac{\left[\sum_i \sum_j \alpha_i \beta_j Y_{ij}\right]^2}{\sum_i \alpha_i^2 \sum_j \beta_j^2}$$

with l degrees of freedom. The sum of squares due to non-additivity is given by

$$s_N^2 = \frac{\left[\sum_i \sum_j \alpha_i^* \beta_j^* Y_{ij}\right]^2}{\sum_i \alpha_i^{*2} \sum_j \beta_j^{*2}}.$$

For all given α_i^*, β_j^*, for all i, j, we have that s_N^2/σ^2 and $(s_E^2 - s_N^2)/\sigma^2 = s_R^2$ are independent and have χ^2-distribution with 1 and $(p-1)(q-1) - 1$ degrees of freedom, respectively.

We reject H_0: $\lambda = 0$ at level α if the variance ratio for non-additivity is too large, i.e. if

$$[(p-1)(q-1) - 1]\frac{s_N^2}{s_R^2} > F_{1,(p-1)(q-1)-1;\alpha}$$

and fail to reject otherwise.

Example data

i \ j	1	2	3	4	Y_{i0}	$\bar{Y}_{i0}$
1	14	2	1	2	19	4.75
2	2	0	2	2	6	1.5
3	2	1	5	0	8	2
Y_{0j}	18	3	8	4	33	
$\bar{Y}_{0j}$	6	1	2.7	1.33		

$$\mu = Y_{00} = \frac{33}{12} = 2.75$$

$$\alpha_1^* = 19 - 2.75 = 16.25, \ \alpha_2^* = 3.25, \ \alpha_3^* = 5.25$$

$$\beta_1^* = 18 - 2.75 = 15.25, \ \beta_2^* = 0.25, \ \beta_3^* = 5.25, \ \beta_4^* = 1.25$$

$$\lambda^* = \frac{4023.75}{79\,229.788} = 0.05079, \ s_E^2 = 4568.38, \ s_N^2 = 204.35$$

Let $\sigma^2 = 16$, then $\dfrac{s_E^2}{\sigma^2} = 285.52$ and $\dfrac{s_N^2}{\sigma^2} = 12.77$, $s_R^2 = 272.75$.

Hence $F = \dfrac{12.77/1}{285.52/5} = 0.2236$.

Critical value $F_{1,5;0.05} = 6.61$ [Table 3].

We do not reject the null hypothesis $\lambda = 0$.

Test 78 F-test for testing main effects and interaction effects in a two-way classification

Object

To test the main effects and interaction effects for the case of a two-way classification with an equal number of observations per cell.

Limitations

This test is applicable if the error in different measurements is normally distributed; if the relative size of these errors is unrelated to any factor of the experiment; and if the different measurements themselves are independent.

Method

Suppose we have n observations per cell of the two-way table, the observations being Y_{ijk}, $i = 1, 2, \ldots, p$ (level of A); $j = 1, 2, \ldots, q$ (level of B) and $k = 1, 2, \ldots, r$. We use the model:

$$Y_{ijk} = \mu + \alpha_i + \beta_j + (\alpha\beta)_{ij} + e_{ijk}$$

subject to the conditions that

$$\sum_i \alpha_i = \sum_j \beta_j = \sum_{\substack{j \\ \text{all } j}} (\alpha\beta)_{ij} = \sum_{\substack{i \\ \text{all } i}} (\alpha\beta)_{ij} = 0$$

and that the e_{ij} are independently $N(0, \sigma^2)$. Here $(\alpha\beta)_{ij}$ is the interaction effect due to simultaneous occurrence of the ith level of A and the jth level of B. We are interested in testing:

$$H_{AB}: \text{all } (\alpha\beta)_{ij} = 0,$$

$$H_A: \text{all } \alpha_i = 0,$$

$$H_B: \text{all } \beta_j = 0.$$

Under the present set-up, the sum of squares due to the residual is given by

$$s_E^2 = \sum_i \sum_j \sum_k (Y_{ijk} - Y_{ij0})^2,$$

with $rpq - pjq$ degrees of freedom, and the interaction sum of squares due to H_{AB} is

$$r \sum_i \sum_j (\widehat{\alpha\beta})_{ij}^2,$$

with $(p-1)(q-1)$ degrees of freedom, where

$$(\widehat{\alpha\beta})_{ij} = Y_{ij0} - Y_{i00} - Y_{0j0} + Y_{000}$$

and this is also called the sum of squares due to the interaction effects.

Denoting the interaction and error mean squares by $\bar{s}^2_{AB}$ and $\bar{s}^2_E$ respectively. The null hypothesis H_{AB} is tested at the α level of significance by rejecting H_{AB} if

$$\frac{\bar{s}^2_{AB}}{\bar{s}^2_E} > F_{(p-1)(q-1),\, pq(r-1);\alpha}$$

and failing to reject it otherwise.

For testing H_A: $a_i = \sigma$ for all i, the restricted residual sum of squares is

$$s^2_1 = \sum_i \sum_j \sum_k (Y_{ijk} - Y_{ij0} + Y_{i00} - Y_{000})^2$$

$$= s^2_E + rq \sum_i (Y_{i00} - Y_{000})^2,$$

with $rpq - pq + p - 1$ degrees of freedom, and

$$s^2_A = rq \sum_i (Y_{i00} - Y_{000})^2,$$

with $p - 1$ degrees of freedom. With notation analogous to that for the test for H_{AB}, the test for H_A is then performed at level α by rejecting H_A if

$$\frac{\bar{s}^2_A}{\bar{s}^2_E} > F_{(p-1),\, pq(r-1);\alpha}$$

and failing to reject it otherwise. The test for H_B is similar.

Example data

A	B I	II	III
1	95	60	86
	85	90	77
	74	80	75
	74	70	70
2	90	89	83
	80	90	70
	92	91	75
	82	86	72
3	70	68	74
	80	73	86
	85	78	91
	85	93	89

Table of means

	$\bar{Y}_{ij}$			$\bar{Y}_{i.}$
1	82	75	77	78.0
2	86	89	75	83.3
3	80	78	85	81.0
				$\bar{Y}_{...}$
$\bar{Y}_{.j.}$	82.7	80.7	79.0	80.8

$$s^2_A = 3 \times 4 \times \sum_i (\bar{Y}_{i..} - \bar{Y}_{...})^2 = 3 \times 4 \times 14.13 = 169.56$$

$$s_B^2 = 3 \times 4 \times \sum_j (\bar{Y}_{.j.} - \bar{Y}_{...})^2 = 12 \times 6.86 = 82.32$$

$$s_{AB}^2 = 4 \sum_i \sum_j (\bar{Y}_{ij.} - \bar{Y}_{i..} - \bar{Y}_{.j.} + \bar{Y}_{...})^2 = 4 \times 140.45 = 561.80$$

$$s_E^2 = \sum_i \sum_j \sum_k (Y_{ijk} - \bar{Y}_{ij.})^2 = 1830.0$$

ANOVA table

Source	SS	DF	MS	F ratio
A	169.56	2	84.78	1.25
B	82.32	2	41.16	0.61
AB	561.80	4	140.4	2.07
Error	1830.00	27	67.78	

Critical values $F_{2,27}(0.05) = 3.35$ [Table 3],
$F_{4,27}(0.05) = 2.73$ [Table 3].

Hence we do not reject any of the three hypotheses.

Test 79 *F*-test for testing main effects in a two-way classification

Object

To test the main effects in the case of a two-way classification with unequal numbers of observations per cell.

Limitations

This test is applicable if the error in different measurements is normally distributed; if the relative size of these errors is unrelated to any factor of the experiment; and if the different measurements themselves are independent.

Method

We consider the case of testing the null hypothesis

$$H_A: \alpha_i = 0 \text{ for all } i \qquad \text{and} \qquad H_B: \beta_j = 0 \text{ for all } j$$

under additivity. Under H_A, the model is:

$$Y_{ijk} = \mu + \beta_j + e_{ijk},$$

with the e_{ijk} independently $N(0, \sigma^2)$. The residual sum of squares (SS) under H_A is

$$s_2^2 = \sum_i \sum_j \sum_k Y_{ijk}^2 - \sum_j C_j^2 / n_{.j.}$$

with $n - q$ degrees of freedom, where $n_{.j.} (\mu + \beta_j) + \Sigma_i n_{ij} \alpha_i = C_j$ and n_{ij} is the number of observations in the (i, j)th cell and $\Sigma_j n_{ij} = n_{i.}$ and $\Sigma_i n_{ij} = n_{.j}$. The adjusted SS due to A is

$$\text{SSA}^* = s_2^2 - s_1^2 = \sum_i \left(R_i - \sum_j p_{ij} C_j \right) \hat{\alpha}_i$$

with $p - 1$ degrees of freedom, where $n_{i.} (\mu + \alpha_i) + \Sigma_j n_{ij} \beta_j = R_i$, $p_{ij} = n_{ij}/n_{.j}$. Under additivity, the test statistic for H_A is

$$\frac{\text{SSA}^*}{s_1^2} \frac{n - p - q + 1}{p - 1},$$

which, under H_A, has the F-distribution with $(p - 1, n - p - q + 1)$ degrees of freedom. Similarly, the test statistic for H_B is

$$\frac{\text{SSB}^*}{s_1^2} \frac{n - p - q + 1}{q - 1},$$

which, under H_B, has the F-distribution with $(q - 1, n - p - q + 1)$ degrees of freedom; where $\mathrm{SSB}^* = \Sigma_j(C_j - \Sigma_i q_{ij} R_i)\hat{\beta}_j$ is the adjusted SS due to B, with $q - 1$ degrees of freedom.

Example data

		A		
B	1	2	3	Total
1	88 (172) 84 [0.2500]	22 26 (71) 23 [0.4286]	60 (126) 66 [0.2857]	369
2	108 98 (308) 102 [0.3750]	10 (34) 24 [0.2857]	82 54 (196) 60 [0.4286]	538
3	108 80 (276) 88 [0.3750]	20 (36) 16 [0.2857]	50 (82) 32 [0.2857]	394
Total	756	141	404	1301

Note
1. Values in parentheses are the totals.
2. Values in brackets are the ratio of the number of observations divided by the column total number of observations, e.g. the first column has $2/8 = 0.25$.

$T = 1301$, and $T_2 = $ observation sum of squares $= 100\,021$

$$\text{CF (correction factor)} = \frac{T^2}{N} = 76\,936.41$$

$$\text{Total SS} = T_2 - \frac{T^2}{N} = 23\,084.59$$

SS between cells $= \frac{1}{2}(172)^2 + \frac{1}{3}(71)^2 + \cdots + \frac{1}{2}(82)^2 - \text{CF} = 21\,880.59$

SS within cells (error) $= $ total SS $-$ SS between cells $= 1204.00$

SSA unadjusted $= \frac{1}{8}(756)^2 + \frac{1}{7}(141)^2 + \frac{1}{2}(404)^2 - \text{CF} = 20\,662.30$

SSB unadjusted $= \frac{1}{7}(369)^2 + \frac{1}{8}(538)^2 + \frac{1}{7}(394)^2 - \text{CF} = 872.23$

$C_{11} = 7 - 2(0.2500) - 3(0.4286) - 2(0.2857) = 4.6429$

$C_{12} = -2.4643, Q_1 = 369 - 756(0.2500) - 141(0.4286)$
$\qquad - 404(0.2857) = 4.143$

$Q_2 = 41.071$, $Q_3 = -45.214$, $\hat{\alpha}_1 = 0.8341$, $\hat{\alpha}_2 = 5.4146$, $\hat{\alpha}_3 = -6.2487$

SSB adjusted $= Q_1\hat{\alpha}_1 + Q_2\hat{\alpha}_2 + Q_3\hat{\alpha}_3 = 508.37$

SSA adjusted $=$ SSB adjusted $+$ SSA unadjusted
$\qquad\qquad - $ SSB unadjusted $= 20\,298.44$

SS interaction $=$ SS between cells $-$ SSB adjusted
$\qquad\qquad - $ SSA unadjusted $= 709.92$

ANOVA table

Source	DF	SS	MS	F ratio
SSA adjusted	2	20 298.44	10 149.22	109.58
SSB adjusted	2	508.37	254.18	27.44
Interaction AB	4	709.92	177.48	1.92
Error	13	1 204.00	92.62	

Critical values $F_{2,\,13;\,0.05} = 3.81$ [Table 3]
$\qquad\qquad\quad F_{4,\,13;\,0.05} = 3.18$ [Table 3]

The main effects of A and B are significantly different, whereas the interaction between A and B is not significant.

Test 80 *F*-test for nested or hierarchical classification

Object

To test for nestedness in the case of a nested or hierarchical classification.

Limitations

This test is applicable if the error in different measurements is normally distributed; if the relative size of these errors is unrelated to any factor of the experiment; and if the different measurements themselves are independent.

Method

In the case of a nested classification, the levels of factor B will be said to be nested with the levels of factor A if any level of B occurs with only a single level of A. This means that if A has p levels, then the q levels of B will be grouped into p mutually exclusive and exhaustive groups, such that the ith group of levels of B occurs only with the ith level of A in the observations. Here we shall only consider two-factor nesting, where the number of levels of B associated with the ith level of A is q_i, i.e. we consider the case where there are $\Sigma_i q_i$ levels of B.

For example, consider a chemical experiment where factor A stands for the method of analysing a chemical, there being p different methods. Factor B may represent the different analysts, there being q_i analysts associated with the ith method.

The jth analyst performs the n_{ij} experiments allotted to him. The corresponding fixed effects model is:

$$Y_{ijk} = \mu + \alpha_i + \beta_{ij} + e_{ijk}, \qquad i = 1, 2, \ldots, p; j = 1, 2, \ldots, q_i;$$
$$k = 1, 2, \ldots, n_{ij},$$

$$\sum_{i=l}^{p} n_i \alpha_i = \sum_{\substack{j \\ \text{all } i}} n_{ij} \beta_j = 0$$

$$n_i = \sum_j n_{ij}, n = \sum_i n_i \text{ and } e_{ijk} \text{ are independently } N(0, \sigma^2).$$

We are interested in testing H_A: $\alpha_i = 0$, for all i, and H_B: $\beta_{ij} = 0$, for all i, j.

The residual sum of squares is given by

$$s_E^2 = \sum_i \sum_j \sum_k (Y_{ijk} - Y_{ij0})^2$$

with $\sum_{ij} (n_{ij} - 1)$ degrees of freedom; the sums of squares due respectively to A and B are

$$s_A^2 = \sum_i n_i (Y_{i00} - Y_{000})^2$$

with $p - 1$ degrees of freedom, and

$$s_B^2 = \sum_i \sum_j n_{ij}(Y_{ij0} - Y_{i00})$$

with $\sum_i(q_i - 1)$ degrees of freedom.

To perform the tests for H_A and H_B we first require the mean squares, $\bar{s}_E^2, \bar{s}_A^2$ and $\bar{s}_B^2$, corresponding to these sums of squares; we then calculate $\bar{s}_A^2/\bar{s}_E^2$ to test H_A and $\bar{s}_B^2/\bar{s}_E^2$ to test H_B, each of which, under the respective null hypothesis, follows the F-distribution with appropriate degrees of freedom.

Nested models are frequently used in sample survey investigations.

Example data

Scores of pupils from three teachers in each of four schools are shown in the following table.

						Schools						
	I			II			III			IV		
	Teacher			Teacher			Teacher			Teacher		
	1	2	3	1	2	3	1	2	3	1	2	3
	44	39	39	51	48	44	46	45	43	42	45	39
	41	37	36	49	43	43	43	40	41	39	40	38
	39	35	33	45	42	42	41	38	39	38	37	35
	36	35	31	44	40	39	40	38	37	36	37	35
	35	34	28	40	37	37	36	35	34	34	32	35
	32	30	26	40	34	36	34	34	33	31	32	29
Teacher total	227	210	193	269	244	241	240	230	227	220	223	211
Mean	37.8	35.0	32.17	44.83	40.67	40.16	40.0	38.33	37.83	36.67	37.17	35.17
School total	630			754			697			654		2735
Mean	35.00			41.89			38.72			36.33		

$T = 2735$

CF (correction factor) $= \dfrac{2735^2}{72} = 103\,892.01$

Total sum of squares $= 105\,637.00 - 103\,892.01 = 1744.99$

Between-schools sum of squares

$$= \frac{630^2}{18} + \frac{754^2}{18} + \frac{697^2}{18} + \frac{654^2}{18} - CF = 493.60$$

Between teachers (within school) sum of squares

$$= \frac{227^2}{6} + \frac{210^2}{6} + \frac{193^2}{6} - \frac{630^2}{18} + \text{similar terms for schools II, III and}$$

$$\text{IV} = 203.55$$

Within-group sum of squares $= 1744.99 - 493.60 - 203.55 = 1047.84$.

ANOVA table

	DF	SS	Mean square
Schools	3	493.60	164.53
Teachers within school	8	203.55	25.44
Pupils within teachers	60	1047.84	17.46
Total	71	1744.99	

Teacher differences:

$$F = \frac{25.44}{17.46} = 1.46$$

Critical value $F_{8, 60; 0.05} = 2.10$ [Table 3].

The calculated value is less than the critical value.

Hence the differences between teachers are not significant.

School differences:

$$F = \frac{164.53}{25.44} = 6.47$$

Critical value $F_{3, 8; 0.05} = 4.07$ [Table 3].

The calculated value is greater than the critical value.

Hence the differences between schools are significant.

Test 81   *F*-test for testing regression

Object

To test the presence of regression of variable Y on the observed value X.

Limitations

For given X, the Ys are normally and independently distributed. The error terms are normally and independently distributed with mean zero.

Method

Suppose, corresponding to each value X_i $(i = 1, 2, \ldots, p)$ of the independent random variable X, we have a corresponding array of observations Y_{ij} $(j = 1, 2, \ldots, n_i)$ on the dependent variable Y. Using the model:

$$Y_{ij} = \mu_i + e_{ij}, \qquad i = 1, 2, \ldots, p, \quad j = 1, 2, \ldots, n_i,$$

where the e_{ij} are independently $N(0, \sigma^2)$, we are interested in testing H_0: all μ_i are equal, against H_1: not all μ_i are equal. 'H_0 is true' implies the absence of regression of Y on X. Then the sums of squares are given by

$$s_B^2 = \sum_i n_i (Y_{i0} - Y_{00})^2, \qquad s_E^2 = \sum_i \sum_j (Y_{ij} - Y_{i0})^2.$$

Denoting the corresponding mean squares by $\bar{s}_B^2$ and $\bar{s}_E^2$ respectively, then, under H_0, $F = \bar{s}_B^2 / \bar{s}_E^2$ follows the F-distribution with $(p - 1, n - p)$ degrees of freedom.

Example data

$$Y_{ij}$$

X_1	1	2	3	$n_1 = 3$, where $Y_{i0} = \displaystyle\sum_{j=1}^{n_i} \dfrac{Y_{ij}}{n_i}$,	$i = 1, 2, \ldots, p$
X_2	7	5	6	$n_2 = 3$, and $Y_{00} = \displaystyle\sum_i \sum_j \dfrac{Y_{ij}}{n}$,	$n = \sum n_i$

Hence $Y_{i0} = \dfrac{1 + 2 + 3}{3} = 2$, $Y_{20} = \dfrac{7 + 5 + 6}{3} = 6$,

$$Y_{00} = \frac{1 + 2 + 3 + 7 + 5 + 6}{6} = 4$$

$s_B^2 = 3(2 - 4)^2 + 3(6 - 4)^2 = 24$

$s_E^2 = (1 - 2)^2 + (2 - 2)^2 + (3 - 2)^2 + (7 - 6)^2 + (5 - 6)^2 + (6 - 6)^2 = 4$

$\bar{s}_B^2 = 24/1 = 24$, $\bar{s}_E^2 = 4/4 = 1$, $F = 24/1 = 24$

Critical value $F_{1,4;0.05} = 7.71$ [Table 3].

Hence reject the null hypothesis, indicating the presence of regression.

Test 82 *F*-test for testing linearity of regression

Object

To test the linearity of regression between an X variable and a Y variable.

Limitations

For given X, the Ys are normally and independently distributed. The error terms are normally and independently distributed with mean zero.

Method

Once the relationship between X and Y is established using Test 81, we would further like to know whether the regression is linear or not. Under the same set-up as Test 81, we are interested in testing:

$$H_0: \mu_i = \alpha + \beta X_i, \qquad i = 1, 2, \ldots, n,$$

Under H_0,

$$s_E^2 = \sum_i (y_i - \bar{y})^2 - b^2 \sum_i n_i (x_i - \bar{x})^2,$$

with $n - 2$ degrees of freedom, and the sum of squares due to regression

$$s_R^2 = b^2 \sum_i n_i (x_i - \bar{x})^2,$$

with 1 degree of freedom. The ratio of mean squares

$$F = \bar{s}_R^2 / \bar{s}_E^2 \text{ is used to test } H_0 \text{ with } (1, n - 2) \text{ degrees of freedom.}$$

Example data

i	1	2	3	4	5	6	7	8	9	10	11	12
x_i	150	150	150	200	200	200	250	250	250	300	300	300
y_i	77.4	76.7	78.2	84.1	84.5	83.7	88.9	89.2	89.7	94.8	94.7	95.9

$n = 12$, $n - 2 = 10$. For $\beta = 0$, test $H_0: \beta = 0$ against $H_1: \beta \neq 0$
The total sum of squares is

$$\sum y_i^2 - \left(\sum y_i \right)^2 \bigg/ n = 513.1167,$$

and

$$s_R^2 = b \frac{\left(\sum x_i y_i - \dfrac{1}{n} \sum x_i y_i \right)^2}{\sum x_i^2 - \dfrac{1}{n} (x_i)^2} = 509.10,$$

$s_E^2 = 4.0117$, $\bar{s}_R^2 = 42.425$, $\bar{s}_E^2 = 0.401$, $F = 105.80$
Critical value $F_{1, 10; 0.05} = 4.96$ [Table 3].
Hence reject the null hypothesis and conclude that $\beta \neq 0$.

Test 83 *Z*-test for the uncertainty of events

Object

To test the significance of the reduction of uncertainty of past events.

Limitations

Unlike sequential analyses, this test procedure requires a probability distribution of a variable.

Method

It is well known that the reduction of uncertainty by knowledge of past events is the basic concept of sequential analysis. The purpose here is to test the significance of this reduction of uncertainty using the statistic

$$Z = \frac{P(B_{+k}|A) - P(B)}{\sqrt{\dfrac{P(B)[1 - P(B)][1 - P(A)]}{(n - k)P(A)}}}$$

where $P(A) =$ probability of A, $P(B) =$ probability of B and $P(B_{+k}|A) = P(B|A)$ at lag k.

Example data

Consider a sequence of A and B: $AA\ BA\ BA\ BB\ AB\ AB$

$$n = 12, \quad k = 1, \quad P(A) = \frac{6}{12} = 0.5, \quad P(B) = \frac{6}{12} = 0.5$$

We note that A occurs six times and that of these six times B occurs immediately after A five times. Given that A just occurred we have

$$P(B|A) \text{ at lag one} = P(B_{+1}|A) = \frac{5}{6} = 0.83.$$

Therefore the test statistic is

$$Z = \frac{0.83 - 0.50}{\sqrt{\dfrac{0.50(1 - 0.50)(1 - 0.50)}{(12 - 1)(0.50)}}} = 2.20.$$

The critical value at $\alpha = 0.05$ is 1.96 [Table 1].

The calculated value is greater than the critical value.

Hence it is significant.

Test 84   Z-test for comparing sequential contingencies across two groups using the 'log odds ratio'

Object

To test the significance of the difference in sequential connections across groups.

Limitations

This test is applicable when a logit transformation can be used and 2×2 contingency tables are available.

Method

Consider a person's antecedent behaviour (W_t) taking one of the two values:

$$W_t = \begin{cases} 1 & \text{for negative effect} \\ 0 & \text{for positive effect.} \end{cases}$$

Let us use $H_t + 1$, a similar notation, for the spouse's consequent behaviour. A fundamental distinction may be made between measures of association in contingency tables which are either sensitive or insensitive to the marginal (row) totals. A measure that is invariant to the marginal total is provided by the so-called logit transformation. The logit is defined by:

$$\text{logit}(P) = \log_{e} \frac{P}{1 - P}.$$

We can now define a statistic β as follows:

$$\beta = \text{logit}[P_r(H_{t+k} = 1 \mid W_t = 1)] - \text{logit}[P_r(H_{t+k} = 1 \mid W_t = 0)].$$

Hence β is known as the logarithm of the 'odds ratio' which is the cross product ratio in a 2×2 contingency table, i.e. if we have a table in which first row is (a, b) and second row is (c, d) then

$$\beta = \log\left(\frac{ad}{bc}\right).$$

In order to test whether β is different across groups we use the statistic

$$Z = \frac{\beta_1 - \beta_2}{\sqrt{\sum \left(\frac{1}{f_i}\right)}}$$

where f_i is the frequency in the ith cell and Z is the standard normal variate, i.e. $N(0, 1)$.

Example data

	Distressed couples W_{t+1}		Non-distressed couples W_{t+1}	
H_t	1	0	1	0
1	76	100	80	63
0	79	200	43	39

$$\beta_1 = \log_e \frac{76 \times 200}{79 \times 100} = 0.654; \quad \beta_2 = \log_e \frac{80 \times 39}{43 \times 63} = 0.141$$

$$Z = \frac{0.654 - 0.141}{\sqrt{\dfrac{1}{76} + \dfrac{1}{79} + \dfrac{1}{100} + \dfrac{1}{200} + \dfrac{1}{80} + \dfrac{1}{43} + \dfrac{1}{63} + \dfrac{1}{39}}} = 1.493$$

The critical value at $\alpha = 0.05$ is 1.96 [Table 1].

The calculated value is less than the critical value.

Hence it is not significant and the null hypothesis (that β is not different across groups) cannot be rejected.

Test 85   *F*-test for testing the coefficient of multiple regression

Object

A multiple linear regression model is used in order to test whether the population value of each multiple regression coefficient is zero.

Limitations

This test is applicable if the observations are independent and the error term is normally distributed with mean zero.

Method

Let $X_1, X_2, \ldots, X_k$ be k independent variables and $X_{1i}, X_{2i}, \ldots, X_{ki}$ be their fixed values, corresponding to dependent variables Y_i. We consider the model:

$$Y_i = \beta_0 + \beta_1 X'_{1i} + \cdots + \beta_k X'_{ki} + e_i$$

where $X'_{ji} = X_{ji} - \bar{X}_j$ and the e_i are independently $N(0, \sigma^2)$.

We are interested in testing whether the population value of each multiple regression coefficient is zero. We want to test:

$$H_0: \beta_1 = \beta_2 = \cdots = \beta_k = 0 \qquad \text{against} \qquad H_1: \text{not all } \beta_k = 0$$

for $k = 1, 2, \ldots, p - 1$, where p is the number of parameters. The error sum of squares is

$$s_E^2 = \sum_i (Y_i - \bar{Y})^2 - \sum_j b_j \sum_i Y_i X'_{ji}$$

with $n - k - 1$ degrees of freedom, where b_j is the least-squares estimator of β_j.

The sum of squares due to H_0 is

$$s_H^2 = \sum_j b_j \sum_i Y_i X'_{ji}$$

with k degrees of freedom. Denoting the corresponding mean squares by $\bar{s}_E^2$ and $\bar{s}_H^2$ respectively, then, under H_0, $F = \bar{s}_H^2 / \bar{s}_E^2$ follows the F-distribution with $(k, n - k - 1)$ degrees of freedom and can be used for testing H_0.

The appropriate decision rule is: if the calculated $F \leqslant F_{p-1, n-p; 0.05}$, do not reject H_0; if the calculated $F > F_{p-1, n-p; 0.05}$, reject H_0.

Example data

$n = 16, p = 3, \nu = p - 1, \nu_2 = n - p$

Critical value $F_{2, 13; 0.05} = 3.81$ [Table 3].

From the computer output of a certain set of data

$\bar{s}_H^2 = 96.74439, \bar{s}_E^2 = 0.28935$

$F = 96.74439 / 0.28935 = 334$

Hence reject the null hypothesis.

Test 86 *F*-test for variance of a random effects model

Object

To test for variance in a balanced random effects model of random variables.

Limitations

This test is applicable if the random variables are independently and normally distributed with mean zero.

Method

Let the random variable $Y_{ij\cdots m}$ for a balanced case be such that:

$$Y_{ij\cdots m} = \mu + a_i + b_{ij} + c_{ijk} + \cdots + e_{ijk\cdots m}$$

where μ is a constant and the random variables $a_i, b_{ij}, c_{ijk}, \ldots, e_{ijk\cdots m}$ are completely independent and $a_i \sim N(0, \sigma_a^2), \ldots, b_{ij} \sim N(0, \sigma_b^2),\ c_{ijk} \sim N(0, \sigma_c^2), \ldots, e_{ijk\cdots m} \sim N(0, \sigma^2)$.

Then the test for $H_0 = \sigma_i^2 = \sigma_j^2 (i \neq j)$ against $H_1 = \sigma_i^2 > \sigma_j^2$ is given by s_i^2/s_j^2 which is distributed as $(\sigma_i^2/\sigma_j^2)F$ and follows the F-distribution with (f_i, f_j) degrees of freedom. Here s_i^2 and s_j^2 are the estimates of σ_i^2 and σ_j^2.

Example data

$s_1^2 = 5.69,\ s_2^2 = 4.45, f_1 = 2, f_2 = 3$

$H_0: \sigma_1^2 = \sigma_2^2;\ H_1: \sigma_1^2 > \sigma_2^2$

$$F = \frac{s_1^2}{s_2^2} = \frac{5.69}{4.45} = 1.279$$

Critical value $F_{2, 3; 0.05} = 9.55$ [Table 3]

Hence we do not reject the null hypothesis H_0.

$f_i = n_1 - 1$

$f_i = 2n_2 - 1$

Test 87   *F*-test for factors *A* and *B* and an interaction effect

Object

To test for the homogeneity of factors *A* and *B* and the absence of an interaction effect.

Limitations

This test is applicable if the random variables and interaction effects are jointly normal with mean zero and the error terms are independently normally distributed with mean zero.

Method

Let the factor having fixed levels be labelled *A* and represented by the columns of the table and let the randomly sampled factor be *B* and represented by the rows. Let

$$Y_{ijk} = \mu + \alpha_i + b_k + c_{jk} + e_{ijk}$$

where
α_i is the fixed effect of the treatment indicated by the column *i*;
b_k = random variable associated with the *k*th row;
c_{jk} = random interaction effect operating on the (j, k)th cell; and
e_{ijk} = random error associated with observation *i* in the (j, k)th cell.

We make the following assumptions:
1. b_k and c_{jk} are jointly normal with mean zero and with variance σ_B^2 and σ_{AB}^2, respectively;
2. e_{ijk} are normally distributed with mean zero and variance σ_E^2;
3. e_{ijk} are independent of b_k and c_{jk};
4. e_{ijk} are independent of each other.
  Denoting the column, interaction, row and error mean squares by $\bar{s}_C^2, \bar{s}_I^2, \bar{s}_R^2$ and $\bar{s}_E^2$ respectively, then $\bar{s}_C^2/\bar{s}_I^2 \sim F_{c-1, (r-1)(c-1)}$ provides an appropriate test for the column effects, i.e. $H_0: \sigma_A^2 = 0$; $\bar{s}_R^2/\bar{s}_E^2 \sim F_{r-1, rc(n-1)}$ provides a test for $H_0: \sigma_B^2 = 0$; and $\bar{s}_I^2/\bar{s}_E^2 \sim F_{(r-1)(c-1), r(n-1)}$ provides a test for $H_0: \sigma_{AB}^2 = 0$.

Example data

In the following table the values are a combination of classroom and task and represent the independent performance of two subjects in each cell.

Classroom	Tasks I	II	III	Total
1	7.8 (16.5) 8.7	11.1 (23.1) 12.0	11.7 (21.7) 10.0	61.3
2	8.0 (17.2) 9.2	11.3 (21.9) 10.6	9.8 (21.7) 11.9	60.8
3	4.0 (10.9) 6.9	9.8 (19.9) 10.1	11.7 (24.3) 12.6	55.1
4	10.3 (19.7) 9.4	11.4 (21.9) 10.5	7.9 (16.0) 8.1	57.6
5	9.3 (19.9) 10.6	13.0 (24.7) 11.7	8.3 (16.2) 7.9	60.8
6	9.5 (19.3) 9.8	12.2 (24.5) 12.3	8.6 (19.1) 10.5	62.9
Total	103.5	136.0	119.0	358.5

CF (correction factor) $= 358.5^2/36 = 3570.0625$

TSS $= 7.8^2 + \cdots + 10.5^2 - (3570.0625) = 123.57$

The sums of squares are given by

$$s_C^2 = \frac{(103.5)^2 + (136.0)^2 + (119.0)^2}{12} - CF = 44.04$$

$$s_R^2 = \frac{61.3^2 + \cdots + 62.9^2}{6} - CF = 6.80$$

$$s_E^2 = 7.8^2 + \cdots + 10.5^2 - \frac{16.5^2 + \cdots + 19.1^2}{2} = 14.54$$

$$s_I^2 = 123.57 - 44.04 - 6.8 - 14.54 = 58.19$$

ANOVA table

Source	DF	SS	MS	F
Column	2	44.04	22.02	3.78
Row	5	6.80	1.36	1.68
Interaction	10	58.19	5.82	7.19
Error	18	14.54	0.81	
Total	35	123.57		

Critical values $F_{10, 18; 0.05} = 2.41$ [Table 3]

$\qquad\qquad F_{2, 10; 0.05} = 4.10$

$\qquad\qquad F_{5, 18; 0.05} = 2.77$

Hence $H_0: \sigma_{AB} = 0$ is rejected.

$\qquad H_0: \sigma_A^2 = 0$ is not rejected.

$\qquad H_0: \sigma_B^2 = 0$ is not rejected.

Test 88   Likelihood ratio test for the parameter of a rectangular population

Object

To test for one of the parameters of a rectangular population with probability density function

$$f_0(X) = \begin{cases} \dfrac{1}{2\beta}, & \alpha - \beta \leqslant X \leqslant \alpha + \beta \\ 0, & \text{otherwise.} \end{cases}$$

Limitations

This test is applicable if the observations are a random sample from a rectangular distribution.

Method

Let $X_1, X_2, \ldots, X_n$ be a random sample from the above rectangular population. We are interested in testing $H_0\colon \alpha = 0$ against $H_1\colon \alpha \neq 0$. Then, the likelihood ratio test criterion for testing H_0 is:

$$\lambda = \left(\frac{X_{(n)} - X_{(1)}}{2Z} \right)^n = \left(\frac{R}{2Z} \right)^n,$$

where R is the sample range and $Z = \max[-X_{(1)}, X_{(n)}]$. Then the asymptotic distribution of $2\log_e \lambda$ is χ_2^2.

Example data

Consider $(-0.2, -0.3, -0.4, 0.4, 0.3, 0.5)$ as a random sample from a rectangular distribution. Here,
$n = 6$

$R = 0.5 - (-0.2) = 0.7, Z = \max[0.4, 0.5] = 0.5$

$$\lambda = \left(\frac{R}{2Z} \right)^6 = (0.7)^6 = 0.1176, \qquad 2\log_e \lambda = -4.2809$$

Critical value $\chi_{2;0.05}^2 = 5.99$ [Table 5].

Hence we reject the null hypothesis that $\alpha = 0$.

Test 89   Uniformly most powerful test for the parameter of an exponential population

Object

To test the parameter (θ) of the exponential population with probability density function

$$f(X, \theta) = \theta \, e^{-\theta X}, \qquad X > 0.$$

Limitations

The test is applicable if the observations are a random sample from an exponential distribution.

Method

Let $X_1, X_2, \ldots, X_n$ be a random sample from an exponential distribution with parameter θ. Let our null hypothesis be H_0: $\theta = \theta_0$ against the alternative H_1: $\theta = \theta_1 (\theta_1 \neq \theta_0)$.

Case (a) $\theta_1 > \theta_0$: The most powerful critical region is given by:

$$W_0 = \left[X = \sum_i X_i \leqslant \chi^2_{2n; \, 1-\alpha} / 2\theta_0 \right].$$

Since W_0 is independent of θ_1, so W_0 is uniformly most powerful for testing H_0: $\theta = \theta_0$ against H_1: $\theta > \theta_0$.

Case (b) $\theta_1 < \theta_0$: The most powerful critical region is given by:

$$W_1 = \left[X = \sum X_i > \chi^2_{2n; \, \alpha} / 2\theta_0 \right].$$

Again W_1 is independent of θ_1 and so it is also uniformly most powerful for testing H_0: $\theta = \theta_0$ against H_1: $\theta < \theta_0$.

Example data

Let us consider a sample of size 2 from the population $f(X_1\theta) = \theta \, e^{-\theta X}$, $X > 0$. Consider testing H_0: $\theta = 1$ against H_1: $\theta = 2$, i.e. $\theta > \theta_0$. The critical region is

$$W = \left\{ \mathbf{X} / \sum X_i \leqslant \chi^2_{0.95, \, 4} / 2 \right\}$$

$$= \left\{ \mathbf{X} / \sum X_i \leqslant 0.71 / 2 \right\} \text{ [Table 5]}$$

$$= \left\{ \mathbf{X} / \sum X_i \leqslant 0.36 \right\}$$

Test 90   Sequential test for the parameter of a Bernoulli population

Object

To test the parameter of the Bernoulli population by the sequential method.

Limitations

This test is applicable if the observations are independent and identically follow the Bernoulli distribution.

Method

Let $X_1, X_2, \ldots, X_m$ be independent and identically distributed random variables having the distribution with probability density function (PDF)

$$f_0^{(x)} = \begin{cases} \theta^x(1-\theta)^{1-x}, & X = 0, 1 \\ 0, & \text{otherwise.} \end{cases}$$

where $0 < \theta < 1$. We want to test H_0: $\theta = \theta_0$ against H_1: $\theta = \theta_1$.

We fail to reject H_0 if $S_m \leqslant a_m$, and we reject H_0 if $S_m \geqslant r_m$. We continue sampling, i.e. taking observations, if $a_m < S_m < r_m$, where $S_m = \sum_{i=1}^{m} X_i$ and

$$a_m = \frac{\log \dfrac{\beta}{1-\alpha}}{\log \dfrac{\theta_1}{\theta_0} - \log\left(\dfrac{1-\theta_1}{1-\theta_0}\right)} + \frac{m \log\left(\dfrac{1-\theta_0}{1-\theta_1}\right)}{\log\left(\dfrac{\theta_1}{\theta_0}\right) - \log\left(\dfrac{1-\theta_1}{1-\theta_0}\right)}$$

$$r_m = \frac{\log \dfrac{1-\beta}{\alpha}}{\log \dfrac{\theta_1}{\theta_0} - \log\left(\dfrac{1-\theta_1}{1-\theta_0}\right)} + \frac{m \log\left(\dfrac{1-\theta_0}{1-\theta_1}\right)}{\log\left(\dfrac{\theta_1}{\theta_0}\right) - \log\left(\dfrac{1-\theta_1}{1-\theta_0}\right)}.$$

Example data

While dealing with the sampling of manufactured products, θ may be looked upon as the true proportion of defectives under a new production process. A manufacturer may be willing to adopt the new process if $\theta \leqslant \theta_0$ and will reject it if if $\theta \geqslant \theta_1$ and he may not be decisive if $\theta_0 < \theta < \theta_1$. To reach a decision, he may use a sequential sampling plan, taking one item at each stage and at random. Here S_m will be the number of defectives up to the mth stage, a_m the corresponding acceptance number and r_m the rejection number. If $\theta_0 = 0.04$ and $\theta_1 = 0.08$, $\alpha = 0.15$, $\beta = 0.25$, then the graphical representation of the sequential plan is:

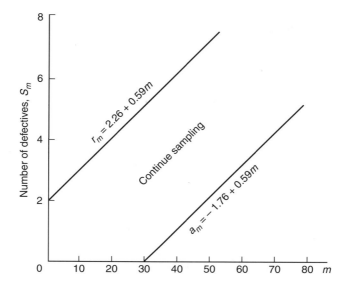

As soon as (m, S_m) lies on or below the line for a_m or on or above the line for r_m, sampling is to be stopped; the new process is to be considered in the former case and rejected in the latter.

Test 91   Sequential probability ratio test

Object

A sequential test for the ratio between the mean and the standard deviation of a normal population where both are unknown.

Limitations

This test is applicable if the observations are normally distributed with unknown mean and variance.

Method

Let $X \sim N(\mu, \sigma^2)$, where both μ and σ^2 are unknown. We want to find a sequential test for testing H_0: $\mu/\sigma = r_0$ against H_1: $\mu/\sigma = r_1$. The sequential probability ratio test procedure is as follows.

1. Continue sampling if $b_n < t_n < a_n$, where

$$t_n = \frac{\sum_{i=1}^{n} X_i}{\sqrt{\sum_{i=1}^{n} X_i^2}} = \frac{\sum_{i=1}^{n} y_i}{\sqrt{\sum_{i=1}^{n} y_i^2}}$$

where $y_i = X_i/|X_i|$, $i = 1, 2, \ldots, n$,

$$a_n = \log \frac{1-\beta}{\alpha} \quad \text{and} \quad b_n = \log \frac{\beta}{1-\alpha}.$$

2. Fail to reject H_0 if $t_n \leqslant b_n$ and reject H_0 if $t_n \geqslant a_n$.

Example data

Consider a sample from $N(\mu, \sigma^2)$ where μ and σ are both unknown. Then we want a sequential test for testing H_0: $\mu/\sigma = 0.2$ against H_1: $\mu/\sigma = 0.4$.

Let $\alpha = 0.25$, $\beta = 0.35$, $a_n = \log(0.65/0.25)$, $b_n = \log(0.35/0.75)$.

If $\log 7/15 < t_n < \log 13/5$ then continue sampling.

If $t_n \leqslant \log 7/15$ do not reject H_0, and if $t_n \geqslant \log 13/5$ reject H_0.

Test 92   Durbin–Watson test

Object

To test whether the error terms in a regression model are autocorrelated.

Limitations

This test is applicable if the autocorrelation parameter and error terms are independently normally distributed with mean zero and variance s^2.

Method

This test is based on the first-order autoregressive error model $\varepsilon_t = \varphi \varepsilon_{t-1} + u_t$ where φ is the autocorrelation parameter and the u_t are independently normally distributed with zero mean and variance σ^2. When one is concerned with positive autocorrelation the alternatives are given as follows:

$$H_0: \varphi \leqslant 0 \qquad H_1: \varphi > 0.$$

Here H_0 implies that error terms are uncorrelated or negatively correlated, while H_1 implies that they are positively autocorrelated. This test is based on the difference between adjacent residuals $\varepsilon_t - \varepsilon_{t-1}$ and is given by

$$d = \frac{\sum_{t=2}^{n} (e_t - e_{t-1})^2}{\sum_{t=1}^{n} e_t^2}$$

where e_t is the regression residual for period t, and n is the number of time periods used in fitting the regression model.

When the error terms are positively autocorrelated the adjacent residuals will tend to be of similar magnitude and the numerator of the test statistic d will be small. If the error terms are either not correlated or negatively correlated e_t and e_{t-1} will tend to differ and the numerator of the test statistic will be larger. The exact action limit for this test is difficult to calculate and the test is used with lower bound d_L and the upper bound d_U. When the statistic d is less than the lower bound d_L, we conclude that positive autocorrelation is present. Similarly, when the test statistic exceeds the upper bound d_U, we conclude that positive autocorrelation is not present. When $d_L < d < d_U$, the test is inconclusive.

Example data

$n = 20$, $\alpha = 0.05$

Quarter-t	Company sale Y_i	Industry sales X_i
1	77.044	746.512
2	78.613	762.345
3	80.124	778.179
4	–	–
–	–	–
–	–	–
–	–	–
–	–	–
20	102.481	1006.882

A computer run of a regression package provided us with the value of the test statistic $d = 0.4765$: $d_L = 1.20$ and $d_U = 1.41$ from Table 33. Since $d = 0.4765 < 1.20$, the error terms are positively autocorrelated.

Test 93 Duckworth's test for comparing the medians of two populations

Object

A quick and easy test for comparing the medians of two populations which could be used for a wide range of m and n observations.

Limitations

This is not a powerful test but it is easy to use and the table values can be easily obtained. It works only on the largest and the smallest values of the observations from different populations.

Method

Consider the smallest observation from the X population and the largest from the Y population. Then the test statistic, D, is the sum of the overlaps, the number of X observations that are smaller than the smallest Y, plus the number of Y observations that are larger than the largest X. If either $3 + 4n/3 \leqslant m \leqslant 2n$ or vice versa we subtract 1 from D. Under these circumstances, the table of critical values consists of the three numbers; 7, 10, and 13. If $D \leqslant 7$ we reject the hypothesis of equal medians at $\alpha = 0.05$.

Example data

$m = n = 12$

1	2	3	4	5	6	7	8	9	10	11	12
66.3	68.3	68.5	69.2	70.0	70.1	70.4	70.9	71.1	71.2	72.1	72.1
X	X	X	Y	Y	X	X	Y	X	X	Y	Y

13	14	15	16	17	18	19	20	21	22	23	24
72.1	72.7	72.8	73.3	73.6	74.1	74.2	74.6	74.7	74.8	75.5	75.8
X	X	Y	Y	X	X	Y	Y	Y	X	Y	Y

We note that there are three X observations below all the Y observations and two Ys above all the Xs. The total is $D = 5$, which is less than 7 and so not significant.

Test 94 χ^2-test for a suitable probabilistic model

Object

Many experiments yield a set of data, say $X_1, X_2, \ldots, X_n$, and the experimenter is often interested in determining whether the data can be treated as the observed values of the random sample $X_1, X_2, \ldots, X_n$ from a given distribution. That is, would this proposed distribution be a reasonable probabilistic model for these sample items?

Limitations

This test is applicable if both distributions have the same interval classification and the same number of elements. The observed data are observed by random sampling.

Method

Let X_1 denote the number of heads that occur when coins are tossed at random, under the assumptions that the coins are independent and the probability of heads for each coin has a binomial distribution. An experiment resulted in certain observed values at Y_i corresponding to 0, 1, 2, 3 and 4 heads.

Let $A_1 = \{0\}$, $A_2 = \{1\}$, $A_3 = \{2\}$, $A_4 = \{3\}$, $A_5 = \{4\}$ be the corresponding heads and if $\pi_i = P(X \in A_i)$ when X is $B(4, \frac{1}{2})$, then we have

$$\pi_1 = \pi_5 = \binom{4}{0}\left(\frac{1}{2}\right)^4 = 0.0625$$

$$\pi_2 = \pi_4 = \binom{4}{1}\left(\frac{1}{2}\right)^4 = 0.25$$

$$\pi_3 = \binom{4}{2}\left(\frac{1}{2}\right)^4 = 0.375.$$

If $\alpha = 0.05$, then the null hypothesis

$$H_0\colon p_1 = \pi_1, \ p_2 = \pi_2, \ p_3 = \pi_3, \ p_4 = \pi_4, \ p_5 = \pi_5$$

is rejected if the calculated value is greater than the tabulated value using

$$\left[q_{k-1} = \sum_{i=1}^{k} \frac{(y_i - n\pi_i)^2}{n\pi_i} \right] \sim \chi_{k-1}^2.$$

Example data

In this case $y_1 = 7$, $y_2 = 18$, $y_3 = 40$, $y_4 = 31$ and $y_5 = 4$. The computed value is

$$q_4 = \frac{(7 - 6.25)^2}{6.25} + \frac{(18 - 25)^2}{25} + \frac{(40 - 37.5)^2}{37.5} + \frac{(31 - 25)^2}{25}$$

$$+ \frac{(4 - 6.25)^2}{6.25} = 4.47.$$

Critical value $\chi_4^2(0.05) = 9.49$ [Table 5].

Hence the hypothesis is not rejected. Thus the data support the hypothesis that $B\left(4, \frac{1}{2}\right)$ is a reasonable probabilistic model for X.

Test 95   V-test (modified Rayleigh)

Object

To test whether the observed angles have a tendency to cluster around a given angle indicating a lack of randomness in the distribution.

Limitations

For grouped data the length of the mean vector must be adjusted, and for axial data all angles must be doubled.

Method

Given a random sample of n angular values $\Phi_1, \Phi_2, \ldots, \Phi_n$ and a given theoretical direction determined by an angle θ_0, then the test statistic for the test of randomness is:

$$V = (2n)^{\frac{1}{2}}\vartheta$$

where $\vartheta = r\cos(\bar{\Phi} - \theta_0)$ and r is the length of the mean vector

$$r = \frac{1}{n}\left[\left(\sum \cos \Phi_i\right)^2 + \left(\sum \sin \Phi_i\right)^2\right] = (\bar{x}^2 + \bar{y}^2)^{\frac{1}{2}}$$

$$\bar{\Phi} = \begin{cases} \arctan\left(\dfrac{\bar{y}}{\bar{x}}\right) & \text{if } \bar{x} > 0 \\ 180° + \arctan\left(\dfrac{\bar{y}}{\bar{x}}\right) & \text{if } \bar{x} < 0. \end{cases}$$

If V is greater than or equal to the critical $V(\alpha)$, the null hypothesis, that the parent population is uniformly distributed (randomness), is rejected.

Example data

$n = 15$

$\Phi_1 = 250°$, $\Phi_2 = 275°$, $\Phi_3 = 285°$, $\Phi_4 = 285°$, $\Phi_5 = 290°$, $\Phi_6 = 290°$, $\Phi_7 = 295°$, $\Phi_8 = 300°$, $\Phi_9 = 305°$, $\Phi_{10} = 310°$, $\Phi_{11} = 315°$, $\Phi_{12} = 320°$, $\Phi_{13} = 330°$, $\Phi_{14} = 330°$, $\Phi_{15} = 5°$, $\theta_0 = 265°$

$$\bar{x} = \frac{1}{n}(\cos \Phi_1 + \cdots + \cos \Phi_{15}) = \frac{7.287}{15} = 0.4858$$

$$\bar{y} = \frac{1}{n}(\sin \Phi_1 + \cdots + \sin \Phi_{15}) = \frac{-11.367}{15} = -0.7578$$

$$r = (\bar{x}^2 + \bar{y}^2)^{\frac{1}{2}} = (0.4858^2 + 0.7578^2)^{\frac{1}{2}} = 0.9001$$

$$\bar{\Phi} = \arctan\left(\frac{-0.7578}{0.4858}\right) = -57.3°, \text{ which is equivalent to } 303°.$$

$$\vartheta = r\cos(\bar{\Phi} - \theta_0) = 0.9001 \times \cos(303° - 265°) = 0.9001 \times 0.7880 = 0.7092$$

$$V = (2 \times 15)^{\frac{1}{2}} \times 0.7092 = 5.4772 \times 0.7092 = 3.884$$

Critical value $V_{15;0.01} = 2.302$ [Table 34].

Hence reject the null hypothesis of randomness.

Test 96 Watson's U_n^2-test

Object

To test whether the given distribution fits a random sample of angular values.

Limitations

This test is suitable for both unimodal and the multimodal cases. The test is very practical if a computer program is available. It can be used as a test for randomness.

Method

Given a random sample of n angular values $\Phi_1, \Phi_2, \ldots, \Phi_n$ rearranged in ascending order: $\Phi_1 \leqslant \Phi_2 \leqslant \cdots \leqslant \Phi_n$. Suppose $F(\Phi)$ is the distribution function of the given theoretical distribution and let

$$V_i = F(\Phi_i), \qquad i = 1, 2, \ldots, n$$

$$\bar{V} = \frac{1}{n} \sum V_i \qquad \text{and} \qquad C_i = 2i - 1.$$

Then the test statistic is:

$$U_n^2 = \sum_{i=1}^{n} V_i^2 - \sum_{i=1}^{n} \left(\frac{C_i V_i}{n} \right) + n\left[\tfrac{1}{3} - (\bar{V} - \tfrac{1}{2})^2\right].$$

If the sample value of U_n^2 exceeds the critical value the null hypothesis is rejected. Otherwise the fit is satisfactory.

Example data

$n = 13$, $F(\Phi) = \Phi/360°$, $\Phi_1 = 20°$, $\Phi_2 = 135°$, $\Phi_3 = 145°$, $\Phi_4 = 165°$, $\Phi_5 = 170°$, $\Phi_6 = 200°$, $\Phi_7 = 300°$, $\Phi_8 = 325°$, $\Phi_9 = 335°$, $\Phi_{10} = 350°$, $\Phi_{11} = 350°$, $\Phi_{12} = 350°$, $\Phi_{13} = 355°$

$V_i = \Phi_i/13$, $i = 1, \ldots, 13$

$$\sum V_i = 8.8889, \quad \sum V_i^2 = 7.2310, \quad \sum C_i V_i / n = 10.9893, \quad \bar{V} = 0.68376$$

$U_n^2 = 7.2310 - 10.9893 + 13\left[\tfrac{1}{3} - (0.18376)^2\right] = 0.1361$

Critical value $U_{13;0.05}^2 = 0.184$ [Table 35].

Do not reject the null hypothesis. The sample comes from the given theoretical distribution.

Test 97   Watson's U^2-test

Object

To test whether two samples from circular observations differ significantly from each other with regard to mean direction or angular variance.

Limitation

Both samples must come from a continuous distribution. In the case of grouping the class interval should not exceed $5°$.

Method

Given two random samples of n and m circular observations $\Phi_1, \Phi_2, \ldots, \Phi_n$ and $\Psi_1, \Psi_2, \ldots, \Psi_m$, let $n + m = N$ and $d_1, d_2, \ldots, d_N$ $(k = 1, 2, \ldots, N)$ be the differences between the sample distribution function, and let $\bar{d}$ denote the mean of the N differences. Then the test statistic is given by:

$$U^2 = \frac{nm}{N^2} \left[\sum_{k=1}^{N} d_k^2 - \frac{1}{N} \left(\sum_{k=1}^{N} d_k \right)^2 \right].$$

If $U^2 > U^2(\alpha)$, reject the null hypothesis.

Example data

$$n = 8, \ m = 10, \ \sum_{k=1}^{16} d_k = 6.525, \ \sum_{k=1}^{16} d_k^2 = 3.422$$

$$U^2 = \frac{80}{18^2} \left(3.422 - \frac{6.525 \times 6.525}{18} \right) = 0.261$$

Critical value $U^2_{8, 10; 0.05} = 0.185$ [Table 36].

The calculated value is greater than the critical value.

Reject the hypothesis. The two samples deviate significantly from each other.

Test 98   Watson–Williams test

Object

To test whether the mean angles of two independent circular observations differ significantly from each other.

Limitations

Samples are drawn from a von Mises distribution and the concentration parameter k (>2) must have the same value in each population.

Method

Given two independent random samples of n and m circular observations $\Phi_1, \Phi_2, \ldots, \Phi_n$ and $\Psi_1, \Psi_2, \ldots, \Psi_m$, for each sample, calculate the components of the resultant vectors

$$C_1 = \sum_{i=1}^{n} \cos \Phi_i \qquad S_1 = \sum_{i=1}^{n} \sin \Phi_i$$

$$C_2 = \sum_{i=1}^{m} \cos \Psi_i \qquad S_2 = \sum_{i=1}^{m} \sin \Psi_i$$

with the resultant lengths

$$R_1 = (C_1^2 + S_1^2)^{\frac{1}{2}} \qquad R_2 = (C_2^2 + S_2^2)^{\frac{1}{2}}.$$

The directions of the resultant vectors are given by $\bar{\Phi}$ and $\bar{\Psi}$. For the combined sample, the components of the resultant vector are

$$C = C_1 + C_2 \qquad \text{and} \qquad S = S_1 + S_2.$$

Hence, the length of the resultant vector is

$$R = (C^2 + S^2)^{\frac{1}{2}}.$$

To test the unknown mean angles of the population use the test statistic

$$F = g(N-2)\frac{R_1 + R_2 - R}{N - (R_1 + R_2)}$$

where $N = n + m$ and $g = 1 - 3/8\hat{k}$, with k determined from

$$\bar{R} = \frac{R_1 + R_2}{N}$$

and Table 37. Reject the null hypothesis if the calculated value F is greater than the critical value $F_{1, N-2}$.

Example data

$n = 10, m = 10, N = 20, \nu_1 = 1, \nu_2 = N - 2$
$C_1 = 9.833, \quad C_2 = 9.849, \quad C = 19.682$
$S_1 = -1.558, \quad S_2 = 0.342, \quad S = -1.246$
$R_1 = 9.956, \quad R_2 = 9.854, \quad R = 19.721$

$\bar{R} = 0.991$ for $\hat{k}$ greater than 10, $\quad g = 1$
$\hat{k} = 50.241$ [Table 37]

$$F = \frac{18 \times 0.089}{0.190} = 8.432$$

Critical value $F_{1, 18; 0.01} = 8.29$ [Table 3].

Reject the null hypothesis.

Hence the mean directions differ significantly.

Test 99 Mardia–Watson–Wheeler test

Object

To test whether two independent random samples from circular observations differ significantly from each other regarding mean angle, angular variance or both.

Limitation

There are no ties between the samples and the populations have a continuous circular distribution.

Method

Consider two independent samples of n and m circular observations $\Phi_1, \Phi_2, \ldots, \Phi_n$ and $\Psi_1, \Psi_2, \ldots, \Psi_m$. We observe the order in which the random samples are arranged and then alter the space between successive sample points in such a way that all these spaces become the same size. Having spaced the sample points equally, the sample points are then ranked. Let $r_1, r_2, \ldots, r_n$ be the ranks of the first sample and $\beta_i = r_i \delta (i = 1, \ldots, n)$ be the angles, where δ and $N = n + m$ are known as uniform scores. Then the resultant vector of the first sample has components

$$C_1 = \sum \cos \beta_i \qquad S_1 = \sum \sin \beta_i$$

and the length of the resultant vector is

$$R_1 = (C^2 + S^2)^{\frac{1}{2}}.$$

The test statistic is given by

$$B = R_1^2.$$

If $B > B_\alpha$, reject the null hypothesis. When $N > 17$, the quantity $\chi^2 = 2(N - 1)R_1^2/nm$ has a χ^2-distribution with 2 degrees of freedom if H_0 is true.

Example data

$n = 6$, $m = 4$, $N = 10$, $\delta = 360°/10 = 36°$, $\alpha = 0.05$
Here m is the smaller sample size.
For the first sample:

$r_1 = 1,$	$r_2 = 2,$	$r_3 = 3,$	$r_4 = 4,$	$r_5 = 8,$	$r_6 = 9$
$\beta_1 = 36°,$	$\beta_2 = 72°,$	$\beta_3 = 108°,$	$\beta_4 = 144°,$	$\beta_5 = 288°,$	$\beta_6 = 324°$
$C_1 = 1.118$	$S_1 = 1.539$	$R_1 = 1.902$			
$B = 3.618$					

Critical value $B_{N, m; \alpha} = B_{10, 4; 0.05} = 9.47$ [Table 38].

The calculated value B is less than the critical value B_α.

Hence there are no significant differences between the samples. (The second sample would lead to the same result.)

Test 100　Harrison–Kanji–Gadsden test (analysis of variance for angular data)

Object

To test whether the treatment effects of the q independent random samples from von Mises populations differ significantly from each other.

Limitations

1. Samples are drawn from a von Mises population.
2. The concentration parameter k has the same value for each sample.
3. k must be at least 2.

Method

Given a one-way classification situation with μ_0, β_j and e_{ij} denoting the overall mean direction, treatment effect and random error variation respectively, then

$$\Phi_{ij} = \mu_0 + \beta_j + e_{ij}, \qquad i = 1, \ldots, p; \quad j = 1, 2, \ldots, q$$

where each observation Φ_{ij} is an independent observation from a von Mises distribution with mean $\mu_0 + \beta_j$ and concentration parameter k.

For the one-way situation, the components of variation are similarly

$$k\left[N - \frac{R^2}{N} \right] = k\left[\sum_{j=1}^{q} \left(\frac{R_{\cdot j}^2}{N_{\cdot j}} - \frac{R^2}{N} \right) \right] + k\left[N - \sum_{j=1}^{q} \left(\frac{R_{\cdot j}^2}{N_{\cdot j}} \right) \right]$$

(Total variation) = (Between variation) + (Residual variation)

and the test statistic for a large value of k is given by

$$F'_{q-1, N-q} = \beta \left[\frac{(N-q)\left(\sum_{j=1}^{q} \left(\frac{R_{\cdot j}^2}{N_{\cdot j}} \right) - \frac{R^2}{N} \right)}{(q-1)\left\{ N - \sum_{j=1}^{q} \left(\frac{R_{\cdot j}^2}{N_{\cdot j}} \right) \right\}} \right]$$

where $\sum_{i=1}^{p} \sum_{j=1}^{q} \cos(\Phi_{ij} - \hat{\mu}_0) = R$, and $\bar{\Phi}_{\cdot j}$ are the jth mean angles with corresponding resultant length $r_{\cdot j}$.

Let $x_{\cdot j}$ and $y_{\cdot j}$ be the rectangular components of $r_{\cdot j}$. Then:

$$r_{\cdot\cdot} = \left[\left(\frac{1}{q} \sum_{j=1}^{q} r_{\cdot j} \cos \bar{\Phi}_{\cdot j} \right)^2 + \left(\frac{1}{q} \sum_{j=1}^{q} r_{\cdot j} \sin \bar{\Phi}_{\cdot j} \right)^2 \right]^{\frac{1}{2}}$$

and $R = N r_{\cdot\cdot}$, $R_{\cdot j} = \sum_{j=1}^{q} \cos(\Phi_{ij} - \bar{\Phi}_{\cdot j})$,

$$\bar{\Phi}_{\cdot j} = \arctan\left(\frac{\bar{y}}{\bar{x}} \right), \qquad r_{\cdot j} = [(\bar{x}^2 + \bar{y}^2)]^{\frac{1}{2}}$$

where

$$\bar{x} = \frac{1}{q}[\cos \Phi_{1j} + \cos \Phi_{2j} + \cdots + \cos \Phi_{qj}]$$

$$\bar{y} = \frac{1}{q}[\sin \Phi_{1j} + \sin \Phi_{2j} + \cdots + \sin \Phi_{qj}]$$

$\hat{k}$ is found by calculating the resultant $\bar{R}$ and using Table 37. Here $\bar{R} = R/N$.

Example data

Magnification	
100	82, 71, 85, 89, 78, 77, 74, 71, 68, 83, 72, 73, 81, 65, 62, 90, 92, 80, 77, 93, 75, 80, 69, 74, 77, 75, 71, 82, 84, 79, 78, 81, 89, 79, 82, 81, 85, 76, 71, 80, 94, 68, 72, 70, 59, 80, 86, 98, 82, 73
200	75, 74, 71, 63, 83, 74, 82, 78, 87, 87, 82, 71, 60, 66, 63, 85, 81, 78, 80, 89, 82, 82, 92, 80, 81, 74, 90, 78, 73, 72, 80, 59, 64, 78, 73, 70, 79, 79, 77, 81, 72, 76, 69, 73, 75, 84, 81, 51, 76, 88
400	70, 76, 79, 86, 77, 86, 77, 90, 88, 82, 84, 70, 87, 61, 71, 89, 72, 90, 74, 88, 82, 68, 83, 75, 90, 79, 89, 78, 74, 73, 71, 80, 83, 89, 68, 81, 47, 88, 69, 76, 71, 67, 76, 90, 84, 70, 80, 77, 93, 89
1200	78, 90, 72, 91, 73, 79, 82, 87, 78, 83, 74, 82, 85, 75, 67, 72, 78, 88, 89, 71, 73, 77, 90, 82, 80, 81, 89, 87, 78, 73, 78, 86, 73, 84, 68, 75, 70, 89, 54, 80, 90, 88, 81, 82, 88, 82, 75, 79, 83, 82
400 × 1.3	88, 69, 64, 78, 71, 68, 54, 80, 73, 72, 65, 73, 93, 84, 80, 49, 78, 82, 95, 69, 87, 83, 52, 79, 85, 67, 82, 84, 87, 83, 88, 79, 83, 77, 78, 89, 75, 72, 88, 78, 62, 86, 89, 74, 71, 73, 84, 56, 77, 71

$q = 5$, $N_{.1} = N_{.2} = \cdots = N_{.q} = 50$, $N = 250$

$\nu_1 = q - 1 = 4$, $\nu_2 = N - q = 245$

$R = 238.550$, $\sum_{j=1}^{q}\left[\frac{R_{.j}^2}{N_{.j}}\right] = 228.1931$, $\frac{R^2}{N} = 227.6244$

Between variation = 0.5687, within variation = 21.8069

$$F'_{q-1, N-q} = \beta\left[\frac{0.142175}{0.089007}\right] = \beta\,(1.597337)$$

$\hat{k} = 11.02$, $\frac{1}{\beta} = 1 - \frac{1}{5\hat{k}} - \frac{1}{10\hat{k}^2}$ or $\beta = 1.01959$,

where $\bar{R} = \frac{R}{N} = 0.954$ [Table 37]

Modified $F' = \beta \times F_{4, 245} = 1.01959 \times 1.597337$ or $F'_{4, 245} = 1.628$

Critical value $F_{4, 245; 0.05} = 2.37$ [Table 3].

Hence there are no significant differences between the treatments.

LIST OF TABLES

TABLES

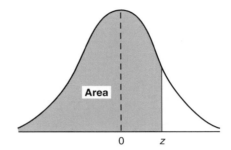

Area

Table 1   The normal curve

(a) Area under the normal curve

z	0.00	0.01	0.02	0.03	0.04	0.05	0.06	0.07	0.08	0.09
−3.4	0.0003	0.0003	0.0003	0.0003	0.0003	0.0003	0.0003	0.0003	0.0003	0.0002
−3.3	0.0005	0.0005	0.0005	0.0004	0.0004	0.0004	0.0004	0.0004	0.0004	0.0003
−3.2	0.0007	0.0007	0.0006	0.0006	0.0006	0.0006	0.0006	0.0005	0.0005	0.0005
−3.1	0.0010	0.0009	0.0009	0.0009	0.0008	0.0008	0.0008	0.0008	0.0007	0.0007
−3.0	0.0013	0.0013	0.0013	0.0012	0.0012	0.0011	0.0011	0.0011	0.0010	0.0010
−2.9	0.0019	0.0018	0.0017	0.0017	0.0016	0.0016	0.0015	0.0015	0.0014	0.0014
−2.8	0.0026	0.0025	0.0024	0.0023	0.0023	0.0022	0.0021	0.0021	0.0020	0.0019
−2.7	0.0035	0.0034	0.0033	0.0032	0.0031	0.0030	0.0029	0.0028	0.0027	0.0026
−2.6	0.0047	0.0045	0.0044	0.0043	0.0041	0.0040	0.0039	0.0038	0.0037	0.0036
−2.5	0.0062	0.0060	0.0059	0.0057	0.0055	0.0054	0.0052	0.0051	0.0049	0.0048
−2.4	0.0082	0.0080	0.0078	0.0075	0.0073	0.0071	0.0069	0.0068	0.0066	0.0064
−2.3	0.0107	0.0104	0.0102	0.0099	0.0096	0.0094	0.0091	0.0089	0.0087	0.0084
−2.2	0.0139	0.0136	0.0132	0.0129	0.0124	0.0122	0.0119	0.0116	0.0113	0.0110
−2.1	0.0179	0.0174	0.0170	0.0166	0.0162	0.0158	0.0154	0.0150	0.0146	0.0143
−2.0	0.0228	0.0222	0.0217	0.0212	0.0207	0.0202	0.0197	0.0192	0.0188	0.0183
−1.9	0.0287	0.0281	0.0274	0.0268	0.0262	0.0256	0.0250	0.0244	0.0239	0.0233
−1.8	0.0359	0.0352	0.0344	0.0336	0.0329	0.0322	0.0314	0.0307	0.0301	0.0294
−1.7	0.0446	0.0436	0.0427	0.0418	0.0409	0.0401	0.0392	0.0384	0.0375	0.0367
−1.6	0.0548	0.0537	0.0526	0.0516	0.0505	0.0495	0.0485	0.0475	0.0465	0.0455
−1.5	0.0668	0.0655	0.0643	0.0630	0.0618	0.0606	0.0594	0.0582	0.0571	0.0559
−1.4	0.0808	0.0793	0.0778	0.0764	0.0749	0.0735	0.0722	0.0708	0.0694	0.0681
−1.3	0.0968	0.0951	0.0934	0.0918	0.0901	0.0885	0.0869	0.0853	0.0838	0.0823
−1.2	0.1151	0.1131	0.1112	0.1093	0.1075	0.1056	0.1038	0.1020	0.1003	0.0985
−1.1	0.1357	0.1335	0.1314	0.1292	0.1271	0.1251	0.1230	0.1210	0.1190	0.1170
−1.0	0.1587	0.1562	0.1539	0.1515	0.1492	0.1469	0.1446	0.1423	0.1401	0.1379
−0.9	0.1841	0.1814	0.1788	0.1762	0.1736	0.1711	0.1685	0.1660	0.1635	0.1611
−0.8	0.2119	0.2090	0.2061	0.2033	0.2005	0.1977	0.1949	0.1922	0.1894	0.1867
−0.7	0.2420	0.2389	0.2358	0.2327	0.2296	0.2266	0.2236	0.2206	0.2177	0.2148
−0.6	0.2743	0.2709	0.2676	0.2643	0.2611	0.2578	0.2546	0.2514	0.2483	0.2451
−0.5	0.3085	0.3050	0.3015	0.2981	0.2946	0.2912	0.2877	0.2843	0.2810	0.2776
−0.4	0.3446	0.3409	0.3372	0.3336	0.3300	0.3264	0.3228	0.3192	0.3156	0.3121
−0.3	0.3821	0.3783	0.3745	0.3707	0.3669	0.3632	0.3594	0.3557	0.3520	0.3483
−0.2	0.4207	0.4168	0.4129	0.4090	0.4052	0.4013	0.3974	0.3936	0.3897	0.3859
−0.1	0.4602	0.4562	0.4522	0.4483	0.4443	0.4404	0.4364	0.4325	0.4286	0.4247
−0.0	0.5000	0.4960	0.4920	0.4880	0.4840	0.4801	0.4761	0.4721	0.4681	0.4641

Table 1(a) continued

z	0.00	0.01	0.02	0.03	0.04	0.05	0.06	0.07	0.08	0.09
0.0	0.5000	0.5040	0.5080	0.5120	0.5160	0.5199	0.5239	0.5279	0.5319	0.5359
0.1	0.5398	0.5438	0.5478	0.5517	0.5557	0.5596	0.5636	0.5675	0.5714	0.5753
0.2	0.5793	0.5832	0.5871	0.5910	0.5948	0.5987	0.6026	0.6064	0.6103	0.6141
0.3	0.6179	0.6217	0.6255	0.6293	0.6331	0.6368	0.6406	0.6443	0.6480	0.6517
0.4	0.6554	0.6591	0.6628	0.6664	0.6700	0.6736	0.6772	0.6808	0.6844	0.6879
0.5	0.6915	0.6950	0.6985	0.7019	0.7054	0.7088	0.7123	0.7157	0.7190	0.7224
0.6	0.7257	0.7291	0.7324	0.7357	0.7389	0.7422	0.7454	0.7486	0.7517	0.7549
0.7	0.7580	0.7611	0.7642	0.7673	0.7704	0.7734	0.7764	0.7794	0.7823	0.7852
0.8	0.7881	0.7910	0.7939	0.7967	0.7995	0.8023	0.8051	0.8078	0.8106	0.8133
0.9	0.8159	0.8186	0.8212	0.8238	0.8264	0.8289	0.8315	0.8340	0.8365	0.8389
1.0	0.8413	0.8438	0.8461	0.8485	0.8508	0.8531	0.8554	0.8577	0.8599	0.8621
1.1	0.8643	0.8665	0.8686	0.8708	0.8729	0.8749	0.8770	0.8790	0.8810	0.8830
1.2	0.8849	0.8869	0.8888	0.8907	0.8925	0.8944	0.8962	0.8980	0.8997	0.9015
1.3	0.9032	0.9049	0.9066	0.9082	0.9099	0.9115	0.9131	0.9147	0.9162	0.9177
1.4	0.9192	0.9207	0.9222	0.9236	0.9251	0.9265	0.9278	0.9292	0.9306	0.9319
1.5	0.9332	0.9345	0.9357	0.9370	0.9382	0.9394	0.9406	0.9418	0.9429	0.9441
1.6	0.9452	0.9463	0.9474	0.9484	0.9495	0.9505	0.9515	0.9525	0.9535	0.9545
1.7	0.9554	0.9564	0.9573	0.9582	0.9591	0.9599	0.9608	0.9616	0.9625	0.9633
1.8	0.9641	0.9649	0.9656	0.9664	0.9671	0.9678	0.9686	0.9693	0.9699	0.9706
1.9	0.9713	0.9719	0.9726	0.9732	0.9738	0.9744	0.9750	0.9756	0.9761	0.9767
2.0	0.9772	0.9778	0.9783	0.9788	0.9793	0.9798	0.9803	0.9808	0.9812	0.9817
2.1	0.9821	0.9826	0.9830	0.9834	0.9838	0.9842	0.9846	0.9850	0.9854	0.9857
2.2	0.9861	0.9864	0.9868	0.9871	0.9875	0.9878	0.9881	0.9884	0.9887	0.9890
2.3	0.9893	0.9896	0.9898	0.9901	0.9904	0.9906	0.9909	0.9911	0.9913	0.9916
2.4	0.9918	0.9920	0.9922	0.9925	0.9927	0.9929	0.9931	0.9932	0.9934	0.9936
2.5	0.9938	0.9940	0.9941	0.9943	0.9945	0.9946	0.9948	0.9949	0.9951	0.9952
2.6	0.9953	0.9955	0.9956	0.9957	0.9959	0.9960	0.9961	0.9962	0.9963	0.9964
2.7	0.9965	0.9966	0.9967	0.9968	0.9969	0.9970	0.9971	0.9972	0.9973	0.9974
2.8	0.9974	0.9975	0.9976	0.9977	0.9977	0.9978	0.9979	0.9979	0.9980	0.9981
2.9	0.9981	0.9982	0.9982	0.9983	0.9984	0.9984	0.9985	0.9985	0.9986	0.9986
3.0	0.9987	0.9987	0.9987	0.9988	0.9988	0.9989	0.9989	0.9989	0.9990	0.9990
3.1	0.9990	0.9991	0.9991	0.9991	0.9992	0.9992	0.9992	0.9992	0.9993	0.9993
3.2	0.9993	0.9993	0.9994	0.9994	0.9994	0.9994	0.9994	0.9995	0.9995	0.9995
3.3	0.9995	0.9995	0.9995	0.9996	0.9996	0.9996	0.9996	0.9996	0.9996	0.9997
3.4	0.9997	0.9997	0.9997	0.9997	0.9997	0.9997	0.9997	0.9997	0.9997	0.9998

Source: Walpole and Myers, 1989

(b) critical values for a standard normal distribution

The normal distribution is symmetrical with respect to $\mu = 0$.

Level of significance α		z
Two-sided	One-sided	
0.001	0.0005	3.29
0.002	0.001	3.09
0.0026	0.0013	3.00
0.01	0.05	2.58
0.02	0.01	2.33
0.0456	0.0228	2.00
0.05	0.025	1.96
0.10	0.05	1.64
0.20	0.10	1.28
0.318	0.159	1.00

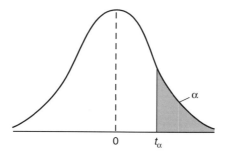

Table 2   Critical values of the *t*-distribution

ν	Level of significance α				
	0.10	0.05	0.025	0.01	0.005
1	3.078	6.314	12.706	31.821	63.657
2	1.886	2.920	4.303	6.965	9.925
3	1.638	2.353	3.182	4.541	5.841
4	1.533	2.132	2.776	3.747	4.604
5	1.476	2.015	2.571	3.365	4.032
6	1.440	1.943	2.447	3.143	3.707
7	1.415	1.895	2.365	2.998	3.499
8	1.397	1.860	2.306	2.896	3.355
9	1.383	1.833	2.262	2.821	3.250
10	1.372	1.812	2.228	2.764	3.169
11	1.363	1.796	2.201	2.718	3.106
12	1.356	1.782	2.179	2.681	3.055
13	1.350	1.771	2.160	2.650	3.012
14	1.345	1.761	2.145	2.624	2.977
15	1.341	1.753	2.131	2.602	2.947
16	1.337	1.746	2.120	2.583	2.921
17	1.333	1.740	2.110	2.567	2.898
18	1.330	1.734	2.101	2.552	2.878
19	1.328	1.729	2.093	2.539	2.861
20	1.325	1.725	2.086	2.528	2.845
21	1.323	1.721	2.080	2.518	2.831
22	1.321	1.717	2.074	2.508	2.819
23	1.319	1.714	2.069	2.500	2.807
24	1.318	1.711	2.064	2.492	2.797
25	1.316	1.708	2.060	2.485	2.787
26	1.315	1.706	2.056	2.479	2.779
27	1.314	1.703	2.052	2.473	2.771
28	1.313	1.701	2.048	2.467	2.763
29	1.311	1.699	2.045	2.462	2.756
30	1.310	1.697	2.042	2.457	2.750
∞	1.282	1.645	1.960	2.326	2.576

Source: Fisher and Yates, 1974

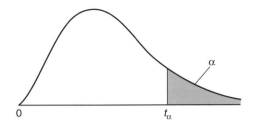

0 t_α

Table 3   Critical values of the *F*-distribution

Level of significance $\alpha = 0.05$

ν_2 \ ν_1	1	2	3	4	5	6	7	8	9
1	161.4	199.5	215.7	224.6	230.2	234.0	236.8	238.9	240.5
2	18.51	19.00	19.16	19.25	19.30	19.33	19.35	19.37	19.38
3	10.13	9.55	9.28	9.12	9.01	8.94	8.89	8.85	8.81
4	7.71	6.94	6.59	6.39	6.26	6.16	6.09	6.04	6.00
5	6.61	5.79	5.41	5.19	5.05	4.95	4.88	4.82	4.77
6	5.99	5.14	4.76	4.53	4.39	4.28	4.21	4.15	4.10
7	5.59	4.74	4.35	4.12	3.97	3.87	3.79	3.73	3.68
8	5.32	4.46	4.07	3.84	3.69	3.58	3.50	3.44	3.39
9	5.12	4.26	3.86	3.63	3.48	3.37	3.29	3.23	3.18
10	4.96	4.10	3.71	3.48	3.33	3.22	3.14	3.07	3.02
11	4.84	3.98	3.59	3.36	3.20	3.09	3.01	2.95	2.90
12	4.75	3.89	3.49	3.26	3.11	3.00	2.91	2.85	2.80
13	4.67	3.81	3.41	3.18	3.03	2.92	2.83	2.77	2.71
14	4.60	3.74	3.34	3.11	2.96	2.85	2.76	2.70	2.65
15	4.54	3.68	3.29	3.06	2.90	2.79	2.71	2.64	2.59
16	4.49	3.63	3.24	3.01	2.85	2.74	2.66	2.59	2.54
17	4.45	3.59	3.20	2.96	2.81	2.70	2.61	2.55	2.49
18	4.41	3.55	3.16	2.93	2.77	2.66	2.58	2.51	2.46
19	4.38	3.52	3.13	2.90	2.74	2.63	2.54	2.48	2.42
20	4.35	3.49	3.10	2.87	2.71	2.60	2.51	2.45	2.39
21	4.32	3.47	3.07	2.84	2.68	2.57	2.49	2.42	2.37
22	4.30	3.44	3.05	2.82	2.66	2.55	2.46	2.40	2.34
23	4.28	3.42	3.03	2.80	2.64	2.53	2.44	2.37	2.32
24	4.26	3.40	3.01	2.78	2.62	2.51	2.42	2.36	2.30
25	4.24	3.39	2.99	2.76	2.60	2.49	2.40	2.34	2.28
26	4.23	3.37	2.98	2.74	2.59	2.47	2.39	2.32	2.27
27	4.21	3.35	2.96	2.73	2.57	2.46	2.37	2.31	2.25
28	4.20	3.34	2.95	2.71	2.56	2.45	2.36	2.29	2.24
29	4.18	3.33	2.93	2.70	2.55	2.43	2.35	2.28	2.22
30	4.17	3.32	2.92	2.69	2.53	2.42	2.33	2.27	2.21
40	4.08	3.23	2.84	2.61	2.45	2.34	2.25	2.18	2.12
60	4.00	3.15	2.76	2.53	2.37	2.25	2.17	2.10	2.04
120	3.92	3.07	2.68	2.45	2.29	2.17	2.09	2.02	1.96
∞	3.84	3.00	2.60	2.37	2.21	2.10	2.01	1.94	1.88

Table 3 continued

Level of significance $\alpha = 0.05$

ν_2 \ ν_1	10	12	15	20	24	30	40	60	120	∞
1	241.9	243.9	245.9	248.0	249.1	250.1	251.1	252.2	253.3	254.3
2	19.40	19.41	19.43	19.45	19.45	19.46	19.47	19.48	19.49	19.50
3	8.79	8.74	8.70	8.66	8.64	8.62	8.59	8.57	8.55	8.53
4	5.96	5.91	5.86	5.80	5.77	5.75	5.72	5.69	5.66	5.63
5	4.74	4.68	4.62	4.56	4.53	4.50	4.46	4.43	4.40	4.36
6	4.06	4.00	3.94	3.87	3.84	3.81	3.77	3.74	3.70	3.67
7	3.64	3.57	3.51	3.44	3.41	3.38	3.34	3.30	3.27	3.23
8	3.35	3.28	3.22	3.15	3.12	3.08	3.04	3.01	2.97	2.93
9	3.14	3.07	3.01	2.94	2.90	2.86	2.83	2.79	2.75	2.71
10	2.98	2.91	2.85	2.77	2.74	2.70	2.66	2.62	2.58	2.54
11	2.85	2.79	2.72	2.65	2.61	2.57	2.53	2.49	2.45	2.40
12	2.75	2.69	2.62	2.54	2.51	2.47	2.43	2.38	2.34	2.30
13	2.67	2.60	2.53	2.46	2.42	2.38	2.34	2.30	2.25	2.21
14	2.60	2.53	2.46	2.39	2.35	2.31	2.27	2.22	2.18	2.13
15	2.54	2.48	2.40	2.33	2.29	2.25	2.20	2.16	2.11	2.07
16	2.49	2.42	2.35	2.28	2.24	2.19	2.15	2.11	2.06	2.01
17	2.45	2.38	2.31	2.23	2.19	2.15	2.10	2.06	2.01	1.96
18	2.41	2.34	2.27	2.19	2.15	2.11	2.06	2.02	1.97	1.92
19	2.38	2.31	2.23	2.16	2.11	2.07	2.03	1.98	1.93	1.88
20	2.35	2.28	2.20	2.12	2.08	2.04	1.99	1.95	1.90	1.84
21	2.32	2.25	2.18	2.10	2.05	2.01	1.96	1.92	1.87	1.81
22	2.30	2.23	2.15	2.07	2.03	1.98	1.94	1.89	1.84	1.78
23	2.27	2.20	2.13	2.05	2.01	1.96	1.91	1.86	1.81	1.76
24	2.25	2.18	2.11	2.03	1.98	1.94	1.89	1.84	1.79	1.73
25	2.24	2.16	2.09	2.01	1.96	1.92	1.87	1.82	1.77	1.71
26	2.22	2.15	2.07	1.99	1.95	1.90	1.85	1.80	1.75	1.69
27	2.20	2.13	2.06	1.97	1.93	1.88	1.84	1.79	1.73	1.67
28	2.19	2.12	2.04	1.96	1.91	1.87	1.82	1.77	1.71	1.65
29	2.18	2.10	2.03	1.94	1.90	1.85	1.81	1.75	1.70	1.64
30	2.16	2.09	2.01	1.93	1.89	1.84	1.79	1.74	1.68	1.62
40	2.08	2.00	1.92	1.84	1.79	1.74	1.69	1.64	1.58	1.51
60	1.99	1.92	1.84	1.75	1.70	1.65	1.59	1.53	1.47	1.39
120	1.91	1.83	1.75	1.66	1.61	1.55	1.50	1.43	1.35	1.25
∞	1.83	1.75	1.67	1.57	1.52	1.46	1.39	1.32	1.22	1.00

Table 3 continued

Level of significance $\alpha = 0.01$

ν_2 \ ν_1	1	2	3	4	5	6	7	8	9
1	4052	4999	5403	5625	5764	5859	5928	5981	6022
2	98.50	99.00	99.17	99.25	99.30	99.33	99.36	99.37	99.39
3	34.12	30.82	29.46	28.71	28.24	27.91	27.67	27.49	27.35
4	21.20	18.00	16.69	15.98	15.52	15.21	14.98	14.80	14.66
5	16.26	13.27	12.06	11.39	10.97	10.67	10.46	10.29	10.16
6	13.75	10.92	9.78	9.15	8.75	8.47	8.26	8.10	7.98
7	12.25	9.55	8.45	7.85	7.46	7.19	6.99	6.84	6.72
8	11.26	8.65	7.59	7.01	6.63	6.37	6.18	6.03	5.91
9	10.56	8.02	6.99	6.42	6.06	5.80	5.61	5.47	5.35
10	10.04	7.56	6.55	5.99	5.64	5.39	5.20	5.06	4.94
11	9.65	7.21	6.22	5.67	5.32	5.07	4.89	4.74	4.63
12	9.33	6.93	5.95	5.41	5.06	4.82	4.64	4.50	4.39
13	9.07	6.70	5.74	5.21	4.86	4.62	4.44	4.30	4.19
14	8.86	6.51	5.56	5.04	4.69	4.46	4.28	4.14	4.03
15	8.68	6.36	5.42	4.89	4.56	4.32	4.14	4.00	3.89
16	8.53	6.23	5.29	4.77	4.44	4.20	4.03	3.89	3.78
17	8.40	6.11	5.18	4.67	4.34	4.10	3.93	3.79	3.68
18	8.29	6.01	5.09	4.58	4.25	4.01	3.84	3.71	3.60
19	8.18	5.93	5.01	4.50	4.17	3.94	3.77	3.63	3.52
20	8.10	5.85	4.94	4.43	4.10	3.87	3.70	3.56	3.46
21	8.02	5.78	4.87	4.37	4.04	3.81	3.64	3.51	3.40
22	7.95	5.72	4.82	4.31	3.99	3.76	3.59	3.45	3.35
23	7.88	5.66	4.76	4.26	3.94	3.71	3.54	3.41	3.30
24	7.82	5.61	4.72	4.22	3.90	3.67	3.50	3.36	3.26
25	7.77	5.57	4.68	4.18	3.85	3.63	3.46	3.32	3.22
26	7.72	5.53	4.64	4.14	3.82	3.59	3.42	3.29	3.18
27	7.68	5.49	4.60	4.11	3.78	3.56	3.39	3.26	3.15
28	7.64	5.45	4.57	4.07	3.75	3.53	3.36	3.23	3.12
29	7.60	5.42	4.54	4.04	3.73	3.50	3.33	3.20	3.09
30	7.56	5.39	4.51	4.02	3.70	3.47	3.30	3.17	3.07
40	7.31	5.18	4.31	3.83	3.51	3.29	3.12	2.99	2.89
60	7.08	4.98	4.13	3.65	3.34	3.12	2.95	2.82	2.72
120	6.85	4.79	3.95	3.48	3.17	2.96	2.79	2.66	2.56
∞	6.63	4.61	3.78	3.32	3.02	2.80	2.64	2.51	2.41

Table 3 continued

Level of significance $\alpha = 0.01$

ν_2 \ ν_1	10	12	15	20	24	30	40	60	120	∞
1	6056	6106	6157	6209	6235	6261	6287	6313	6339	6366
2	99.40	99.42	99.43	99.45	99.46	99.47	99.47	99.48	99.49	99.50
3	27.23	27.05	26.87	26.69	26.60	26.50	26.41	26.32	26.22	26.13
4	14.55	14.37	14.20	14.02	13.93	13.84	13.75	13.65	13.56	13.46
5	10.05	9.89	9.72	9.55	9.47	9.38	9.29	9.20	9.11	9.02
6	7.87	7.72	7.56	7.40	7.31	7.23	7.14	7.06	6.97	6.88
7	6.62	6.47	6.31	6.16	6.07	5.99	5.91	5.82	5.74	5.65
8	5.81	5.67	5.52	5.36	5.28	5.20	5.12	5.03	4.95	4.86
9	5.26	5.11	4.96	4.81	4.73	4.65	4.57	4.48	4.40	4.31
10	4.85	4.71	4.56	4.41	4.33	4.25	4.17	4.08	4.00	3.91
11	4.54	4.40	4.25	4.10	4.02	3.94	3.86	3.78	3.69	3.60
12	4.30	4.16	4.01	3.86	3.78	3.70	3.62	3.54	3.45	3.36
13	4.10	3.96	3.82	3.66	3.59	3.51	3.43	3.34	3.25	3.17
14	3.94	3.80	3.66	3.51	3.43	3.35	3.27	3.18	3.09	3.00
15	3.80	3.67	3.52	3.37	3.29	3.21	3.13	3.05	2.96	2.87
16	3.69	3.55	3.41	3.26	3.18	3.10	3.02	2.93	2.84	2.75
17	3.59	3.46	3.31	3.16	3.08	3.00	2.92	2.83	2.75	2.65
18	3.51	3.37	3.23	3.08	3.00	2.92	2.84	2.75	2.66	2.57
19	3.43	3.30	3.15	3.00	2.92	2.84	2.76	2.67	2.58	2.49
20	3.37	3.23	3.09	2.94	2.86	2.78	2.69	2.61	2.52	2.42
21	3.31	3.17	3.03	2.88	2.80	2.72	2.64	2.55	2.46	2.36
22	3.26	3.12	2.98	2.83	2.75	2.67	2.58	2.50	2.40	2.31
23	3.21	3.07	2.93	2.78	2.70	2.62	2.54	2.45	2.35	2.26
24	3.17	3.03	2.89	2.74	2.66	2.58	2.49	2.40	2.31	2.21
25	3.13	2.99	2.85	2.70	2.62	2.54	2.45	2.36	2.27	2.17
26	3.09	2.96	2.81	2.66	2.58	2.50	2.42	2.33	2.23	2.13
27	3.06	2.93	2.78	2.63	2.55	2.47	2.38	2.29	2.20	2.10
28	3.03	2.90	2.75	2.60	2.52	2.44	2.35	2.26	2.17	2.06
29	3.00	2.87	2.73	2.57	2.49	2.41	2.33	2.23	2.14	2.03
30	2.98	2.84	2.70	2.55	2.47	2.39	2.30	2.21	2.11	2.01
40	2.80	2.66	2.52	2.37	2.29	2.20	2.11	2.02	1.92	1.80
60	2.63	2.50	2.35	2.20	2.12	2.03	1.94	1.84	1.73	1.60
120	2.47	2.34	2.19	2.03	1.95	1.86	1.76	1.66	1.53	1.38
∞	2.32	2.18	2.04	1.88	1.79	1.70	1.59	1.47	1.32	1.00

Source: Pearson and Hartley, 1970

Table 4   Fisher *z*-transformation

$$z(r) = \tfrac{1}{2}\log_e\left(\frac{1+r}{1-r}\right) = \tanh^{-1} r = 1.1513\log_{10}\left(\frac{1+r}{1-r}\right)$$

z	0	1	2	3	4	5	6	7	8	9
0.0	0.0000	0.0100	0.0200	0.0300	0.0400	0.0500	0.0601	0.0701	0.0802	0.0902
0.1	0.1003	0.1104	0.1206	0.1307	0.1409	0.1511	0.1614	0.1717	0.1820	0.1923
0.2	0.2027	0.2132	0.2237	0.2342	0.2448	0.2554	0.2661	0.2769	0.2877	0.2986
0.3	0.3095	0.3205	0.3316	0.3428	0.3541	0.3654	0.3769	0.3884	0.4001	0.4118
0.4	0.4236	0.4356	0.4477	0.4599	0.4722	0.4847	0.4973	0.5101	0.5230	0.5361
0.5	0.5493	0.5627	0.5763	0.5901	0.6042	0.6184	0.6328	0.6475	0.6625	0.6777
0.6	0.6931	0.7089	0.7250	0.7414	0.7582	0.7753	0.7928	0.8107	0.8291	0.8480
0.7	0.8673	0.8872	0.9076	0.9287	0.9505	0.9730	0.9962	1.0203	1.0454	1.0714
0.8	1.0986	1.1270	1.1568	1.1881	1.2212	1.2562	1.2933	1.3331	1.3758	1.4219
0.90	1.4722	1.4775	1.4828	1.4882	1.4937	1.4992	1.5047	1.5103	1.5160	1.5217
0.91	1.5275	1.5334	1.5393	1.5453	1.5513	1.5574	1.5636	1.5698	1.5762	1.5826
0.92	1.5890	1.5956	1.6022	1.6089	1.6157	1.6226	1.6296	1.6366	1.6438	1.6510
0.93	1.6584	1.6658	1.6734	1.6811	1.6888	1.6967	1.7047	1.7129	1.7211	1.7295
0.94	1.7380	1.7467	1.7555	1.7645	1.7736	1.7828	1.7923	1.8019	1.8117	1.8216
0.95	1.8318	1.8421	1.8527	1.8635	1.8745	1.8857	1.8972	1.9090	1.9210	1.9333
0.96	1.9459	1.9588	1.9721	1.9857	1.9996	2.0139	2.0287	2.0439	2.0595	2.0756
0.97	2.0923	2.1095	2.1273	2.1457	2.1649	2.1847	2.2054	2.2269	2.2494	2.2729
0.98	2.2976	2.3235	2.3507	2.3796	2.4101	2.4427	2.4774	2.5147	2.5550	2.5987
0.99	2.6467	2.6996	2.7587	2.8257	2.9031	2.9945	3.1063	3.2504	3.4534	3.8002

Source: Neave, 1978

Table 5   Critical values for the χ^2-distribution

Columns a denote the lower boundaries or the left-sided critical values.
Columns b denote the upper boundaries or the right-sided critical values.

	Level of significance α							
Two-sided	0.20		0.10		0·05		0.01	
One-sided	0.10		0.05		0.025		0.005	
ν	a	b	a	b	a	b	a	b
1	0.016	2.71	39.10^{-4}	3.84	98.10^{-5}	5.02	16.10^{-5}	6.63
2	0.21	4.61	0.10	5.99	0.05	7.38	0.02	9.21
3	0.58	6.25	0.35	7.81	0.22	9.35	0.11	11.34
4	1.06	7.78	0.71	9.49	0.48	11.14	0.30	13.28
5	1.61	9.24	1.15	11.07	0.83	12.83	0.55	15.09
6	2.20	10.64	1.64	12.59	1.24	14.45	0.87	16.81
7	2.83	12.02	2.17	14.07	1.69	16.01	1.24	18.48
8	3.49	13.36	2.73	15.51	2.18	17.53	1.65	20.09
9	4.17	14.68	3.33	16.92	2.70	19.02	2.09	21.67
10	4.87	15.99	3.94	18.31	3.25	20.48	2.56	23.21
11	5.58	17.28	4.57	19.68	3.82	21.92	3.05	24.73
12	6.30	18.55	5.23	21.03	4.40	23.34	3.57	26.22
13	7.04	19.81	5.89	22.36	5.01	24.74	4.11	27.69
14	7.79	21.06	6.57	23.68	5.63	26.12	4.66	29.14
15	8.55	22.31	7.26	25.00	6.26	27.49	5.23	30.58
16	9.31	23.54	7.96	26.30	6.91	28.85	5.81	32.00
17	10.09	24.77	8.67	27.59	7.56	30.19	6.41	33.41
18	10.86	25.99	9.39	28.87	8.23	31.53	7.01	34.81
19	11.65	27.20	10.12	30.14	8.91	32.85	7.63	36.19
20	12.44	28.41	10.85	31.41	9.59	34.17	8.26	37.57
21	13.24	29.62	11.59	32.67	10.28	35.48	8.90	38.93
22	14.04	30.81	12.34	33.92	10.98	36.78	9.54	40.29
23	14.85	32.01	13.09	35.17	11.69	38.08	10.20	41.64
24	15.66	33.20	13.85	36.42	12.40	39.36	10.86	42.98
25	16.47	34.38	14.61	37.65	13.12	40.65	11.52	44.31
26	17.29	35.56	15.38	38.89	13.84	41.92	12.20	45.64
27	18.11	36.74	16.15	40.11	14.57	43.19	12.88	46.96
28	18.94	37.92	16.93	41.34	15.31	44.46	13.56	48.28
29	19.77	39.09	17.71	42.56	16.05	45.72	14.26	49.59
30	20.60	40.26	18.49	43.77	16.79	46.98	14.95	50.89
40	29.05	51.81	26.51	55.76	24.43	59.34	22.16	63.69
50	37.69	63.17	34.76	67.50	32.36	71.42	29.71	76.15
60	46.46	74.40	43.19	79.08	40.48	83.30	37.48	88.38
70	55.33	85.53	51.74	90.53	48.76	95.02	45.44	100.43
80	64.28	96.58	60.39	101.88	57.15	106.63	53.54	112.33
90	73.29	107.57	69.13	113.15	65.65	118.14	61.75	124.12
100	82.36	118.50	77.93	124.34	74.22	129.56	70.06	135.81

Table 6 Critical values of *r* for the correlation test with $\rho = 0$

The distribution is symmetrical with respect to $\rho = 0$.

	Level of significance α				
Two-sided	0.10	0.05	0.02	0.01	0.001
One-sided	0.05	0.025	0.01	0.005	0.0005
$\nu = n - 2$					
1	0.988	0.997	0.9995	0.9999	1.000
2	0.900	0.950	0.980	0.990	0.999
3	0.805	0.878	0.934	0.959	0.991
4	0.729	0.811	0.882	0.917	0.974
5	0.669	0.754	0.833	0.874	0.951
6	0.622	0.707	0.789	0.834	0.925
7	0.582	0.666	0.750	0.798	0.898
8	0.549	0.632	0.716	0.765	0.872
9	0.521	0.602	0.685	0.735	0.847
10	0.497	0.576	0.658	0.708	0.823
11	0.476	0.553	0.634	0.684	0.801
12	0.458	0.532	0.612	0.661	0.780
13	0.441	0.514	0.592	0.641	0.760
14	0.426	0.497	0.574	0.623	0.742
15	0.412	0.482	0.558	0.606	0.725
16	0.400	0.468	0.542	0.590	0.708
17	0.389	0.456	0.528	0.575	0.693
18	0.378	0.444	0.516	0.561	0.679
19	0.369	0.433	0.503	0.549	0.665
20	0.360	0.423	0.492	0.537	0.652
22	0.344	0.404	0.472	0.515	0.629
24	0.330	0.388	0.453	0.496	0.607
25	0.323	0.381	0.445	0.487	0.597
30	0.296	0.349	0.409	0.449	0.554
35	0.275	0.325	0.381	0.418	0.519
40	0.257	0.304	0.358	0.372	0.490
45	0.243	0.288	0.338	0.372	0.415
50	0.231	0.273	0.322	0.354	0.443
55	0.220	0.261	0.307	0.338	0.424
60	0.211	0.250	0.295	0.325	0.408
65	0.203	0.240	0.284	0.312	0.393
70	0.195	0.232	0.274	0.302	0.380
75	0.189	0.224	0.264	0.292	0.368
80	0.183	0.217	0.256	0.283	0.357
85	0.178	0.211	0.249	0.275	0.347
90	0.173	0.205	0.242	0.267	0.338
95	0.168	0.200	0.236	0.260	0.329
100	0.164	0.195	0.230	0.254	0.321
125	0.147	0.174	0.206	0.228	0.288
150	0.134	0.159	0.189	0.208	0.264
175	0.124	0.148	0.174	0.194	0.248
200	0.116	0.138	0.164	0.181	0.235
300	0.095	0.113	0.134	0.148	0.188
500	0.074	0.088	0.104	0.115	0.148
1000	0.052	0.062	0.073	0.081	0.104
2000	0.037	0.044	0.056	0.058	0.074

Source: De Jonge, 1963–4

Table 7   Critical values of g_1 and g_2 for Fisher's cumulant test

The g_1 distribution may be considered as symmetrical with respect to 0;
the g_2 distribution has to be considered as asymmetrical.
The columns a denote the lower boundaries or left-sided critical values.
The columns b denote the upper boundaries or right-sided critical values.

	g_1		g_2			
	Level of significance α					
Two-sided	0.10	0.02	0.10		0.02	
One-sided	0.05	0.01	0.05		0.01	
n			a	b	a	b
50	0.550	0.812	–	–	–	–
75	0.454	0.664	–	–	–	–
100	0.395	0.576	−0.62	1.53	−0.80	1.53
125	0.354	0.514	−0.57	1.34	−0.74	1.34
150	0.324	0.469	−0.53	1.22	−0.69	1.22
175	0.301	0.434	−0.50	1.11	−0.66	1.11
200	0.282	0.406	−0.47	1.04	−0.62	1.04
250	0.253	0.362	−0.44	0.91	−0.57	0.91
300	0.231	0.331	−0.40	0.82	−0.53	0.82
350	0.214	0.306	−0.37	0.75	−0.49	0.75
400	0.201	0.286	−0.35	0.69	−0.48	0.69
450	0.189	0.270	−0.33	0.65	−0.44	0.65
500	0.180	0.256	−0.32	0.62	−0.42	0.62
550	0.171	0.244	−0.30	0.59	−0.41	0.59
600	0.163	0.234	−0.29	0.55	−0.39	0.55
650	0.157	0.225	−0.28	0.53	−0.38	0.53
700	0.151	0.215	−0.27	0.51	−0.37	0.51
750	0.146	0.208	−0.26	0.49	−0.35	0.49
800	0.142	0.202	−0.25	0.47	−0.34	0.47
850	0.138	0.196	−0.25	0.46	−0.33	0.46
900	0.134	0.190	−0.24	0.44	−0.33	0.44
950	0.130	0.185	−0.23	0.43	−0.32	0.43
1000	0.127	0.180	−0.23	0.42	−0.31	0.42

Source: Geary and Pearson, n.d.; Bennett and Franklin, 1961

Table 8   Critical values for the Dixon test of outliers

Test statistic	n	Level of significance α						
		0.30	0.20	0.10	0.05	0.02	0.01	0.005
$r_{10} = \dfrac{x_2 - x_1}{x_n - x_1}$	3	0.684	0.781	0.886	0.941	0.976	0.988	0.994
	4	0.471	0.560	0.679	0.765	0.846	0.889	0.926
	5	0.373	0.451	0.557	0.642	0.729	0.780	0.821
	6	0.318	0.386	0.482	0.560	0.644	0.698	0.740
	7	0.281	0.344	0.434	0.507	0.586	0.637	0.680
$r_{11} = \dfrac{x_2 - x_1}{x_{n-1} - x_1}$	8	0.318	0.385	0.479	0.554	0.631	0.683	0.725
	9	0.288	0.352	0.441	0.512	0.587	0.635	0.677
	10	0.265	0.325	0.409	0.477	0.551	0.597	0.639
$r_{21} = \dfrac{x_3 - x_1}{x_{n-1} - x_1}$	11	0.391	0.442	0.517	0.576	0.638	0.679	0.713
	12	0.370	0.419	0.490	0.546	0.605	0.642	0.675
	13	0.351	0.399	0.467	0.521	0.578	0.615	0.649
$r_{22} = \dfrac{x_3 - x_1}{x_{n-2} - x_1}$	14	0.370	0.421	0.492	0.546	0.602	0.641	0.674
	15	0.353	0.402	0.472	0.525	0.579	0.616	0.647
	16	0.338	0.386	0.454	0.507	0.559	0.595	0.624
	17	0.325	0.373	0.438	0.490	0.542	0.577	0.605
	18	0.314	0.361	0.424	0.475	0.527	0.561	0.589
	19	0.304	0.350	0.412	0.462	0.514	0.547	0.575
	20	0.295	0.340	0.401	0.450	0.502	0.535	0.562
	21	0.287	0.331	0.391	0.440	0.491	0.524	0.551
	22	0.280	0.323	0.382	0.430	0.481	0.514	0.541
	23	0.274	0.316	0.374	0.421	0.472	0.505	0.532
	24	0.268	0.310	0.367	0.413	0.464	0.497	0.524
	25	0.262	0.304	0.360	0.406	0.457	0.489	0.516

Source: Dixon and Massey, 1957

Table 9 Critical values of the Studentized range for multiple comparison

Level of significance $\alpha = 0.05$

v_2 \ K	2	3	4	5	6	7	8	9	10	11	12	13	14	15	16	17	18	19	20
1	17.969	26.98	32.82	37.08	40.41	43.12	45.40	47.36	49.07	50.59	51.96	53.20	54.33	55.36	56.32	57.22	58.04	58.83	59.56
2	6.085	8.33	9.80	10.88	11.74	12.44	13.03	13.54	13.99	14.39	14.75	15.08	15.38	15.65	15.91	16.14	16.37	16.57	16.77
3	4.501	5.91	6.82	7.50	8.04	8.48	8.85	9.18	9.46	9.72	9.95	10.15	10.35	10.52	10.69	10.84	10.98	11.11	11.24
4	3.926	5.04	5.76	6.29	6.71	7.05	7.35	7.60	7.83	8.03	8.21	8.37	8.52	8.66	8.79	8.91	9.03	9.13	9.23
5	3.635	4.60	5.22	5.67	6.03	6.33	6.58	6.80	6.99	7.17	7.32	7.47	7.60	7.72	7.83	7.93	8.03	8.12	8.21
6	3.460	4.34	4.90	5.30	5.63	5.90	6.12	6.32	6.49	6.65	6.79	6.92	7.03	7.14	7.24	7.34	7.43	7.51	7.59
7	3.344	4.16	4.68	5.06	5.36	5.61	5.82	6.00	6.16	6.30	6.43	6.55	6.66	6.76	6.85	6.94	7.02	7.10	7.17
8	3.261	4.04	4.53	4.89	5.17	5.40	5.60	5.77	5.92	6.05	6.18	6.29	6.39	6.48	6.57	6.65	6.73	6.80	6.87
9	3.199	3.95	4.41	4.76	5.02	5.24	5.43	5.59	5.74	5.87	5.98	6.09	6.19	6.28	6.36	6.44	6.51	6.58	6.64
10	3.151	3.88	4.33	4.65	4.91	5.12	5.30	5.46	5.60	5.72	5.83	5.93	6.03	6.11	6.19	6.27	6.34	6.40	6.47
11	3.113	3.82	4.26	4.57	4.82	5.03	5.20	5.35	5.49	5.61	5.71	5.81	5.90	5.98	6.06	6.13	6.20	6.27	6.33
12	3.081	3.77	4.20	4.51	4.75	4.95	5.12	5.27	5.39	5.51	5.61	5.71	5.80	5.88	5.95	6.02	6.09	6.15	6.21
13	3.055	3.73	4.15	4.45	4.69	4.88	5.05	5.19	5.32	5.43	5.53	5.63	5.71	5.79	5.85	5.93	5.99	6.05	6.11
14	3.033	3.70	4.11	4.41	4.64	4.83	4.99	5.13	5.25	5.36	5.46	5.55	5.64	5.71	5.79	5.85	5.91	5.97	6.03
15	3.014	3.67	4.08	4.37	4.59	4.78	4.94	5.08	5.20	5.31	5.40	5.49	5.57	5.65	5.72	5.78	5.85	5.90	5.96
16	2.998	3.65	4.05	4.33	4.56	4.74	4.90	5.03	5.15	5.26	5.35	5.44	5.52	5.59	5.66	5.73	5.79	5.84	5.90
17	2.984	3.63	4.02	4.30	4.52	4.70	4.86	4.99	5.11	5.21	5.31	5.39	5.47	5.54	5.61	5.67	5.73	5.79	5.84
18	2.971	3.61	4.00	4.28	4.49	4.67	4.82	4.96	5.07	5.17	5.27	5.35	5.43	5.50	5.57	5.63	5.69	5.74	5.79
19	2.960	3.59	3.98	4.25	4.47	4.65	4.79	4.92	5.04	5.14	5.23	5.31	5.39	5.46	5.53	5.59	5.65	5.70	5.75
20	2.950	3.58	3.96	4.23	4.45	4.62	4.77	4.90	5.01	5.11	5.20	5.28	5.36	5.43	5.49	5.55	5.61	5.66	5.71
21	2.941	3.56	3.94	4.21	4.43	4.60	4.74	4.87	4.98	5.08	5.17	5.25	5.33	5.40	5.46	5.52	5.58	5.62	5.67
22	2.933	3.55	3.93	4.20	4.41	4.58	4.72	4.85	4.96	5.05	5.15	5.23	5.30	5.37	5.43	5.49	5.55	5.59	5.64
23	2.926	3.54	3.91	4.18	4.39	4.56	4.70	4.83	4.94	5.03	5.12	5.20	5.27	5.34	5.40	5.46	5.52	5.57	5.62
24	2.919	3.53	3.90	4.17	4.37	4.54	4.68	4.81	4.92	5.01	5.10	5.18	5.25	5.32	5.38	5.44	5.49	5.55	5.59

Table 9 continued

ν_2 \ K	2	3	4	5	6	7	8	9	10	11	12	13	14	15	16	17	18	19	20
25	2.913	3.52	3.89	4.16	4.36	4.52	4.66	4.79	4.90	4.99	5.08	5.16	5.23	5.30	5.36	5.42	5.48	5.52	5.57
26	2.907	3.51	3.88	4.14	4.34	4.51	4.65	4.78	4.89	4.97	5.06	5.14	5.21	5.28	5.34	5.40	5.46	5.50	5.55
27	2.902	3.51	3.87	4.13	4.33	4.50	4.63	4.76	4.87	4.96	5.04	5.12	5.19	5.26	5.32	5.38	5.43	5.48	5.53
28	2.897	3.50	3.86	4.12	4.32	4.48	4.62	4.75	4.86	4.94	5.03	5.11	5.18	5.24	5.30	5.36	5.42	5.46	5.51
29	2.892	3.49	3.85	4.11	4.31	4.47	4.61	4.73	4.84	4.93	5.01	5.09	5.16	5.23	5.29	5.35	5.40	5.44	5.49
30	2.888	3.49	3.85	4.10	4.30	4.46	4.60	4.72	4.82	4.92	5.00	5.08	5.15	5.21	5.27	5.33	5.38	5.43	5.47
31	2.884	3.48	3.83	4.09	4.29	4.45	4.59	4.71	4.82	4.91	4.99	5.07	5.14	5.20	5.26	5.32	5.37	5.41	5.46
32	2.881	3.48	3.83	4.09	4.28	4.44	4.58	4.70	4.81	4.89	4.98	5.06	5.13	5.19	5.24	5.30	5.35	5.40	5.45
33	2.877	3.47	3.82	4.08	4.27	4.44	4.57	4.69	4.80	4.88	4.97	5.04	5.11	5.17	5.23	5.29	5.34	5.39	5.44
34	2.874	3.47	3.82	4.07	4.27	4.43	4.56	4.68	4.79	4.87	4.96	5.03	5.10	5.16	5.22	5.28	5.33	5.37	5.42
35	2.871	3.46	3.81	4.07	4.26	4.42	4.55	4.67	4.78	4.86	4.95	5.02	5.09	5.15	5.21	5.27	5.32	5.36	5.41
36	2.868	3.46	3.81	4.06	4.25	4.41	4.55	4.66	4.77	4.85	4.94	5.01	5.08	5.14	5.20	5.26	5.31	5.35	5.40
37	2.865	3.45	3.80	4.05	5.25	4.41	4.54	4.65	4.76	4.84	4.93	5.00	5.08	5.14	5.19	5.25	5.30	5.34	5.39
38	2.863	3.45	3.80	4.05	4.24	4.40	4.53	4.64	4.75	4.84	4.92	5.00	5.07	5.13	5.18	5.24	5.29	5.33	5.38
39	2.861	3.44	3.79	4.04	4.24	4.40	4.53	4.64	4.75	4.83	4.92	4.99	5.06	5.12	5.17	5.23	5.28	5.32	5.37
40	2.858	3.44	3.79	4.04	4.23	4.39	4.52	4.63	4.73	4.82	4.90	4.98	5.04	5.11	5.16	5.22	5.27	5.22	5.36
50	2.841	3.41	3.76	4.00	4.19	4.34	4.47	4.58	4.69	4.76	4.85	4.92	4.99	5.05	5.10	5.15	5.20	5.24	5.29
60	2.829	3.40	3.74	3.98	4.16	4.31	4.44	4.55	4.65	4.73	4.81	4.88	4.94	5.00	5.06	5.11	5.15	5.20	5.24
120	2.800	3.36	3.68	3.92	4.10	4.24	4.36	4.47	4.56	4.64	4.71	4.78	4.84	4.90	4.95	5.00	5.04	5.09	5.13
∞	2.772	3.31	3.63	3.86	4.03	4.17	4.29	4.39	4.47	4.55	4.62	4.68	4.74	4.80	4.85	4.89	4.93	4.97	5.01

100 STATISTICAL TESTS

Table 9 continued

Level of significance $\alpha = 0.01$

ν_2 \ K	2	3	4	5	6	7	8	9	10	11	12	13	14	15	16	17	18	19	20
1	90.025	135.0	164.3	185.6	202.2	215.8	227.2	237.0	245.6	253.2	260.0	266.2	271.8	277.0	281.8	286.3	290.4	294.3	298.0
2	14.036	19.02	22.29	24.72	26.63	28.20	29.53	30.68	31.69	32.59	33.40	34.13	34.81	35.43	36.00	36.53	37.03	37.50	37.95
3	8.260	10.62	12.17	13.33	14.24	15.00	15.64	16.20	16.69	17.13	17.53	17.89	18.22	18.52	18.81	19.07	19.32	19.55	19.77
4	6.511	8.12	9.17	9.96	10.58	11.10	11.55	11.93	12.27	12.57	12.84	13.09	13.32	13.53	13.73	13.91	14.08	14.24	14.40
5	5.702	6.98	7.80	8.42	8.91	9.32	9.67	9.97	10.24	10.48	10.70	10.89	11.08	11.24	11.40	11.55	11.68	11.81	11.93
6	5.243	6.33	7.08	7.56	7.97	8.32	8.61	8.87	9.10	9.30	9.48	9.65	9.81	9.95	10.08	10.21	10.32	10.43	10.54
7	4.949	5.92	6.54	7.01	7.37	7.68	7.94	8.17	8.37	8.55	8.71	8.86	9.00	9.12	9.24	9.35	9.46	9.55	9.65
8	4.745	5.64	6.20	6.62	6.96	7.24	7.47	7.68	7.86	8.03	8.18	8.31	8.44	8.55	8.66	8.76	8.85	8.94	9.03
9	4.596	5.43	5.96	6.35	6.66	6.91	7.13	7.33	7.49	7.65	7.78	7.91	8.03	8.13	8.23	8.33	8.41	8.49	8.57
10	4.482	5.27	5.77	6.14	6.43	6.67	6.87	7.05	7.21	7.36	7.49	7.60	7.71	7.81	7.91	7.99	8.08	8.15	8.23
11	4.392	5.15	5.62	5.97	6.25	6.48	6.67	6.84	6.99	7.13	7.25	7.36	7.46	7.56	7.65	7.73	7.81	7.88	7.95
12	4.320	5.05	5.50	5.84	6.10	6.32	6.51	6.67	6.81	6.94	7.06	7.17	7.26	7.36	7.44	7.52	7.59	7.66	7.73
13	4.260	4.96	5.40	5.73	5.98	6.19	6.37	6.53	6.67	6.79	6.90	7.01	7.10	7.19	7.27	7.35	7.42	7.48	7.55
14	4.210	4.89	5.32	5.63	5.88	6.08	6.26	6.41	6.54	6.66	6.77	6.87	6.96	7.05	7.13	7.20	7.27	7.33	7.39
15	4.167	4.84	5.25	5.56	5.80	5.99	6.16	6.31	6.44	6.55	6.66	6.76	6.84	6.93	7.00	7.07	7.14	7.20	7.26
16	4.131	4.79	5.19	5.49	5.72	5.92	6.08	6.22	6.35	6.46	6.56	6.66	6.74	6.82	6.90	6.97	7.03	7.09	7.15
17	4.099	4.74	5.14	5.43	5.66	5.85	6.01	6.15	6.27	6.38	6.48	6.57	6.66	6.73	6.81	6.87	6.94	7.00	7.05
18	4.071	4.70	5.09	5.38	5.60	5.79	5.94	6.08	6.20	6.31	6.41	6.50	6.58	6.65	6.73	6.79	6.85	6.91	6.97
19	4.045	4.67	5.05	5.33	5.55	5.73	5.89	6.02	6.14	6.25	6.34	6.43	6.51	6.58	6.65	6.72	6.78	6.84	6.89
20	4.024	4.64	5.02	5.29	5.51	5.69	5.84	5.97	6.09	6.19	6.28	6.37	6.45	6.52	6.59	6.65	6.71	6.77	6.82
21	4.004	4.61	4.99	5.26	5.47	5.65	5.80	5.92	6.04	6.14	6.24	6.32	6.39	6.47	6.53	6.59	6.65	6.70	6.76
22	3.986	4.58	4.96	5.22	5.43	5.61	5.76	5.88	6.00	6.10	6.19	6.27	6.35	6.42	6.48	6.54	6.60	6.65	6.70
23	3.970	4.56	4.93	5.20	5.40	5.57	5.72	5.84	5.96	6.06	6.15	6.23	6.30	6.37	6.43	6.49	6.55	6.60	6.65
24	3.955	4.55	4.91	5.17	5.37	5.54	5.69	5.81	5.92	6.02	6.11	6.19	6.26	6.33	6.39	6.45	6.51	6.56	6.61

Table 9 continued

ν_2 \ K	2	3	4	5	6	7	8	9	10	11	12	13	14	15	16	17	18	19	20
25	3.942	4.52	4.89	5.15	5.34	5.51	5.66	5.78	5.89	5.99	6.07	6.15	6.22	6.29	6.35	6.41	6.47	6.52	6.57
26	3.930	4.50	4.87	5.12	5.32	5.49	5.63	5.75	5.86	5.95	6.04	6.12	6.19	6.26	6.32	6.38	6.43	6.48	6.53
27	3.918	4.49	4.85	5.10	5.30	5.46	5.61	5.72	5.83	5.93	6.01	6.09	6.16	6.22	6.28	6.34	6.40	6.45	6.50
28	3.908	4.47	4.83	5.08	5.28	5.44	5.58	5.70	5.80	5.90	5.98	6.06	6.13	6.19	6.25	6.31	6.37	6.42	6.47
29	3.889	4.45	4.80	5.05	5.24	5.40	5.54	5.65	5.76	5.85	5.93	6.01	6.08	6.14	6.20	6.26	6.31	6.36	6.41
30	3.889	4.45	4.80	5.05	5.24	5.40	5.54	5.65	5.76	5.85	5.93	6.01	6.08	6.14	6.20	6.26	6.31	6.36	6.41
31	3.881	4.44	4.79	5.03	5.22	5.38	5.52	5.63	5.74	5.83	5.91	5.99	6.06	6.12	6.18	6.23	6.29	6.34	6.38
32	3.873	4.43	4.78	5.02	5.21	5.37	5.50	5.61	5.72	5.81	5.89	5.97	6.03	6.09	6.16	6.21	6.26	6.31	6.36
33	3.865	4.42	4.76	5.01	5.19	5.35	5.48	5.59	5.70	5.79	5.87	5.95	6.01	6.07	6.13	6.19	6.24	6.29	6.34
34	3.859	4.41	4.75	4.99	5.18	5.34	5.47	5.58	5.68	5.77	5.86	5.93	5.99	6.05	6.12	6.17	6.22	6.27	6.31
35	3.852	4.41	4.74	4.98	5.16	5.33	5.45	5.56	5.67	5.76	5.84	5.91	5.98	6.04	6.10	6.15	6.20	6.25	6.29
36	3.846	4.40	4.73	4.97	5.15	5.31	5.44	5.55	5.65	5.74	5.82	5.90	5.96	6.02	6.08	6.13	6.18	6.23	6.28
37	3.841	4.39	4.72	4.96	5.14	5.30	5.43	5.54	5.64	5.73	5.81	5.88	5.94	6.00	6.06	6.12	6.17	6.22	6.26
38	3.835	4.38	4.72	4.95	5.13	5.29	5.41	5.52	5.62	5.72	5.80	5.87	5.93	5.99	6.05	6.10	6.15	6.20	6.24
39	3.830	4.38	4.71	4.94	5.12	5.28	5.40	5.51	5.62	5.70	5.78	5.85	5.91	5.97	6.03	6.08	6.13	6.18	6.23
40	3.825	4.37	4.70	4.93	5.11	5.26	5.39	5.50	5.60	5.69	5.76	5.83	5.90	5.96	6.02	6.07	6.12	6.16	6.21
50	3.787	4.32	4.64	4.86	5.04	5.19	5.30	5.41	5.51	5.59	5.67	5.74	5.80	5.86	5.91	5.96	6.01	6.06	6.09
60	3.762	4.28	4.59	4.82	4.99	5.13	5.25	5.36	5.45	5.53	5.60	5.67	5.73	5.78	5.84	5.89	5.93	5.97	6.01
120	3.702	4.20	4.50	4.71	4.87	5.01	5.12	5.21	5.30	5.37	5.44	5.50	5.56	5.61	5.66	5.71	5.75	5.79	5.83
∞	3.643	4.12	4.40	4.60	4.76	4.88	4.99	5.08	5.16	5.23	5.29	5.35	5.40	5.45	5.49	5.54	5.57	5.61	5.65

Source: Sachs, 1972

Table 10 Critical values of K for the Link–Wallace test

Level of significance α = 0.05

n＼K	2	3	4	5	6	7	8	9	10	11	12	13	14	15	16	17	18	19	20	30	40	50
2	3.43	2.35	1.74	1.39	1.15	0.99	0.87	0.77	0.70	0.63	0.58	0.54	0.50	0.47	0.443	0.418	0.396	0.376	0.358	0.245	0.187	0.151
3	1.90	1.44	1.14	0.94	0.80	0.70	0.62	0.56	0.51	0.47	0.43	0.40	0.38	0.35	0.335	0.317	0.301	0.287	0.274	0.189	0.146	0.119
4	1.62	1.25	1.01	0.84	0.72	0.63	0.57	0.51	0.47	0.43	0.40	0.37	0.35	0.33	0.310	0.294	0.279	0.266	0.254	0.177	0.136	0.112
5	1.53	1.19	0.96	0.81	0.70	0.61	0.55	0.50	0.45	0.42	0.39	0.36	0.34	0.32	0.303	0.287	0.273	0.260	0.249	0.173	0.134	0.110
6	1.50	1.17	0.95	0.80	0.69	0.61	0.55	0.49	0.45	0.42	0.39	0.36	0.34	0.32	0.302	0.287	0.273	0.260	0.249	0.174	0.135	0.110
7	1.49	1.17	0.95	0.80	0.69	0.61	0.55	0.50	0.45	0.42	0.39	0.36	0.34	0.32	0.304	0.289	0.275	0.262	0.251	0.175	0.136	0.111
8	1.49	1.18	0.96	0.81	0.70	0.62	0.55	0.50	0.46	0.42	0.39	0.37	0.35	0.33	0.308	0.292	0.278	0.265	0.254	0.178	0.138	0.113
9	1.50	1.19	0.97	0.82	0.71	0.62	0.56	0.51	0.47	0.43	0.40	0.37	0.35	0.33	0.312	0.297	0.282	0.269	0.258	0.180	0.140	0.115
10	1.52	1.20	0.98	0.83	0.72	0.63	0.57	0.52	0.47	0.44	0.41	0.38	0.36	0.34	0.317	0.301	0.287	0.274	0.262	0.183	0.142	0.117
11	1.54	1.22	0.99	0.84	0.73	0.64	0.58	0.52	0.48	0.44	0.41	0.38	0.36	0.34	0.322	0.306	0.291	0.278	0.266	0.186	0.145	0.119
12	1.56	1.23	1.01	0.85	0.74	0.65	0.58	0.53	0.49	0.45	0.42	0.39	0.37	0.35	0.327	0.311	0.296	0.282	0.270	0.189	0.147	0.121
13	1.58	1.25	1.02	0.86	0.75	0.66	0.59	0.54	0.49	0.46	0.42	0.40	0.37	0.35	0.332	0.316	0.300	0.287	0.274	0.192	0.149	0.122
14	1.60	1.26	1.03	0.87	0.76	0.67	0.60	0.55	0.50	0.46	0.43	0.40	0.38	0.36	0.337	0.320	0.305	0.291	0.279	0.195	0.152	0.124
15	1.62	1.28	1.05	0.89	0.77	0.68	0.61	0.55	0.51	0.47	0.44	0.41	0.38	0.36	0.342	0.325	0.310	0.295	0.283	0.198	0.154	0.126
16	1.64	1.30	1.06	0.90	0.78	0.69	0.62	0.56	0.52	0.48	0.44	0.41	0.39	0.37	0.348	0.330	0.314	0.300	0.287	0.201	0.156	0.128
17	1.66	1.32	1.08	0.91	0.79	0.70	0.63	0.57	0.52	0.48	0.45	0.42	0.39	0.37	0.352	0.335	0.319	0.304	0.291	0.204	0.158	0.130
18	1.68	1.33	1.09	0.92	0.80	0.71	0.64	0.58	0.53	0.49	0.46	0.43	0.40	0.38	0.357	0.339	0.323	0.308	0.295	0.207	0.161	0.132
19	1.70	1.35	1.10	0.93	0.81	0.72	0.64	0.59	0.54	0.50	0.46	0.43	0.41	0.38	0.362	0.344	0.327	0.312	0.299	0.210	0.163	0.134
20	1.72	1.36	1.12	0.95	0.82	0.73	0.65	0.59	0.54	0.50	0.47	0.44	0.41	0.39	0.367	0.348	0.332	0.317	0.303	0.212	0.165	0.135
30	1.92	1.52	1.24	1.05	0.91	0.81	0.73	0.66	0.60	0.56	0.52	0.49	0.46	0.43	0.408	0.387	0.369	0.352	0.337	0.237	0.184	0.151
40	2.08	1.66	1.35	1.14	0.99	0.88	0.79	0.72	0.66	0.61	0.57	0.53	0.50	0.47	0.444	0.422	0.402	0.384	0.367	0.258	0.201	0.165
50	2.23	1.77	1.45	1.22	1.06	0.94	0.85	0.77	0.71	0.65	0.61	0.57	0.53	0.50	0.476	0.453	0.431	0.412	0.394	0.277	0.216	0.177
100	2.81	2.23	1.83	1.55	1.34	1.19	1.07	0.97	0.89	0.83	0.77	0.72	0.67	0.64	0.60	0.573	0.546	0.521	0.499	0.351	0.273	0.224
200	3.61	2.88	2.35	1.99	1.73	1.53	1.38	1.25	1.15	1.06	0.99	0.93	0.87	0.82	0.78	0.74	0.70	0.67	0.64	0.454	0.353	0.290
500	5.15	4.10	3.35	2.84	2.47	2.19	1.97	1.79	1.64	1.52	1.42	1.32	1.24	1.17	1.11	1.06	1.01	0.96	0.92	0.65	0.504	0.414
1000	6.81	5.43	4.44	3.77	3.28	2.90	2.61	2.37	2.18	2.22	1.88	1.76	1.65	1.56	1.47	1.40	1.33	1.27	1.22	0.86	0.669	0.549

Table 10   continued

Level of significance $\alpha = 0.01$

ν_2 \ K	2	3	4	5	6	7	8	9	10	11	12	13	14	15	16	17	18	19	20	30	40	50
2	7.92	4.32	2.84	2.10	1.66	1.38	1.17	1.02	0.91	0.82	0.74	0.68	0.63	0.58	0.54	0.51	0.480	0.454	0.430	0.285	0.214	0.172
3	3.14	2.12	1.57	1.25	1.04	0.89	0.78	0.69	0.62	0.57	0.52	0.48	0.45	0.42	0.39	0.37	0.352	0.334	0.318	0.217	0.165	0.134
4	2.48	1.74	1.33	1.08	0.91	0.78	0.69	0.62	0.56	0.51	0.47	0.44	0.41	0.38	0.36	0.34	0.323	0.307	0.293	0.200	0.153	0.125
5	2.24	1.60	1.24	1.02	0.86	0.75	0.66	0.59	0.54	0.49	0.46	0.42	0.40	0.37	0.35	0.33	0.314	0.299	0.285	0.196	0.151	0.123
6	2.14	1.55	1.21	0.99	0.85	0.74	0.65	0.59	0.53	0.49	0.45	0.42	0.39	0.37	0.35	0.33	0.313	0.298	0.284	0.196	0.151	0.123
7	2.10	1.53	1.20	0.99	0.84	0.73	0.65	0.59	0.53	0.49	0.45	0.42	0.39	0.37	0.35	0.33	0.314	0.299	0.286	0.198	0.152	0.124
8	2.09	1.53	1.20	0.99	0.85	0.74	0.66	0.59	0.54	0.49	0.46	0.43	0.40	0.37	0.35	0.33	0.318	0.303	0.289	0.200	0.154	0.126
9	2.09	1.54	1.21	1.00	0.85	0.75	0.66	0.60	0.54	0.50	0.46	0.43	0.40	0.38	0.36	0.34	0.322	0.307	0.293	0.200	0.156	0.127
10	2.10	1.55	1.22	1.01	0.86	0.76	0.67	0.61	0.55	0.51	0.47	0.44	0.41	0.38	0.36	0.34	0.327	0.311	0.297	0.206	0.159	0.129
11	2.11	1.56	1.23	1.02	0.87	0.76	0.68	0.61	0.56	0.51	0.48	0.44	0.42	0.39	0.37	0.35	0.332	0.316	0.302	0.209	0.161	0.132
12	2.13	1.58	1.25	1.04	0.89	0.78	0.69	0.62	0.57	0.52	0.48	0.45	0.42	0.40	0.37	0.35	0.337	0.321	0.306	0.213	0.164	0.134
13	2.15	1.60	1.26	1.05	0.90	0.79	0.70	0.63	0.58	0.53	0.49	0.46	0.43	0.40	0.38	0.36	0.342	0.326	0.311	0.216	0.166	0.136
14	2.18	1.62	1.28	1.06	0.91	0.80	0.71	0.64	0.58	0.54	0.50	0.46	0.43	0.41	0.39	0.36	0.347	0.330	0.316	0.219	0.169	0.138
15	2.20	1.63	1.30	1.08	0.92	0.81	0.72	0.65	0.59	0.54	0.50	0.47	0.44	0.41	0.39	0.37	0.352	0.335	0.320	0.222	0.171	0.140
16	2.22	1.65	1.31	1.09	0.93	0.82	0.73	0.66	0.60	0.55	0.51	0.48	0.45	0.42	0.40	0.38	0.357	0.340	0.325	0.226	0.174	0.142
17	2.25	1.67	1.33	1.10	0.95	0.83	0.74	0.67	0.61	0.56	0.52	0.48	0.45	0.43	0.40	0.38	0.362	0.345	0.329	0.229	0.176	0.144
18	2.27	1.69	1.34	1.12	0.96	0.84	0.75	0.68	0.62	0.57	0.53	0.49	0.46	0.43	0.41	0.39	0.367	0.350	0.334	0.232	0.179	0.146
19	2.30	1.71	1.36	1.13	0.97	0.85	0.76	0.68	0.62	0.57	0.53	0.50	0.46	0.44	0.41	0.39	0.372	0.354	0.338	0.235	0.181	0.148
20	2.32	1.73	1.38	1.14	0.98	0.86	0.77	0.69	0.63	0.58	0.54	0.50	0.47	0.44	0.42	0.40	0.376	0.359	0.343	0.238	0.184	0.150
30	2.59	1.95	1.54	1.27	1.09	0.96	0.85	0.77	0.70	0.65	0.60	0.56	0.52	0.49	0.46	0.44	0.419	0.399	0.381	0.266	0.205	0.168
40	2.80	2.11	1.66	1.38	1.18	1.04	0.93	0.84	0.76	0.70	0.65	0.61	0.57	0.54	0.51	0.48	0.456	0.435	0.415	0.289	0.223	0.183
50	2.99	2.25	1.78	1.48	1.27	1.11	0.99	0.90	0.82	0.75	0.70	0.65	0.61	0.57	0.54	0.51	0.489	0.466	0.446	0.310	0.240	0.196
100	3.74	2.83	2.24	1.86	1.60	1.40	1.25	1.13	1.03	0.95	0.88	0.82	0.77	0.73	0.69	0.65	0.62	0.590	0.564	0.393	0.304	0.248
200	4.79	3.63	2.88	2.39	2.06	1.81	1.61	1.46	1.33	1.23	1.14	1.06	0.99	0.94	0.88	0.84	0.80	0.76	0.73	0.507	0.392	0.320
500	6.81	5.16	4.10	3.41	2.93	2.58	2.30	2.08	1.90	1.75	1.62	1.52	1.42	1.34	1.26	1.20	1.14	1.09	1.04	0.73	0.560	0.458
1000	9.01	6.83	5.42	4.52	3.88	3.41	3.05	2.76	2.52	2.32	2.15	2.01	1.88	1.77	1.68	1.59	1.51	1.44	1.38	0.96	0.743	0.608

Source: Sachs, 1972

Table 11 Critical values for the Dunnett test

Level of significance $\alpha = 0.01$

ν \ K	2	3	4	5	6	7	8	9
5	3.90	4.21	4.43	4.60	4.73	4.85	4.94	5.03
6	3.61	3.88	4.07	4.21	4.33	4.43	4.51	4.59
7	3.42	3.66	3.83	3.96	4.07	4.15	4.23	4.30
8	3.29	3.51	3.67	3.79	3.88	3.96	4.03	4.09
9	3.19	3.40	3.55	3.66	3.75	3.82	3.89	3.94
10	3.11	3.31	3.45	3.56	3.64	3.71	3.78	3.83
11	3.06	3.25	3.38	3.48	3.56	3.63	3.69	3.74
12	3.01	3.19	3.32	3.42	3.50	3.56	3.62	3.67
13	2.97	3.15	3.27	3.37	3.44	3.51	3.56	3.61
14	2.94	3.11	3.23	3.32	3.40	3.46	3.51	3.56
15	2.91	3.08	3.20	3.29	3.36	3.42	3.47	3.52
16	2.88	3.05	3.17	3.26	3.33	3.39	3.44	3.48
17	2.86	3.03	3.14	3.23	3.30	3.36	3.41	3.43
18	2.84	3.01	3.12	3.21	3.27	3.33	3.38	3.42
20	2.81	2.97	3.08	3.17	3.23	3.29	3.34	3.38
24	2.77	2.92	3.03	3.11	3.17	3.22	3.27	3.31
30	2.72	2.87	2.97	3.05	3.11	3.16	3.21	3.24
40	2.68	2.82	2.92	2.99	3.05	3.10	3.14	3.18
60	2.64	2.78	2.87	2.94	3.00	3.04	3.08	3.12
120	2.60	2.73	2.82	2.89	2.94	2.99	3.03	3.06
∞	2.56	2.68	2.77	2.84	2.89	2.93	2.97	3.00

Level of significance $\alpha = 0.05$

ν \ K	2	3	4	5	6	7	8	9
5	2.44	2.68	2.85	2.98	3.08	3.16	3.24	3.30
6	2.34	2.56	2.71	2.83	2.92	3.00	3.07	3.12
7	2.27	2.48	2.62	2.73	2.82	2.89	2.95	3.01
8	2.22	2.42	2.55	2.66	2.74	2.81	2.87	2.92
9	2.18	2.37	2.50	2.60	2.68	2.75	2.81	2.86
10	2.15	2.34	2.47	2.56	2.64	2.70	2.76	2.81
11	2.13	2.31	2.44	2.53	2.60	2.67	2.72	2.77
12	2.11	2.29	2.41	2.50	2.58	2.64	2.69	2.74
13	2.09	2.27	2.39	2.48	2.55	2.61	2.66	2.71
14	2.08	2.25	2.37	2.46	2.53	2.59	2.64	2.69
15	2.07	2.24	2.36	2.44	2.51	2.57	2.62	2.67
16	2.06	2.23	2.34	2.43	2.50	2.56	2.61	2.65
17	2.05	2.22	2.33	2.42	2.49	2.54	2.59	2.64
18	2.04	2.21	2.32	2.41	2.48	2.53	2.58	2.62
20	2.03	2.19	2.30	2.39	2.46	2.51	2.56	2.60
24	2.01	2.17	2.28	2.36	2.43	2.48	2.53	2.57
30	1.99	2.15	2.25	2.33	2.40	2.45	2.50	2.54
40	1.97	2.13	2.23	2.31	2.37	2.42	2.47	2.51
60	1.95	2.10	2.21	2.28	2.35	2.39	2.44	2.48
120	1.93	2.08	2.18	2.26	2.32	2.37	2.41	2.45
∞	1.92	2.06	2.16	2.23	2.29	2.34	2.38	2.46

Source: De Jonge, 1963–4

Table 12 Critical values of *M* for the Bartlett test

C = constant values.

Level of significance $\alpha = 0.01$

K \ C_i	0.0	0.5	1.0	1.5	2.0	2.5	3.0	3.5	4.0	4.5	5.0	6.0	7.0	8.0	9.0	10.0
3	9.21	9.92	10.47	10.78	10.81	10.50	9.83	—	—	—	—	—	—	—	—	—
4	11.34	11.95	12.46	12.86	13.11	13.18	13.03	12.65	12.03	—	—	—	—	—	—	—
5	13.28	13.81	14.30	14.71	15.03	15.25	15.34	15.28	15.06	14.66	14.07	—	—	—	—	—
6	15.09	15.58	16.03	16.44	16.79	17.07	17.27	17.37	17.37	17.24	16.98	16.03	—	—	—	—
7	16.81	17.27	17.70	18.10	18.46	18.77	19.02	19.21	19.32	19.35	19.28	18.84	17.92	—	—	—
8	18.48	18.91	19.32	19.71	20.07	20.39	20.67	20.90	21.08	21.20	21.35	21.13	20.64	19.76	—	—
9	20.09	20.50	20.90	21.28	21.64	21.97	22.26	22.52	22.74	22.91	23.03	23.10	22.91	22.41	21.56	—
10	21.67	22.06	22.45	22.82	23.17	23.50	23.80	24.08	24.32	24.52	24.69	24.90	24.90	24.66	24.15	23.33
11	23.21	23.59	23.97	24.33	24.67	25.00	25.31	25.59	25.85	26.08	26.28	26.57	26.70	26.65	26.38	25.86
12	24.72	25.10	25.46	25.81	26.15	26.48	26.79	27.08	27.35	27.59	27.81	28.16	28.39	28.46	28.37	28.07
13	26.22	26.58	26.93	27.28	27.62	27.94	28.25	28.54	28.81	29.07	29.30	29.70	29.99	30.16	30.19	30.06
14	27.69	28.04	28.39	28.73	29.06	29.38	29.69	29.98	30.26	30.52	30.77	31.19	31.53	31.77	31.89	31.88
15	29.14	29.39	29.83	30.16	30.49	30.80	30.11	31.40	31.68	31.95	32.20	32.66	33.03	33.32	33.51	33.59

Table 12 continued

Level of significance $\alpha = 0.05$

K \ C_i	0.0	0.5	1.0	1.5	2.0	2.5	3.0	3.5	4.0	4.5	5.0	6.0	7.0	8.0	9.0	10.0
3	5.99	6.47	5.89	7.20	7.38	7.39	7.22	—	—	—	—	—	—	—	—	—
4	7.81	8.24	8.63	8.96	9.21	9.38	9.43	9.37	9.18	—	—	—	—	—	—	—
5	9.49	9.88	10.24	10.57	10.86	11.08	11.24	11.32	11.31	11.21	11.02	—	—	—	—	—
6	11.07	11.43	11.78	12.11	12.40	12.65	12.86	13.01	13.11	13.14	13.10	12.78	—	—	—	—
7	12.59	12.94	13.27	13.59	13.88	14.15	14.38	14.58	14.73	14.83	14.88	14.81	14.49	—	—	—
8	14.07	14.40	14.72	15.03	15.32	15.60	15.84	16.06	16.25	16.40	16.51	16.60	16.49	16.16	—	—
9	15.51	15.83	16.14	16.44	16.73	17.01	17.26	17.49	17.70	17.88	18.03	18.22	18.26	18.12	17.79	—
10	16.92	17.23	17.54	17.83	18.12	18.39	18.65	18.89	19.11	19.31	19.48	19.75	19.89	19.89	19.73	19.40
11	18.31	18.61	18.91	19.20	19.48	19.76	20.02	20.26	20.49	20.70	20.89	21.21	21.42	21.52	21.49	21.32
12	19.68	19.97	20.26	20.55	20.83	21.10	21.36	21.61	21.84	22.06	22.27	22.62	22.88	23.06	23.12	23.07
13	21.03	21.32	21.60	21.89	22.16	22.43	22.69	22.94	23.18	23.40	23.62	23.99	24.30	24.53	24.66	24.70
14	22.36	22.65	22.93	23.21	23.48	23.75	24.01	24.26	24.50	24.73	24.95	25.34	25.68	25.95	26.14	26.25
15	23.68	23.97	24.24	24.52	24.79	25.05	25.31	25.56	25.80	26.04	26.26	26.67	27.03	27.33	27.56	27.73

Source: Merrington and Thompson, 1946

Table 13   Critical values for the Hartley test (right-sided)

Level of significance α = 0.01

$n-1$ \ K	2	3	4	5	6	7	8	9	10	11	12
2	199	448	729	1036	1362	1705	2063	2432	2813	3204	3605
3	47.5	85	120	151	184	216*	249*	281*	310*	337*	361*
4	23.2	37	49	59	69	79	89	97	106	113	120
5	14.9	22	28	33	38	42	46	50	54	57	60
6	11.1	15.5	19.1	22	25	27	30	32	34	36	37
7	8.89	12.1	14.5	16.5	18.4	20	22	23	24	26	27
8	7.50	9.9	11.7	13.2	14.5	15.8	16.9	17.9	18.9	19.8	21
9	6.54	8.5	9.9	11.1	12.1	13.1	13.9	14.7	15.3	16.0	16.6
10	5.85	7.4	8.6	9.6	10.4	11.1	11.8	12.4	12.9	13.4	13.9
12	4.91	6.1	6.9	7.6	8.2	8.7	9.1	9.5	9.9	10.2	10.6
15	4.07	4.9	5.5	6.0	6.4	6.7	7.1	7.3	7.5	7.8	8.0
20	3.32	3.8	4.3	4.6	4.9	5.1	5.3	5.5	5.6	5.8	5.9
30	2.63	3.0	3.3	3.4	3.6	3.7	3.8	3.9	4.0	4.1	4.2
60	1.96	2.2	2.3	2.4	2.4	2.5	2.5	2.6	2.6	2.7	2.7
∞	1.0	1.0	1.0	1.0	1.0	1.0	1.0	1.0	1.0	1.0	1.0

* The unit digit is uncertain.

Table 13 continued

Level of significance α = 0.05

$n-1$ \ K	2	3	4	5	6	7	8	9	10	11	12
2	39.0	87.5	142	202	266	333	403	475	550	626	704
3	15.4	27.8	39.2	50.7	62.0	72.9	83.5	93.9	104	114	124
4	9.60	15.5	20.6	25.2	29.5	33.6	37.5	41.1	44.6	48.0	51.4
5	7.15	10.8	13.7	16.3	18.7	20.8	22.9	24.7	26.5	28.2	29.9
6	5.82	8.38	10.4	12.1	13.7	15.0	16.3	17.5	18.6	19.7	20.7
7	4.99	6.94	8.44	9.70	10.8	11.8	12.7	13.5	14.3	15.1	15.8
8	4.43	6.00	7.18	8.12	9.03	9.78	10.5	11.1	11.7	12.2	12.7
9	4.03	5.34	6.31	7.11	7.80	8.41	8.95	9.45	9.91	10.3	10.7
10	3.72	4.85	5.67	6.34	6.92	7.42	7.87	8.28	8.66	9.01	9.34
12	3.28	4.16	4.79	5.30	5.72	6.09	6.42	6.72	7.00	7.25	7.48
15	2.86	3.54	4.01	4.37	4.68	4.95	5.19	5.40	5.59	5.77	5.93
20	2.46	2.95	3.29	3.54	3.76	3.94	4.10	4.24	4.37	4.49	4.59
30	2.07	2.40	2.61	2.78	2.91	3.02	3.12	3.21	3.29	3.36	3.39
60	1.67	1.85	1.96	2.04	2.11	2.17	2.22	2.26	2.30	2.33	2.36
∞	1.00	1.00	1.00	1.00	1.00	1.00	1.00	1.00	1.00	1.00	1.00

Source: De Jonge, 1963–4

Table 14   Critical values of w/s for the normality test

Columns a denote the lower boundaries or the left-sided critical values.
Columns b denote the upper boundaries or the right-sided critical values.

| | Level of significance α | | | | | | | | | | |
| n | 0.000 | | 0.005 | | 0.01 | | 0.025 | | 0.05 | | 0.10 | |
	a	b	a	b	a	b	a	b	a	b	a	b
3	1.732	2.000	1.735	2.000	1.737	2.000	1.745	2.000	1.758	1.999	1.782	1.997
4	1.732	2.449	1.82	2.447	1.87	2.445	1.93	2.439	1.98	2.429	2.04	2.409
5	1.826	2.828	1.98	2.813	2.02	2.803	2.09	2.782	2.15	2.753	2.22	2.712
6	1.826	3.162	2.11	3.115	2.15	3.095	2.22	3.056	2.28	3.012	2.37	2.949
7	1.871	3.464	2.22	3.369	2.26	3.338	2.33	3.282	2.40	3.222	2.49	3.143
8	1.871	3.742	2.31	3.585	2.35	3.543	2.43	3.471	2.50	3.399	2.59	3.308
9	1.897	4.000	2.39	3.772	2.44	3.720	2.51	3.634	2.59	3.552	2.68	3.449
10	1.897	4.243	2.46	3.935	2.51	3.875	2.59	3.777	2.67	3.685	2.76	3.57
11	1.915	4.472	2.53	4.079	2.58	4.012	2.66	3.903	2.74	3.80	2.84	3.68
12	1.915	4.690	2.59	4.208	2.64	4.134	2.72	4.02	2.80	3.91	2.90	3.78
13	1.927	4.899	2.64	4.325	2.70	4.244	2.78	4.12	2.86	4.00	2.96	3.87
14	1.927	5.099	2.70	4.431	2.75	4.34	2.83	4.21	2.92	4.09	3.02	3.95
15	1.936	5.292	2.74	4.53	2.80	4.44	2.88	4.29	2.97	4.17	3.07	4.02
16	1.936	5.477	2.79	4.62	2.84	4.52	2.93	4.37	3.01	4.24	3.12	4.09
17	1.944	5.657	2.83	4.70	2.88	4.60	2.97	4.44	3.06	4.31	3.17	4.15
18	1.944	5.831	2.87	4.78	2.92	4.67	3.01	4.51	3.10	4.37	3.21	4.21
19	1.949	6.000	2.90	4.85	2.96	4.74	3.05	4.56	3.14	4.43	3.25	4.27
20	1.949	6.164	2.94	4.91	2.99	4.80	3.09	4.63	3.18	4.49	3.29	4.32
25	1.961	6.93	3.09	5.19	3.15	5.06	3.24	4.87	3.34	4.71	3.45	4.53
30	1.966	7.62	3.21	5.40	3.27	5.26	3.37	5.06	3.47	4.89	3.59	4.70
35	1.972	8.25	3.32	5.57	3.38	5.42	3.48	5.21	3.58	5.04	3.70	4.84
40	1.975	8.83	3.41	5.71	3.47	5.56	3.57	5.34	3.67	5.16	3.79	4.96
45	1.978	9.38	3.49	5.83	3.55	5.67	3.66	5.45	3.75	5.26	3.88	5.06
50	1.980	9.90	3.56	5.93	3.62	5.77	3.73	5.54	3.83	5.35	3.95	5.14
55	1.982	10.39	3.62	6.02	3.69	5.86	3.80	5.63	3.90	5.43	4.02	5.22
60	1.983	10.86	3.68	6.10	3.75	5.94	3.86	5.70	3.96	5.51	4.08	5.29
65	1.985	11.31	3.74	6.17	3.80	6.01	3.91	5.77	4.01	5.57	4.14	5.35
70	1.986	11.75	3.79	6.24	3.85	6.07	3.96	5.83	4.06	5.63	4.19	5.41
75	1.987	12.17	3.83	6.30	3.90	6.13	4.01	5.88	4.11	5.68	4.24	5.46
80	1.987	12.57	3.88	6.35	3.94	6.18	4.05	5.93	4.16	5.73	4.28	5.51
85	1.988	12.96	3.92	6.40	3.99	6.23	4.09	5.98	4.20	5.78	4.33	5.56
90	1.989	13.34	3.96	6.45	4.02	6.27	4.13	6.03	4.24	5.82	4.36	5.60
95	1.990	13.71	3.99	6.49	4.06	6.32	4.17	6.07	4.27	5.86	4.40	5.64
100	1.990	14.07	4.03	6.53	4.10	6.36	4.21	6.11	4.31	5.90	4.44	5.68
150	1.993	17.26	4.32	6.82	4.38	6.64	4.48	6.39	4.59	6.18	4.72	5.96
200	1.995	19.95	4.53	7.01	4.59	6.84	4.68	6.60	4.78	6.39	4.90	6.15
500	1.998	31.59	5.06	7.60	5.13	7.42	5.25	7.15	5.47	6.94	5.49	6.72
1000	1.999	44.70	5.50	7.99	5.57	7.80	5.68	7.54	5.79	7.33	5.92	7.11

Source: Sachs, 1972

Table 15 Critical values for the Cochran test for variance outliers

Degrees of freedom $\nu = n - 1$.

Level of significance $\alpha = 0.01$

K \ ν_x	1	2	3	4	5	6	7	8	9	10	16	36	144	∞
2	0.9999	0.9950	0.9794	0.9586	0.9373	0.9172	0.8988	0.8823	0.8674	0.8539	0.7949	0.7067	0.6062	0.5000
3	0.9933	0.9423	0.8831	0.8335	0.7933	0.7606	0.7335	0.7107	0.6912	0.6743	0.6059	0.5153	0.4230	0.3333
4	0.9676	0.8643	0.7814	0.7212	0.6761	0.6410	0.6129	0.5897	0.5702	0.5536	0.4884	0.4057	0.3251	0.2500
5	0.9279	0.7885	0.6957	0.6329	0.5875	0.5531	0.5259	0.5037	0.4854	0.4697	0.4094	0.3351	0.2644	0.2000
6	0.8828	0.7218	0.6258	0.5635	0.5195	0.4866	0.4608	0.4401	0.4229	0.4084	0.3529	0.2858	0.2229	0.1667
7	0.8376	0.6644	0.5685	0.5080	0.4659	0.4347	0.4105	0.3911	0.3751	0.3616	0.3105	0.2494	0.1929	0.1429
8	0.7945	0.6152	0.5209	0.4627	0.4226	0.3932	0.3704	0.3522	0.3373	0.3248	0.2779	0.2214	0.1700	0.1250
9	0.7544	0.5727	0.4810	0.4251	0.3870	0.3592	0.3378	0.3207	0.3067	0.2950	0.2514	0.1992	0.1521	0.1111
10	0.7175	0.5358	0.4469	0.3934	0.3572	0.3308	0.3106	0.2945	0.2813	0.2704	0.2297	0.1811	0.1376	0.1000
12	0.6528	0.4751	0.3919	0.3428	0.3099	0.2861	0.2680	0.2535	0.2419	0.2320	0.1961	0.1535	0.1157	0.0833
15	0.5747	0.4069	0.3317	0.2882	0.2593	0.2386	0.2228	0.2104	0.2002	0.1918	0.1612	0.1251	0.0934	0.0667
20	0.4799	0.3297	0.2654	0.2288	0.2048	0.1877	0.1748	0.1646	0.1567	0.1501	0.1248	0.0960	0.0709	0.0500
24	0.4247	0.2871	0.2295	0.1970	0.1759	0.1608	0.1495	0.1406	0.1338	0.1283	0.1060	0.0810	0.0595	0.0417
30	0.3632	0.2412	0.1913	0.1635	0.1454	0.1327	0.1232	0.1157	0.1100	0.1054	0.0867	0.0658	0.0480	0.0333
40	0.2940	0.1915	0.1508	0.1281	0.1135	0.1033	0.0957	0.0898	0.0853	0.0816	0.0668	0.0503	0.0363	0.0250
60	0.2151	0.1371	0.1069	0.0902	0.0796	0.0722	0.0668	0.0625	0.0594	0.0567	0.0461	0.0344	0.0245	0.0167
120	0.1225	0.0759	0.0585	0.0489	0.0429	0.0387	0.0357	0.0334	0.0316	0.0302	0.0242	0.0178	0.0125	0.0083
∞	0	0	0	0	0	0	0	0	0	0	0	0	0	0

Table 15 continued

Level of significance α = 0.05

K \ ν_x	1	2	3	4	5	6	7	8	9	10	16	36	144	∞
2	0.9985	0.9750	0.9392	0.9057	0.8772	0.8534	0.8332	0.8159	0.8010	0.7880	0.7341	0.6602	0.5813	0.5000
3	0.9669	0.8709	0.7977	0.7457	0.7071	0.6771	0.6530	0.6333	0.6167	0.6025	0.5466	0.4748	0.4031	0.3333
4	0.9065	0.7679	0.6841	0.6287	0.5895	0.5598	0.5365	0.5175	0.5017	0.4884	0.4366	0.3720	0.3093	0.2500
5	0.8412	0.6838	0.5981	0.5441	0.5065	0.4783	0.4564	0.4387	0.4241	0.4118	0.3645	0.3066	0.2513	0.2000
6	0.7808	0.6161	0.5321	0.4803	0.4447	0.4184	0.3980	0.3817	0.3682	0.3568	0.3135	0.2612	0.2119	0.1667
7	0.7271	0.5612	0.4800	0.4307	0.3974	0.3726	0.3535	0.3384	0.3259	0.3154	0.2756	0.2278	0.1833	0.1429
8	0.6798	0.5157	0.4377	0.3910	0.3595	0.3362	0.3185	0.3043	0.2926	0.2829	0.2462	0.2022	0.1616	0.1250
9	0.6385	0.4775	0.4027	0.3584	0.3286	0.3067	0.2901	0.2768	0.2659	0.2568	0.2226	0.1820	0.1446	0.1111
10	0.6020	0.4450	0.3733	0.3311	0.3029	0.2823	0.2666	0.2541	0.2439	0.2353	0.2032	0.1655	0.1308	0.1000
12	0.5410	0.3924	0.3264	0.2880	0.2624	0.2439	0.2299	0.2187	0.2098	0.2020	0.1737	0.1403	0.1100	0.0833
15	0.4709	0.3346	0.2758	0.2419	0.2195	0.2034	0.1911	0.1815	0.1736	0.1671	0.1429	0.1144	0.0889	0.0667
20	0.3894	0.2705	0.2205	0.1921	0.1735	0.1602	0.1501	0.1422	0.1357	0.1303	0.1108	0.0879	0.0675	0.0500
24	0.3434	0.2354	0.1907	0.1656	0.1493	0.1374	0.1286	0.1216	0.1160	0.1113	0.0942	0.0743	0.0567	0.0417
30	0.2929	0.1980	0.1593	0.1377	0.1237	0.1137	0.1061	0.1002	0.0958	0.0921	0.0771	0.0604	0.0457	0.0333
40	0.2370	0.1576	0.1259	0.1082	0.0968	0.0887	0.0827	0.0780	0.0745	0.0713	0.0595	0.0462	0.0347	0.0250
60	0.1737	0.1131	0.0895	0.0765	0.0682	0.0623	0.0583	0.0552	0.0520	0.0497	0.0411	0.0316	0.0234	0.0167
120	0.0998	0.0632	0.0495	0.0419	0.0371	0.0337	0.0312	0.0292	0.0279	0.0266	0.0218	0.0165	0.0120	0.0083
∞	0	0	0	0	0	0	0	0	0	0	0	0	0	0

Source: Dixon and Massey, 1957

Table 16   Critical values of *D* for the Kolmogorov–Smirnov one-sample test

D = maximum values of the differences.

n	Level of significance α				
	0.20	0.15	0.10	0.05	0.01
1	0.900	0.925	0.950	0.975	0.995
2	0.684	0.726	0.776	0.842	0.929
3	0.565	0.597	0.642	0.708	0.823
4	0.494	0.525	0.564	0.624	0.733
5	0.446	0.474	0.510	0.565	0.669
6	0.410	0.436	0.470	0.521	0.618
7	0.381	0.405	0.438	0.486	0.577
8	0.358	0.381	0.411	0.457	0.543
9	0.339	0.360	0.388	0.432	0.514
10	0.322	0.342	0.368	0.410	0.490
11	0.307	0.326	0.352	0.391	0.468
12	0.295	0.313	0.338	0.375	0.450
13	0.284	0.302	0.325	0.361	0.433
14	0.274	0.292	0.314	0.349	0.418
15	0.266	0.283	0.304	0.338	0.404
16	0.258	0.274	0.295	0.328	0.392
17	0.250	0.266	0.286	0.318	0.381
18	0.244	0.259	0.278	0.309	0.371
19	0.237	0.252	0.272	0.301	0.363
20	0.231	0.246	0.264	0.294	0.356
25	0.21	0.22	0.24	0.27	0.32
30	0.19	0.20	0.22	0.24	0.29
35	0.18	0.19	0.21	0.23	0.27
Over 35	$\dfrac{1.07}{\sqrt{n}}$	$\dfrac{1.14}{\sqrt{n}}$	$\dfrac{1.22}{\sqrt{n}}$	$\dfrac{1.36}{\sqrt{n}}$	$\dfrac{1.63}{\sqrt{n}}$

Source: Massey, 1951

Table 17   Critical values of *T* for the sign test

	Level of significance α					Level of significance α			
Two-sided	0.10	0.05	0.02	0.01	Two-sided	0.10	0.05	0.02	0.01
One-sided	0.05	0.025	0.01	0.005	One-sided	0.05	0.025	0.01	0.005
n					n				
1	–	–	–	–	31	11	13	15	17
2	–	–	–	–	32	12	14	16	16
3	–	–	–	–	33	11	13	15	17
4	–	–	–	–	34	12	14	16	16
5	5	–	–	–	35	11	13	15	17
6	6	6	–	–	36	12	14	16	18
7	7	7	7	–	37	11	13	17	17
8	6	8	8	8	38	12	14	16	18
9	7	7	9	9	39	13	15	17	17
10	8	8	10	10	40	12	14	16	18
11	7	9	9	11	45	13	15	17	19
12	8	8	10	10	46	14	16	18	20
13	7	9	11	11	49	13	15	19	19
14	8	10	10	12	50	14	16	18	20
15	9	9	11	11	55	15	17	19	21
16	8	10	12	12	56	14	16	18	20
17	9	9	11	13	59	15	17	19	21
18	8	10	12	12	60	14	18	20	22
19	9	11	11	13	65	15	17	21	23
20	10	10	12	14	66	16	18	20	22
21	9	11	13	13	69	15	19	23	25
22	10	12	12	14	70	16	18	22	24
23	9	11	13	15	75	17	19	23	25
24	10	12	14	14	76	16	20	22	24
25	11	11	13	15	79	17	19	23	25
26	10	12	14	14	80	16	20	22	24
27	11	13	13	15	89	17	21	23	27
28	10	12	14	16	90	18	20	24	26
29	11	13	15	15	99	19	21	25	27
30	10	12	14	16	100	18	22	26	28

Source: Wijvekate, 1962

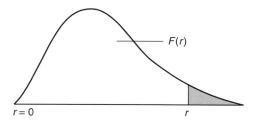

Table 18   Critical values of *r* for the sign test for paired observations

N is the total number of equally probable dichotomous events, r the smaller of the number of events of either kind. If $r \leq r_{N;\alpha}$ then there are too few events of one kind at the $1 - \alpha$ confidence level.

For large values of N, r is approximately distributed as z.
Use $\mu = N/2$, $\sigma = \sqrt{N}/2$ and $Z_\alpha = (\mu - r_{N;\alpha})/\sigma$.

N	$r_{N;0.10}$	$r_{N;0.05}$	$r_{N;0.01}$	$r_{N;0.005}$	$r_{N;0.001}$
8	1	0	0		
10	1	1	0	0	
12	2	2	1	0	0
14	3	2	1	0	0
16	4	3	1	0	0
18	5	4	3	2	1
20	5	5	3	3	2
22	6	5	4	4	3
25	7	7	5	5	4
30	10	9	7	6	5
35	12	11	9	8	7
40	14	13	11	10	9
45	16	15	13	12	11
50	18	17	15	15	13
55	20	19	17	17	15

Source: Dixon and Massey, 1957

Table 19 Critical values of *T* for the signed rank test for paired differences

n is the number of pairs of observations.

n	Two-sided 0.05	Two-sided 0.01	Two-sided 0.001	One-sided 0.05	One-sided 0.01	*n*	Two-sided 0.05	Two-sided 0.01	Two-sided 0.001	One-sided 0.05	One-sided 0.01
6	0			2		36	208	171	130	227	185
7	2			3	0	37	221	182	140	241	198
8	3	0		5	1	38	235	194	150	256	211
9	5	1		8	3	39	249	207	161	271	224
10	8	3		10	5	40	264	220	172	286	238
11	10	5	0	13	7	41	279	233	183	302	252
12	13	7	1	17	9	42	294	247	195	319	266
13	17	9	2	21	12	43	310	261	207	336	281
14	21	12	4	25	15	44	327	276	220	353	296
15	25	15	6	30	19	45	343	291	233	371	312
16	29	19	8	35	23	46	361	307	246	389	328
17	34	23	11	41	27	47	378	322	260	407	345
18	40	27	14	47	32	48	396	339	274	426	362
19	46	32	18	53	37	49	415	355	289	446	379
20	52	37	21	60	43	50	434	373	304	466	397
21	58	42	25	67	49	51	453	390	319	486	416
22	65	48	30	75	55	52	473	408	335	507	434
23	73	54	35	83	62	53	494	427	351	429	454
24	81	61	40	91	69	54	514	445	368	550	473
25	89	68	45	100	76	55	536	465	385	573	493
26	98	75	51	110	84	56	557	484	402	595	514
27	107	83	57	119	92	57	579	504	420	618	535
28	116	91	64	130	101	58	602	525	438	642	556
29	126	100	71	140	110	59	625	546	457	666	578
30	137	109	78	151	120	60	648	567	476	690	600
31	147	118	86	163	130	61	672	589	495	715	623
32	159	128	94	175	140	62	697	611	515	741	646
33	170	138	102	187	151	63	721	634	535	767	669
34	182	148	111	200	162	64	747	657	556	793	693
35	195	159	120	213	173	65	772	681	577	820	718

Source: Sachs, 1972

Table 20 Critical values of *U* for the Wilcoxon inversion test

n_1 = number of elements in the largest sample;
n_2 = number of elements in the smallest sample.

		Level of significance α						Level of significance α			
Two-sided		0.10	0.05	0.02	0.01	Two-sided		0.10	0.05	0.02	0.01
One-sided		0.05	0.025	0.01	0.005	One-sided		0.05	0.025	0.01	0.005
n_1	n_2					n_1	n_2				
3	3	0	–	–	–	9	2	1	0	–	–
4	3	0	–	–	–	9	3	4	2	1	0
4	4	1	0	–	–	9	4	6	4	3	1
						9	5	9	7	5	3
5	2	0	–	–	–	9	6	12	10	7	5
5	3	1	0	–	–	9	7	15	12	9	7
5	4	2	1	0	–	9	8	18	15	12	9
5	5	4	2	1	0	9	9	21	17	14	11
6	2	0	–	–	–	10	2	1	0	–	–
6	3	2	1	–	–	10	3	4	3	1	0
6	4	3	2	1	0	10	4	7	5	3	2
6	5	5	3	2	1	10	5	11	8	6	4
6	6	7	5	3	2	10	6	14	11	8	6
7	2	0	–	–	–	10	7	17	14	11	9
7	3	2	1	0	–	10	8	20	17	13	11
7	4	4	3	1	0	10	9	24	20	16	13
7	5	6	5	3	1	10	10	27	23	19	16
7	6	8	6	4	3						
7	7	11	8	6	4						
8	2	1	0	–	–						
8	3	3	2	0	–						
8	4	5	4	2	1						
8	5	8	6	4	2						
8	6	10	8	6	4						
8	7	13	10	7	6						
8	8	15	13	9	7						

Source: Wijvekate, 1962

Table 21 Critical values of the smallest rank sum for the Wilcoxon–Mann–Whitney test

n_1 = number of elements in the largest sample;
n_2 = number of elements in the smallest sample.

		Level of significance α						Level of significance α			
Two-sided		0.20	0.10	0.05	0.01	Two-sided		0.20	0.10	0.05	0.01
One-sided		0.10	0.05	0.025	0.005	One-sided		0.10	0.05	0.025	0.005
n_1	n_2					n_1	n_2				
3	2	3	–	–	–	10	6	38	35	32	27
3	3	7	6	–	–	10	7	49	45	42	37
4	2	3	–	–	–	10	8	60	56	53	47
4	3	7	6	–	–	10	9	73	69	65	58
4	4	13	11	10	–	10	10	87	82	78	71
5	2	4	3	–	–	11	1	1	–	–	–
5	3	8	7	6	–	11	2	6	4	3	–
5	4	14	12	11	–	11	3	13	11	9	6
5	5	20	19	17	15	11	4	21	18	16	12
						11	5	30	27	24	20
6	2	4	3	–	–	11	6	40	37	34	28
6	3	9	8	7	–	11	7	51	47	44	38
6	4	15	13	12	10	11	8	63	59	55	49
6	5	22	20	18	16	11	9	76	72	68	61
6	6	30	28	26	13	11	10	91	86	81	73
7	2	4	3	–	–	11	11	106	100	96	87
7	3	10	8	7	–	12	1	1	–	–	–
7	4	16	14	13	10	12	2	7	5	4	–
7	5	23	21	20	16	12	3	14	11	10	7
7	6	32	29	27	24	12	4	22	19	17	13
7	7	41	39	36	32	12	5	32	28	26	21
8	2	5	4	3	–	12	6	42	38	35	30
8	3	11	9	8	–	12	7	54	49	46	40
8	4	17	15	14	11	12	8	66	62	58	51
8	5	25	23	21	17	12	9	80	75	71	63
8	6	34	31	29	25	12	10	94	89	84	76
8	7	44	41	38	34	12	11	110	104	99	90
8	8	55	51	49	43	12	12	127	120	115	105
9	1	1	–	–	–	13	1	–	–	–	–
9	2	5	4	3	–	13	2	7	5	4	–
9	3	11	9	8	6	13	3	15	12	10	7
9	4	19	16	14	11	13	4	23	20	18	14
9	5	27	24	22	18	13	5	33	30	27	22
9	6	36	33	31	26	13	6	44	40	37	31
9	7	46	43	40	35	13	7	56	52	48	44
9	8	58	54	51	45	13	8	69	64	60	53
9	9	70	66	62	56	13	9	83	78	73	65
10	1	1	–	–	–	13	10	98	92	88	79
10	2	6	4	3	–	13	11	114	108	103	93
10	3	12	10	9	6	13	12	131	125	119	109
10	4	20	17	15	12	13	13	149	142	136	125
10	5	28	26	23	19						

Table 21 continued

Two-sided		0.20	0.10	0.05	0.01
One-sided		0.10	0.05	0.025	0.005
n_1	n_2	Level of significance α			
14	1	1	–	–	–
14	2	7	5	4	–
14	3	16	13	11	7
14	4	25	21	19	14
14	5	35	31	28	22
14	6	46	42	38	32
14	7	59	54	50	43
14	8	72	67	62	54
14	9	86	81	76	67
14	10	102	96	91	81
14	11	118	112	106	96
14	12	136	129	123	112
14	13	154	147	141	129
14	14	174	166	160	147
15	1	1	–	–	–
15	2	8	6	4	–
15	3	16	13	11	8
15	4	26	22	20	15
15	5	37	33	29	23
15	6	48	44	40	33
15	7	61	56	52	44
15	8	75	69	65	56
15	9	90	84	79	69
15	10	106	99	94	84
15	11	123	116	110	99
15	12	141	133	127	115
15	13	159	152	145	133
15	14	179	171	164	151
15	15	200	192	184	171
16	1	1	–	–	–
16	2	8	6	4	–
16	3	17	14	12	8
16	4	27	24	21	15
16	5	38	34	30	24
16	6	50	46	42	34
16	7	64	58	54	46
16	8	78	72	67	58
16	9	93	87	82	72
16	10	109	103	97	86
16	11	127	120	113	102
16	12	145	138	131	119
16	13	165	156	150	130
16	14	185	176	169	155
16	15	206	197	190	175
16	16	229	219	211	196
17	1	1	–	–	–
17	2	9	6	5	–
17	3	18	15	12	8
17	4	28	25	21	16
17	5	40	35	32	25
17	6	52	47	43	36
17	7	66	61	56	47
17	8	81	75	70	60
17	9	97	90	84	74
17	10	113	106	100	89
17	11	131	123	117	105
17	12	150	142	135	122
17	13	170	161	154	140
17	14	190	182	174	159
17	15	212	203	195	180
17	16	235	225	217	201
17	17	259	249	240	223
18	1	1	–	–	–
18	2	9	7	5	–
18	3	19	15	13	8
18	4	30	26	22	16
18	5	42	37	33	26
18	6	55	49	45	37
18	7	69	63	58	49
18	8	84	77	72	62
18	9	100	93	87	76
18	10	117	110	103	92
18	11	135	127	121	108
18	12	155	146	139	125
18	13	175	166	158	144
18	14	196	187	179	163
18	15	218	208	200	184
18	16	242	231	222	206
18	17	266	255	246	228
18	18	291	280	270	252
19	1	2	1	–	–
19	2	10	7	5	3
19	3	20	16	13	9
19	4	31	27	23	17
19	5	43	38	34	27
19	6	57	51	46	38
19	7	71	65	60	50
19	8	87	80	74	64
19	9	103	96	90	78
19	10	121	113	107	94
19	11	139	131	124	111
19	12	159	150	143	129
19	13	180	171	163	147
19	14	202	192	182	168
19	15	224	214	205	189
19	16	248	237	228	210

Source: Natrella, 1963

Table 22   The Kruskal–Wallis test

Critical region: $H \geq$ tabulated value.

K = 3 Sample sizes	$\alpha = 0.05$	$\alpha = 0.01$	K = 4 Sample sizes	$\alpha = 0.05$	$\alpha = 0.01$	K = 5 Sample sizes	$\alpha = 0.05$	$\alpha = 0.01$
2 2 2	–	–	2 2 1 1	–	–	2 2 1 1 1	–	–
3 2 1	–	–	2 2 2 1	5.679	–	2 2 2 1 1	6.750	–
3 2 2	4.714	–	2 2 2 2	6.167	6.667	2 2 2 2 1	7.133	7.533
3 3 1	5.143	–				2 2 2 2 2	7.418	8.291
3 3 2	5.361	–	3 1 1 1	–	–			
3 3 3	5.600	7.200	3 2 1 1	–	–	3 1 1 1 1	–	–
			3 2 2 1	5.833	–	3 2 1 1 1	6.583	–
4 2 1	–	–	3 2 2 2	6.333	7.133	3 2 2 1 1	6.800	7.600
4 2 2	5.333	–	3 3 1 1	6.333	–	3 2 2 2 1	7.309	8.127
4 3 1	5.208	–	3 3 2 1	6.244	7.200	3 2 2 2 2	7.682	8.682
4 3 2	5.444	6.444	3 3 2 2	6.527	7.636	3 3 1 1 1	7.111	–
4 3 3	5.791	6.745	3 3 3 1	6.600	7.400	3 3 2 1 1	7.200	8.073
4 4 1	4.967	6.667	3 3 3 2	6.727	8.015	3 3 2 2 1	7.591	8.576
4 4 2	5.455	7.036	3 3 3 3	7.000	8.538	3 3 2 2 2	7.910	9.115
4 4 3	5.598	7.144				3 3 3 1 1	7.576	8.424
4 4 4	5.692	7.654	4 1 1 1	–	–	3 3 3 2 1	7.769	9.051
			4 2 1 1	5.833	–	3 3 3 2 2	8.044	9.505
5 2 1	5.000	–	4 2 2 1	6.133	7.000	3 3 3 3 1	8.000	9.451
5 2 2	5.160	6.533	4 2 2 2	6.545	7.391	3 3 3 3 2	8.200	9.876
5 3 1	4.960	–	4 3 1 1	6.178	7.067	3 3 3 3 3	8.333	10.20
5 3 2	5.251	6.909	4 3 2 1	6.309	7.455			
5.3.3	5.648	7.079	4 3 2 2	6.621	7.871			
5 4 1	4.985	6.955	4 3 3 1	6.545	7.758			
5 4 2	5.273	7.205	4 3 3 2	6.795	8.333			
5 4 3	5.656	7.445	4 3 3 3	6.984	8.659			
5 4 4	5.657	7.760	4 4 1 1	5.945	7.909			
5 5 1	5.127	7.309	4 4 2 1	6.386	7.909			
5 5 2	5.338	7.338	4 4 2 2	6.731	8.346			
5 5 3	5.705	7.578	4 4 3 1	6.635	8.231			
5 5 4	5.666	7.823	4 4 3 2	6.874	8.621			
5 5 5	5.780	8.000	4 4 3 3	7.038	8.876			
			4 4 4 1	6.725	8.588			
6 1 1	–	–	4 4 4 2	6.957	8.871			
6 2 1	4.822	–	4 4 4 3	7.142	9.075			
6 2 2	5.345	6.655	4 4 4 4	7.235	9.287			
6 3 1	4.855	6.873						
6 3 2	5.348	6.970						
6 3 3	5.615	7.410						
6 4 1	4.947	7.106						
6 4 2	5.340	7.340						
6 4 3	5.610	7.500						
6 4 4	5.681	7.795						
6 5 1	4.990	7.182						
6 5 2	5.338	7.376						
6 5 3	5.602	7.590						
6 5 4	5.661	7.936						
6 5 5	5.729	8.028						
6 6 1	4.945	7.121						
6 6 2	5.410	7.467						
6 6 3	5.625	7.725						
6 6 4	5.724	8.000						
6 6 5	5.765	8.124						
6 6 6	5.801	8.222						
7 7 7	5.819	8.378						
8 8 8	5.805	8.465						

Source: Neave, 1978

Table 23   Critical values for the rank sum difference test (two-sided)

Level of significance $\alpha = 0.01$

n \ K	3	4	5	6	7	8	9	10
1	4.1	5.7	7.3	8.9	10.5	12.2	13.9	15.6
2	10.9	15.3	19.7	24.3	28.9	33.6	38.3	43.1
3	19.5	27.5	35.7	44.0	52.5	61.1	69.8	78.6
4	29.7	41.9	54.5	67.3	80.3	93.6	107.0	120.6
5	41.2	58.2	75.8	93.6	111.9	130.4	149.1	168.1
6	53.9	76.3	99.3	122.8	146.7	171.0	195.7	220.6
7	67.6	95.8	124.8	154.4	184.6	215.2	246.3	277.7
8	82.4	116.8	152.2	188.4	225.2	262.6	300.6	339.0
9	98.1	139.2	181.4	224.5	268.5	313.1	358.4	404.2
10	114.7	162.8	212.2	262.7	314.2	366.5	419.5	473.1
11	132.1	187.6	244.6	302.9	362.2	422.6	483.7	545.6
12	150.4	213.5	278.5	344.9	412.5	481.2	551.0	621.4
13	169.4	240.6	313.8	388.7	464.9	542.4	621.0	700.5
14	189.1	268.7	350.5	434.2	519.4	606.0	693.8	782.6
15	209.6	297.8	388.5	481.3	575.8	671.9	769.3	867.7
16	230.7	327.9	427.9	530.1	634.2	740.0	847.3	955.7
17	252.5	359.0	468.4	580.3	694.4	810.2	927.8	1046.5
18	275.0	391.0	510.2	632.1	756.4	882.6	1010.6	1140.0
19	298.1	423.8	553.1	685.4	820.1	957.0	1095.8	1236.2
20	321.8	457.6	597.2	740.0	885.5	1033.3	1183.3	1334.9
21	346.1	492.2	642.4	796.0	952.6	1111.6	1273.0	1436.0
22	371.0	527.6	688.7	853.4	1021.3	1191.8	1364.8	1539.7
23	396.4	563.8	736.0	912.1	1091.5	1273.8	1458.8	1645.7
24	422.4	600.9	784.4	972.1	1163.4	1357.6	1554.8	1754.0
25	449.0	638.7	833.8	1033.3	1236.7	1443.2	1652.8	1864.6

Level of significance $\alpha = 0.05$

n \ K	3	4	5	6	7	8	9	10
1	3.3	4.7	6.1	7.5	9.0	10.5	12.0	13.5
2	8.8	12.6	16.5	20.5	24.7	28.9	33.1	37.4
3	15.7	22.7	29.9	37.3	44.8	52.5	60.3	68.2
4	23.9	34.6	45.6	57.0	68.6	80.4	92.4	104.6
5	33.1	48.1	63.5	79.3	95.5	112.0	128.8	145.8
6	43.3	62.9	83.2	104.0	125.3	147.0	169.1	191.4
7	54.4	79.1	104.6	130.8	157.6	184.9	212.8	240.9
8	66.3	96.4	127.6	159.6	192.4	225.7	259.7	294.1
9	7.89	114.8	152.0	190.2	229.3	269.1	309.6	350.6
10	92.3	134.3	177.8	222.6	268.4	315.0	362.4	410.5
11	106.3	154.8	205.0	256.6	309.4	363.2	417.9	473.3
12	120.9	176.2	233.4	292.2	352.4	413.6	476.0	539.1
13	136.2	198.5	263.0	329.3	397.1	466.2	536.5	607.7

Table 23 continued

Level of significance $\alpha = 0.05$

n \ K	3	4	5	6	7	8	9	10
14	152.1	221.7	293.8	367.8	443.6	520.8	599.4	679.0
15	168.6	245.7	325.7	407.8	491.9	577.4	664.6	752.8
16	185.6	270.6	358.6	449.1	541.7	635.9	732.0	829.2
17	203.1	296.2	392.6	491.7	593.1	696.3	801.5	907.9
18	221.2	322.6	427.6	535.5	646.1	758.5	873.1	989.0
19	239.8	349.7	463.6	580.6	700.5	822.4	946.7	1072.4
20	258.8	377.6	500.5	626.9	756.4	888.1	1022.3	1158.1
21	278.4	406.1	538.4	674.4	813.7	955.4	1099.8	1245.9
22	298.4	435.3	577.2	723.0	872.3	1024.3	1179.1	1335.7
23	318.9	464.2	616.9	772.7	932.4	1094.8	1260.3	1427.7
24	339.8	495.8	657.4	823.5	993.7	1166.8	1343.2	1521.7
25	361.1	527.0	698.8	875.4	1056.3	1240.4	1427.9	1616.6

Level of significance $\alpha = 0.10$

n \ K	3	4	5	6	7	8	9	10
1	2.9	4.2	5.5	6.8	8.2	9.6	11.1	12.5
2	7.6	11.2	14.9	18.7	22.5	26.5	30.5	34.5
3	13.8	20.2	26.9	33.9	40.9	48.1	55.5	63.0
4	20.9	30.9	41.2	51.8	62.6	73.8	85.1	96.5
5	29.0	42.9	57.2	72.1	87.3	102.8	118.6	134.6
6	37.9	56.1	75.0	94.5	114.4	134.8	155.6	176.6
7	47.6	70.5	94.3	118.8	144.0	169.6	195.8	222.3
8	58.0	86.0	115.0	145.0	175.7	207.0	239.0	271.4
9	69.1	102.4	137.0	172.8	209.4	246.8	284.9	323.6
10	80.8	119.8	160.3	202.2	245.1	288.9	333.5	378.8
11	93.1	138.0	184.8	233.1	282.6	333.1	384.6	436.8
12	105.9	157.1	210.4	265.4	321.8	379.3	438.0	497.5
13	119.3	177.0	237.1	299.1	362.7	427.6	493.7	560.8
14	133.2	197.7	264.8	334.1	405.1	477.7	551.6	626.6
15	147.6	219.1	293.6	370.4	449.2	529.6	611.6	694.8
16	162.5	241.3	323.3	407.9	494.7	583.3	673.6	765.2
17	177.9	264.2	353.9	446.6	541.6	638.7	737.6	837.9
18	193.7	287.7	385.5	486.5	590.0	695.7	803.4	912.8
19	210.0	311.9	417.9	527.5	639.7	754.3	871.2	989.7
20	226.7	336.7	451.2	569.5	690.7	814.5	940.7	1068.8
21	243.8	362.2	485.4	612.6	743.0	876.2	1012.0	1149.8
22	261.3	388.2	520.4	656.8	796.6	939.4	1085.0	1232.7
23	279.2	414.9	556.1	702.0	851.4	1004.1	1159.7	1317.6
24	297.5	442.2	592.7	748.1	907.4	1070.2	1236.0	1404.3
25	316.2	470.0	630.0	795.3	964.6	1137.6	1314.0	1492.9

Source: Sachs, 1972

Table 24   Critical values for the rank sum maximum test

n	K	Level of significance α			
		0.10	0.05	0.01	0.001
3	3	22	23		
	4	30	31		
	5	38	39		
	6	46	48	50	
4	2	24	25		
	3	37	38	41	
	4	50	52	55	
	5	63	66	70	73
	6	77	80	85	89
5	2	35	37	39	
	3	55	57	61	64
	4	75	78	83	87
	5	95	98	105	111
	6	115	119	127	134
6	2	49	51	54	
	3	77	79	85	90
	4	104	108	115	122
	5	133	138	149	161
	6	161	167	180	196
7	2	65	68	72	76
	3	102	105	112	119
	4	138	144	154	167
	5	176	182	196	212
	6	213	221	237	257
8	2	84	87	92	97
	3	130	135	144	156
	4	177	183	197	212
	5	225	233	249	269
	6	273	282	302	326

Source: Sachs, 1970

Table 25   Critical values for the Steel test

One-sided testing

n	α	Number of samples K							
		2	3	4	5	6	7	8	9
4	0.05	11	10	10	10	10	–	–	–
	0.01	–	–	–	–	–	–	–	–
5	0.05	18	17	17	16	16	16	16	15
	0.01	15	–	–	–	–	–	–	–
6	0.05	27	26	25	25	24	24	24	23
	0.01	23	22	21	21	–	–	–	–
7	0.05	37	36	35	35	34	34	33	33
	0.01	32	31	30	30	29	29	29	29
8	0.05	49	48	47	46	46	45	45	44
	0.01	43	42	41	40	40	40	39	39
9	0.05	63	62	61	60	59	59	58	58
	0.01	56	55	54	53	52	52	51	51
10	0.05	79	77	76	75	74	74	73	72
	0.01	71	69	68	67	66	66	65	65
11	0.05	97	95	93	92	91	90	90	89
	0.01	87	85	84	83	82	81	81	80
12	0.05	116	114	112	111	110	109	108	108
	0.01	105	103	102	100	99	99	98	98
13	0.05	138	135	133	132	130	129	129	128
	0.01	125	123	121	120	119	118	117	117
14	0.05	161	158	155	154	153	152	151	150
	0.01	147	144	142	141	140	139	138	137
15	0.05	186	182	180	178	177	176	175	174
	0.01	170	167	165	164	162	161	160	160
16	0.05	213	209	206	204	203	201	200	199
	0.01	196	192	190	188	187	186	185	184
17	0.05	241	237	234	232	231	229	228	227
	0.01	223	219	217	215	213	212	211	210
18	0.05	272	267	264	262	260	259	257	256
	0.01	252	248	245	243	241	240	239	238
19	0.05	304	299	296	294	292	290	288	287
	0.01	282	278	275	273	271	270	268	267
20	0.05	339	333	330	327	325	323	322	320
	0.01	315	310	307	305	303	301	300	299

Table 25   continued
Two-sided testing

n	α	Number of samples K							
		2	3	4	5	6	7	8	9
4	0.05	10	–	–	–	–	–	–	–
	0.01	–	–	–	–	–	–	–	–
5	0.05	16	16	16	15	–	–	–	–
	0.01	–	–	–	–	–	–	–	–
6	0.05	25	24	23	23	22	22	22	21
	0.01	21	–	–	–	–	–	–	–
7	0.05	35	33	33	32	32	31	31	30
	0.01	30	29	28	28	–	–	–	–
8	0.05	46	45	44	43	43	42	42	41
	0.01	41	40	39	38	38	37	37	37
9	0.05	60	58	57	56	55	55	54	54
	0.01	53	52	51	50	49	49	49	48
10	0.05	75	73	72	71	70	69	69	68
	0.01	68	66	65	64	63	62	62	62
11	0.05	92	90	88	87	86	85	85	84
	0.01	84	82	80	79	78	78	77	77
12	0.05	111	108	107	105	104	103	103	102
	0.01	101	99	97	96	95	94	94	93
13	0.05	132	129	127	125	124	123	122	121
	0.01	121	118	116	115	114	113	112	112
14	0.05	154	151	149	147	145	144	144	143
	0.01	142	139	137	135	134	133	132	132
15	0.05	179	175	172	171	169	168	167	166
	0.01	165	162	159	158	156	155	154	154
16	0.05	205	201	196	196	194	193	192	191
	0.01	189	186	184	182	180	179	178	177
17	0.05	233	228	225	223	221	219	218	217
	0.01	216	212	210	208	206	205	204	203
18	0.05	263	258	254	252	250	248	247	246
	0.01	244	240	237	235	233	232	231	230
19	0.05	294	289	285	283	280	279	277	276
	0.01	274	270	267	265	262	261	260	259
20	0.05	328	322	318	315	313	311	309	308
	0.01	306	302	298	296	293	292	290	289

Source: De Jonge, 1963–4

Table 26 Critical values of r_S for the Spearman rank correlation test

n	Level of significance α					
	0.001	0.005	0.010	0.025	0.050	0.100
4	–	–	–	–	0.8000	0.8000
5	–	–	0.9000	0.9000	0.8000	0.7000
6	–	0.9429	0.8857	0.8286	0.7714	0.6000
7	0.9643	0.8929	0.8571	0.7450	0.6786	0.5357
8	0.9286	0.8571	0.8095	0.6905	0.5952	0.4762
9	0.9000	0.8167	0.7667	0.6833	0.5833	0.4667
10	0.8667	0.7818	0.7333	0.6364	0.5515	0.4424
11	0.8455	0.7545	0.7000	0.6091	0.5273	0.4182
12	0.8182	0.7273	0.6713	0.5804	0.4965	0.3986
13	0.7912	0.6978	0.6429	0.5549	0.4780	0.3791
14	0.7670	0.6747	0.6220	0.5341	0.4593	0.3626
15	0.7464	0.6536	0.6000	0.5179	0.4429	0.3500
16	0.7265	0.6324	0.5824	0.5000	0.4265	0.3382
17	0.7083	0.6152	0.5637	0.4853	0.4118	0.3260
18	0.6904	0.5975	0.5480	0.4716	0.3994	0.3148
19	0.6737	0.5825	0.5333	0.4579	0.3895	0.3070
20	0.6586	0.5684	0.5203	0.4451	0.3789	0.2977
21	0.6455	0.5545	0.5078	0.4351	0.3688	0.2909
22	0.6318	0.5426	0.4963	0.4241	0.3597	0.2829
23	0.6186	0.5306	0.4852	0.4150	0.3518	0.2767
24	0.6070	0.5200	0.4748	0.4061	0.3435	0.2704
25	0.5962	0.5100	0.4654	0.3977	0.3362	0.2646
26	0.5856	0.5002	0.4564	0.3894	0.3299	0.2588
27	0.5757	0.4915	0.4481	0.3822	0.3236	0.2540
28	0.5660	0.4828	0.4401	0.3749	0.3175	0.2490
29	0.5567	0.4744	0.4320	0.3685	0.3113	0.2443
30	0.5479	0.4665	0.4251	0.3620	0.3059	0.2400

Source: Sachs, 1972

Table 27   Critical values of S for the Kendall rank correlation test

	Level of significance α			
Two-sided	0.10	0.05	0.02	0.05
One-sided	0.05	0.025	0.01	0.005
n				
4	6	–	–	–
5	8	10	10	–
6	11	13	13	15
7	13	15	17	19
8	16	18	20	22
9	18	20	24	26
10	21	23	27	29
11	23	27	31	33
12	26	30	36	38
13	28	34	40	44
14	33	37	43	47
15	35	41	49	53
16	38	46	52	58
17	42	50	58	64
18	45	53	63	69
19	49	57	67	75
20	52	62	72	80
21	56	66	78	86
22	61	71	83	91
23	65	75	89	99
24	68	80	94	104
25	72	86	100	110
26	77	91	107	117
27	81	95	113	125
28	86	100	118	130
29	90	106	126	138
30	95	111	131	145
31	99	117	137	151
32	104	122	144	160
33	108	128	152	166
34	113	133	157	175
35	117	139	165	181
36	122	146	172	190
37	128	152	178	198
38	133	157	185	205
39	139	163	193	213
40	144	170	200	222

Source: De Jonge, 1963–4

Table 28   Critical values of *D* for the adjacency test

Columns *a* denote the lower boundaries or the left-sided critical values.
Columns *b* denote the upper boundaries or the right-sided critical values.

	Level of significance α			
Two-sided	0.10		0.02	
One-sided	0.05		0.01	
n	*a*	*b*	*a*	*b*
4	0.78	3.22	0.63	3.37
5	0.82	3.18	0.54	3.46
6	0.89	3.11	0.56	3.44
7	0.94	3.06	0.61	3.39
8	0.98	3.02	0.66	3.34
9	1.02	2.98	0.71	3.29
10	1.06	2.94	0.75	3.25
11	1.10	2.90	0.79	3.21
12	1.13	2.87	0.83	3.17
15	1.21	2.79	0.92	3.08
20	1.30	2.70	1.04	2.96
25	1.37	2.63	1.13	2.87

Source: Hart, 1942

Table 29   Critical values of *r* for the serial correlation test

Columns *a* denote the lower boundaries or the left-sided critical values.
Columns *b* denote the upper boundaries or the right-sided critical values.

	Level of significance α			
Two-sided	0.10		0.02	
One-sided	0.05		0.01	
n	*a*	*b*	*a*	*b*
5	−0.753	0.253	−0.798	0.297
6	−0.708	0.345	−0.863	0.447
7	−0.674	0.370	−0.799	0.510
8	−0.625	0.371	−0.764	0.531
9	−0.593	0.366	−0.737	0.533
10	−0.564	0.360	−0.705	0.525
11	−0.539	0.353	−0.679	0.515
12	−0.516	0.348	−0.655	0.505
13	−0.497	0.341	−0.634	0.495
14	−0.479	0.335	−0.615	0.485
15	−0.462	0.328	−0.597	0.475
20	−0.399	0.328	−0.524	0.432
25	−0.356	0.276	−0.473	0.398
30	−0.325	0.257	−0.433	0.370

Source: Anderson, 1942

Table 30   Critical values for the run test on successive differences

Columns *a* denote the lower boundaries or the left-sided critical values.
Columns *b* denote the upper boundaries or the right-sided critical values.

	Level of significance α			
Two-sided	0.02		0.10	
One-sided	0.01		0.05	
n	*a*	*b*	*a*	*b*
5	–	–	1	–
6	1	–	1	–
7	1	–	2	–
8	2	–	2	–
9	2	–	3	8
10	3	–	3	9
11	3	–	4	10
12	4	–	4	11
13	4	–	5	12
14	5	13	6	12
15	5	14	6	13
16	6	15	7	14
17	6	16	7	15
18	7	17	8	15
19	7	17	8	16
20	8	18	9	17
21	8	19	10	18
22	9	20	10	18
23	10	21	11	19
24	10	21	11	20
25	11	22	12	21
26	11	23	13	21
27	12	24	13	22
28	12	24	14	23
29	13	25	14	24
30	13	26	15	24
31	14	27	16	25
32	15	27	16	26
33	15	28	17	27
34	16	29	17	27
35	16	30	18	28
36	17	30	19	29
37	18	31	19	29
38	18	32	20	30
39	19	33	20	31
40	19	33	21	32

Source: De Jonge, 1963–4

Table 31   Critical values for the run test (equal sample sizes)

Columns a denote the lower boundaries or the left-sided critical values.
Columns b denote the upper boundaries or the right-sided critical values.

	Level of significance α							
Two-sided	0.10		0.05		0.02		0.01	
One-sided	0.05		0.025		0.01		0.005	
$n_1 = n_2$	a	b	a	b	a	b	a	b
5	3	9			2	10		
6	3	11			2	12		
7	4	12			3	13		
8	5	13			4	14		
9	6	14			4	16		
10	6	16			5	17		
11	7	17	7	16	6	18	5	18
12	8	18	7	18	7	19	6	19
13	9	19	8	19	7	21	7	20
14	10	20	9	20	8	22	7	22
15	11	21	10	21	9	23	8	23
16	11	23	11	22	10	24	9	24
17	12	24	11	24	10	26	10	25
18	13	25	12	25	11	27	10	27
19	14	26	13	26	12	28	11	28
20	15	27	14	27	13	29	12	29
21	16	28			14	30		
22	17	29			14	32		
23	17	31			15	33		
24	18	32			16	34		
25	19	33	18	33	17	35	16	35
26	20	34			18	36		
27	21	35			19	37		
28	22	36			19	39		
29	23	37			20	40		
30	24	38	22	39	21	41	20	41
35	28	43	27	44	25	46	24	47
40	33	48	31	50	30	51	29	52
45	37	54	36	55	34	57	33	58
50	42	59	40	61	38	63	37	64
55	46	65	45	66	43	68	42	69
60	51	70	49	72	47	74	46	75
65	56	75	54	77	52	79	50	81
70	60	81	58	83	56	85	55	86
75	65	86	63	88	61	90	59	92
80	70	91	68	93	65	96	64	97
85	74	97	72	99	70	101	68	103
90	79	102	77	104	74	107	73	108
95	84	107	82	109	79	112	77	114
100	88	117	80	115	84	113	82	119

Source: Dixon and Massey, 1957

Table 32 Critical values for the Wilcoxon–Wilcox test (two-sided)

Level of significance $\alpha = 0.01$

n \ K	3	4	5	6	7	8	9	10
1	4.1	5.7	7.3	8.9	10.5	12.2	13.9	15.6
2	5.8	8.0	10.3	12.6	14.9	17.3	19.7	22.1
3	7.1	9.8	12.6	15.4	18.3	21.2	24.1	27.0
4	8.2	11.4	14.6	17.8	21.1	24.4	27.8	31.2
5	9.2	12.7	16.3	19.9	23.6	27.3	31.1	34.9
6	10.1	13.9	17.8	21.8	25.8	29.9	34.1	38.2
7	10.9	15.0	19.3	23.5	27.9	32.3	36.8	41.3
8	11.7	16.1	20.6	25.2	29.8	34.6	39.3	44.2
9	12.4	17.1	21.8	26.7	31.6	36.6	41.7	46.8
10	13.0	18.0	23.0	28.1	33.4	38.6	44.0	49.4
11	13.7	18.9	24.1	29.5	35.0	40.5	46.1	51.8
12	14.3	19.7	25.2	30.8	36.5	42.3	48.2	54.1
13	14.9	20.5	26.2	32.1	38.0	44.0	50.1	56.3
14	15.4	21.3	27.2	33.3	39.5	45.7	52.0	58.4
15	16.0	22.0	28.2	34.5	40.8	47.3	53.9	60.5
16	16.5	22.7	29.1	35.6	42.2	48.9	55.6	62.5
17	17.0	23.4	30.0	36.7	43.5	50.4	57.3	64.4
18	17.5	24.1	30.9	37.8	44.7	51.8	59.0	66.2
19	18.0	24.8	31.7	38.8	46.0	53.2	60.6	68.1
20	18.4	25.4	32.5	39.8	47.2	54.6	62.2	69.8
21	18.9	26.0	33.4	40.9	48.3	56.0	63.7	71.6
22	19.3	26.7	34.1	41.7	49.5	57.3	65.2	73.2
23	19.8	27.3	34.9	42.7	50.6	58.6	66.7	74.9
24	20.2	27.8	35.7	43.6	51.7	59.8	68.1	76.5
25	20.6	28.4	36.4	44.5	52.7	61.1	69.5	78.1

Level of significance $\alpha = 0.05$

n \ K	3	4	5	6	7	8	9	10
1	3.3	4.7	6.1	7.5	9.0	10.5	12.0	13.5
2	4.7	6.6	8.6	10.7	12.7	14.8	17.0	19.2
3	5.7	8.1	10.6	13.1	15.6	18.2	20.8	23.5
4	6.6	9.4	12.2	15.1	18.0	21.0	24.0	27.1
5	7.4	10.5	13.6	16.9	20.1	23.5	26.9	30.3
6	8.1	11.5	14.9	18.5	22.1	25.7	29.4	33.2
7	8.8	12.4	16.1	19.9	23.9	27.8	31.8	35.8
8	9.4	13.3	17.3	21.3	25.5	29.7	34.0	38.3
9	9.9	14.1	18.3	22.6	27.0	31.5	36.0	40.6
10	10.5	14.8	19.3	23.8	28.5	33.2	38.0	42.8
11	11.0	15.6	20.2	25.0	29.9	34.8	39.8	44.9
12	11.5	16.2	21.1	26.1	31.2	36.4	41.6	46.9
13	11.9	16.9	22.0	27.2	32.5	37.9	43.3	48.8
14	12.4	17.5	22.8	28.2	33.7	39.3	45.0	50.7
15	12.8	18.2	23.6	29.2	34.9	40.7	46.5	52.5

Table 32   continued

Level of significance $\alpha = 0.05$

n \ K	3	4	5	6	7	8	9	10
16	13.3	18.8	24.4	30.2	36.0	42.0	48.1	54.2
17	13.7	19.3	25.2	31.1	37.1	43.3	49.5	55.9
18	14.1	19.9	25.9	32.0	38.2	44.5	51.0	57.5
19	14.4	20.4	26.6	32.9	39.3	45.8	52.4	59.0
20	14.8	21.0	27.3	33.7	40.3	47.0	53.7	60.6
21	15.2	21.5	28.0	34.6	41.3	48.1	55.1	62.1
22	15.5	22.0	28.6	35.4	42.3	49.2	56.4	63.5
23	15.9	22.5	29.3	36.2	43.2	50.3	57.6	65.0
24	16.2	23.0	29.9	36.9	44.1	51.4	58.9	66.4
25	16.6	23.5	30.5	37.7	45.0	52.5	60.1	67.7

Level of significance $\alpha = 0.10$

n \ K	3	4	5	6	7	8	9	10
1	2.9	4.2	5.5	6.8	8.2	9.6	11.1	12.5
2	4.1	5.9	7.8	9.7	11.6	13.6	15.6	17.7
3	5.0	7.2	9.5	11.9	14.2	16.7	19.1	21.7
4	5.8	8.4	11.0	13.7	16.5	19.3	22.1	25.0
5	6.5	9.4	12.3	15.3	18.4	21.5	24.7	28.0
6	7.1	10.2	13.5	16.8	20.2	23.6	27.1	30.6
7	7.7	11.1	14.5	18.1	21.8	25.5	29.3	33.1
8	8.2	11.8	15.6	19.4	23.3	27.2	31.3	35.4
9	8.7	12.5	16.5	20.5	24.7	28.9	33.2	37.5
10	9.2	13.2	17.4	21.7	26.0	30.4	35.0	39.5
11	9.6	13.9	18.2	22.7	27.3	31.9	36.7	41.5
12	10.1	14.5	19.0	23.7	28.5	33.4	38.3	43.3
13	10.5	15.1	19.8	24.7	29.7	34.7	39.9	45.1
14	10.9	15.7	20.6	25.6	30.8	36.0	41.4	46.8
15	11.2	16.2	21.3	26.5	31.9	37.3	42.8	48.4
16	11.6	16.7	22.0	27.4	32.9	38.5	44.2	50.0
17	12.0	17.2	22.7	28.2	33.9	39.7	45.6	51.5
18	12.3	17.7	23.3	29.1	34.9	40.9	46.9	53.0
19	12.6	18.2	24.0	29.9	35.9	42.0	48.2	54.5
20	13.0	18.7	24.6	30.6	36.8	43.1	49.4	55.9
21	13.3	19.2	25.2	31.4	37.7	44.1	50.7	57.3
22	13.6	19.6	25.8	32.1	38.6	45.2	51.9	58.6
23	13.9	20.1	26.4	32.8	39.5	46.2	53.0	60.0
24	14.2	20.5	26.9	33.6	40.3	47.2	54.2	61.2
25	14.5	20.9	27.5	34.2	41.1	48.1	55.3	62.5

Source: Sachs, 1972

Table 33   Durbin–Watson test bounds

d_L denotes the lower boundary or left-sided critical values.
d_U denotes the upper boundary or right-sided critical values.
Example: for $n = 20$, $\alpha = 0.01$, and two independent variables,
$d_L = 0.86$ and $d_U = 1.27$.

Level of significance $\alpha = 0.05$

	Number of independent variables $(p - 1)$									
	1		2		3		4		5	
n	d_L	d_U	d_L	d_U	d_L	d_U	d_L	d_U	d_L	d_U
15	1.08	1.36	0.95	1.54	0.82	1.75	0.69	1.97	0.56	2.21
16	1.10	1.37	0.98	1.54	0.86	1.73	0.74	1.93	0.62	2.15
17	1.13	1.38	1.02	1.54	0.90	1.71	0.78	1.90	0.67	2.10
18	1.16	1.39	1.05	1.53	0.93	1.69	0.82	1.87	0.71	2.06
19	1.18	1.40	1.08	1.53	0.97	1.68	0.86	1.85	0.75	2.02
20	1.20	1.41	1.10	1.54	1.00	1.68	0.90	1.83	0.79	1.99
21	1.22	1.42	1.13	1.54	1.03	1.67	0.93	1.81	0.83	1.96
22	1.24	1.43	1.15	1.54	1.05	1.66	0.96	1.80	0.86	1.94
23	1.26	1.44	1.17	1.54	1.08	1.66	0.99	1.79	0.90	1.92
24	1.27	1.45	1.19	1.55	1.10	1.66	1.01	1.78	0.93	1.90
25	1.29	1.45	1.21	1.55	1.12	1.66	1.04	1.77	0.95	1.89
26	1.30	1.46	1.22	1.55	1.14	1.65	1.06	1.76	0.98	1.88
27	1.32	1.47	1.24	1.56	1.16	1.65	1.08	1.76	1.01	1.86
28	1.33	1.48	1.26	1.56	1.18	1.65	1.10	1.75	1.03	1.85
29	1.34	1.48	1.27	1.56	1.20	1.65	1.12	1.74	1.05	1.84
30	1.35	1.49	1.28	1.57	1.21	1.65	1.14	1.74	1.07	1.83
31	1.36	1.50	1.30	1.57	1.23	1.65	1.16	1.74	1.09	1.83
32	1.37	1.50	1.31	1.57	1.24	1.65	1.18	1.73	1.11	1.82
33	1.38	1.51	1.32	1.58	1.26	1.65	1.19	1.73	1.13	1.81
34	1.39	1.51	1.33	1.58	1.27	1.65	1.21	1.73	1.15	1.81
35	1.40	1.52	1.34	1.58	1.28	1.65	1.22	1.73	1.16	1.80
36	1.41	1.52	1.35	1.59	1.29	1.65	1.24	1.73	1.18	1.80
37	1.42	1.53	1.36	1.59	1.31	1.66	1.25	1.72	1.19	1.80
38	1.43	1.54	1.37	1.59	1.32	1.66	1.26	1.72	1.21	1.79
39	1.43	1.54	1.38	1.60	1.33	1.66	1.27	1.72	1.22	1.79
40	1.44	1.54	1.39	1.60	1.34	1.66	1.27	1.72	1.23	1.79
45	1.48	1.57	1.43	1.62	1.38	1.67	1.34	1.72	1.29	1.78
50	1.50	1.59	1.46	1.63	1.42	1.67	1.38	1.72	1.34	1.77
55	1.53	1.60	1.49	1.64	1.45	1.68	1.41	1.72	1.38	1.77
60	1.55	1.62	1.51	1.65	1.48	1.69	1.44	1.73	1.41	1.77
65	1.57	1.63	1.54	1.66	1.50	1.70	1.47	1.73	1.44	1.77
70	1.58	1.64	1.55	1.67	1.52	1.70	1.49	1.74	1.46	1.77
75	1.60	1.65	1.57	1.68	1.54	1.71	1.51	1.74	1.49	1.77
80	1.61	1.66	1.59	1.69	1.56	1.72	1.53	1.74	1.51	1.77
85	1.62	1.67	1.60	1.70	1.57	1.72	1.55	1.75	1.52	1.77
90	1.63	1.68	1.61	1.70	1.59	1.73	1.57	1.75	1.54	1.78
95	1.64	1.69	1.62	1.71	1.60	1.73	1.58	1.75	1.56	1.78
100	1.65	1.69	1.63	1.72	1.61	1.74	1.59	1.76	1.57	1.78

Table 33 continued

Level of significance $\alpha = 0.01$

	Number of independent variables $(p-1)$									
	1		2		3		4		5	
n	d_L	d_U	d_L	d_U	d_L	d_U	d_L	d_U	d_L	d_U
15	0.81	1.07	0.70	1.25	0.59	1.46	0.49	1.70	0.39	1.96
16	0.84	1.09	0.74	1.25	0.63	1.44	0.53	1.66	0.44	1.90
17	0.87	1.10	0.77	1.25	0.67	1.43	0.57	1.63	0.48	1.85
18	0.90	1.12	0.80	1.26	0.71	1.42	0.61	1.60	0.52	1.80
19	0.93	1.13	0.83	1.26	0.74	1.41	0.65	1.58	0.56	1.77
20	0.95	1.15	0.86	1.27	0.77	1.41	0.68	1.57	0.60	1.74
21	0.97	1.16	0.89	1.27	0.80	1.41	0.72	1.55	0.63	1.71
22	1.00	1.17	0.91	1.28	0.83	1.40	0.75	1.54	0.66	1.69
23	1.02	1.19	0.94	1.29	0.86	1.40	0.77	1.53	0.70	1.67
24	1.04	1.20	0.96	1.30	0.88	1.41	0.80	1.53	0.72	1.66
25	1.05	1.21	0.98	1.30	0.90	1.41	0.83	1.52	0.75	1.65
26	1.07	1.22	1.00	1.31	0.93	1.41	0.85	1.52	0.78	1.64
27	1.09	1.23	1.02	1.32	0.95	1.41	0.88	1.51	0.81	1.63
28	1.10	1.24	1.04	1.32	0.97	1.41	0.90	1.51	0.83	1.62
29	1.12	1.25	1.05	1.33	0.99	1.42	0.92	1.51	0.85	1.61
30	1.13	1.26	1.07	1.34	1.01	1.42	0.94	1.51	0.88	1.61
31	1.15	1.27	1.08	1.34	1.02	1.42	0.96	1.51	0.90	1.60
32	1.16	1.28	1.10	1.35	1.04	1.43	0.98	1.51	0.92	1.60
33	1.17	1.29	1.11	1.36	1.05	1.43	1.00	1.51	0.94	1.59
34	1.18	1.30	1.13	1.36	1.07	1.43	1.01	1.51	0.95	1.59
35	1.19	1.31	1.14	1.37	1.08	1.44	1.03	1.51	0.97	1.59
36	1.21	1.32	1.15	1.38	1.10	1.44	1.04	1.51	0.99	1.59
37	1.22	1.32	1.16	1.38	1.11	1.45	1.06	1.51	1.00	1.59
38	1.23	1.33	1.18	1.39	1.12	1.45	1.07	1.52	1.02	1.58
39	1.24	1.34	1.19	1.39	1.14	1.45	1.09	1.52	1.03	1.58
40	1.25	1.34	1.20	1.40	1.15	1.46	1.10	1.52	1.05	1.58
45	1.29	1.38	1.24	1.42	1.20	1.48	1.16	1.53	1.11	1.58
50	1.32	1.40	1.28	1.45	1.24	1.49	1.20	1.54	1.16	1.59
55	1.36	1.43	1.32	1.47	1.28	1.51	1.25	1.55	1.21	1.59
60	1.38	1.45	1.35	1.48	1.32	1.52	1.28	1.56	1.25	1.60
65	1.41	1.47	1.38	1.50	1.35	1.53	1.31	1.57	1.28	1.61
70	1.43	1.49	1.40	1.52	1.37	1.55	1.34	1.58	1.31	1.61
75	1.45	1.50	1.42	1.53	1.39	1.56	1.37	1.59	1.34	1.62
80	1.47	1.52	1.44	1.54	1.42	1.57	1.39	1.60	1.36	1.62
85	1.48	1.53	1.46	1.55	1.43	1.58	1.41	1.60	1.39	1.63
90	1.50	1.54	1.47	1.56	1.45	1.59	1.43	1.61	1.41	1.64
95	1.51	1.55	1.49	1.57	1.47	1.60	1.45	1.62	1.42	1.64
100	1.52	1.56	1.50	1.58	1.48	1.60	1.46	1.63	1.44	1.65

Source: Durbin and Watson, 1951

Table 34   Modified Rayleigh test (*V*-test)

n	0.10	0.05	0.01	0.005	0.001	0.0001
	Level of significance α					

n	0.10	0.05	0.01	0.005	0.001	0.0001
5	1.3051	1.6524	2.2505	2.4459	2.7938	3.0825
6	1.3009	1.6509	2.2640	2.4695	2.8502	3.2114
7	1.2980	1.6499	2.2734	2.4858	2.8886	3.2970
8	1.2958	1.6492	2.2803	2.4978	2.9164	3.3578
9	1.2942	1.6484	2.2856	2.5070	2.9375	3.4034
10	1.2929	1.6482	2.2899	2.5143	2.9540	3.4387
11	1.2918	1.6479	2.2933	2.5201	2.9672	3.4669
12	1.2909	1.6476	2.2961	2.5250	2.9782	3.4899
13	1.2902	1.6474	2.2985	2.5290	2.9873	3.5091
14	1.2895	1.6472	2.3006	2.5325	2.9950	3.5253
15	1.2890	1.6470	2.3023	2.5355	3.0017	3.5392
16	1.2885	1.6469	2.3039	2.5381	3.0075	3.5512
17	1.2881	1.6467	2.3052	2.5404	3.0126	3.5617
18	1.2877	1.6466	2.3064	2.5424	3.0171	3.5710
19	1.2874	1.6465	2.3075	2.5442	3.0211	3.5792
20	1.2871	1.6464	2.3085	2.5458	3.0247	3.5866
21	1.2868	1.6464	2.3093	2.5473	3.0279	3.5932
22	1.2866	1.6463	2.3101	2.5486	3.0308	3.5992
23	1.2864	1.6462	2.3108	2.5498	3.0335	3.6047
24	1.2862	1.6462	2.3115	2.5509	3.0359	3.6096
25	1.2860	1.6461	2.3121	2.5519	3.0382	3.6142
26	1.2858	1.6461	2.3127	2.5529	3.0402	3.6184
27	1.2856	1.6460	2.3132	2.5538	3.0421	3.6223
28	1.2855	1.6460	2.3136	2.5546	3.0439	3.6258
29	1.2853	1.6459	2.3141	2.5553	3.0455	3.6292
30	1.2852	1.6459	2.3145	2.5560	3.0471	3.6323
40	1.2843	1.6456	2.3175	2.5610	3.0580	3.6545
50	1.2837	1.6455	2.3193	2.5640	3.0646	3.6677
60	1.2834	1.6454	2.3205	2.5660	3.0689	3.6764
70	1.2831	1.6453	2.3213	2.5674	3.0720	3.6826
100	1.2826	1.6452	2.3228	2.5699	3.0775	3.6936
500	1.2818	1.6449	2.3256	2.5747	3.0877	3.7140
1000	1.2817	1.6449	2.3260	2.5752	3.0890	3.7165

Source: Batschelet, 1981; original provided by W.T. Keeton

Table 35   Watson's U_n^2-test

n	Level of significance α				
	0.10	0.05	0.025	0.01	0.005
2	0.143	0.155	0.161	0.164	0.165
3	0.145	0.173	0.194	0.213	0.224
4	0.146	0.176	0.202	0.233	0.252
5	0.148	0.177	0.205	0.238	0.262
6	0.149	0.179	0.208	0.243	0.269
7	0.149	0.180	0.210	0.247	0.274
8	0.150	0.181	0.211	0.250	0.278
9	0.150	0.182	0.212	0.252	0.281
10	0.150	0.182	0.213	0.254	0.283
12	0.150	0.183	0.215	0.256	0.287
14	0.151	0.184	0.216	0.258	0.290
16	0.151	0.184	0.216	0.259	0.291
18	0.151	0.184	0.217	0.259	0.292
20	0.151	0.185	0.217	0.261	0.293
30	0.152	0.185	0.219	0.263	0.296
40	0.152	0.186	0.219	0.264	0.298
50	0.152	0.186	0.220	0.265	0.299
100	0.152	0.186	0.221	0.266	0.301
∞	0.152	0.187	0.221	0.267	0.302

Source: Batschelet, 1981; adapted from Stephens, 1964

Table 36   Watson's two-sample U^2-test

n and m are sample sizes.

| n | m | \multicolumn{9}{c}{Level of significance α} |
		0.50	0.20	0.10	0.05	0.02	0.01	0.005	0.002	0.001
5	5	0.089	0.161	0.225	0.225					
5	6	0.085	0.133	0.182	0.242					
5	7	0.086	0.128	0.171	0.200	0.257				
5	8	0.085	0.131	0.165	0.215	0.269				
5	9	0.080	0.124	0.159	0.191	0.280	0.280			
5	10	0.084	0.124	0.161	0.196	0.241	0.289	0.289		
5	11	0.081	0.124	0.156	0.190	0.229	0.297	0.297		
5	12	0.078	0.124	0.155	0.186	0.226	0.261	0.304		
6	6	0.088	0.132	0.171	0.206	0.264				
6	7	0.081	0.121	0.154	0.194	0.282	0.282			
6	8	0.083	0.127	0.161	0.196	0.246	0.298	0.298		
6	9	0.082	0.126	0.156	0.193	0.232	0.262	0.311		
6	10	0.077	0.126	0.156	0.190	0.231	0.248	0.323	0.323	
6	11	0.078	0.121	0.157	0.187	0.225	0.262	0.289	0.333	
6	12	0.080	0.124	0.155	0.183	0.226	0.259	0.275	0.343	0.343
7	7	0.079	0.135	0.158	0.199	0.251	0.304	0.304		
7	8	0.079	0.120	0.156	0.182	0.225	0.272	0.322		
7	9	0.079	0.122	0.156	0.182	0.222	0.255	0.291	0.339	
7	10	0.077	0.123	0.155	0.187	0.227	0.262	0.277	0.353	0.353
7	11	0.077	0.122	0.155	0.184	0.221	0.253	0.281	0.323	0.366
7	12	0.076	0.122	0.154	0.186	0.226	0.252	0.276	0.308	0.377
8	8	0.078	0.125	0.156	0.184	0.226	0.250	0.296	0.344	
8	9	0.078	0.123	0.155	0.186	0.226	0.258	0.283	0.363	0.363
8	10	0.078	0.122	0.155	0.185	0.222	0.249	0.280	0.336	0.380
8	11	0.077	0.122	0.154	0.184	0.225	0.252	0.280	0.319	0.353
8	12	0.077	0.121	0.156	0.185	0.223	0.252	0.281	0.317	0.340
9	9	0.077	0.125	0.155	0.187	0.225	0.266	0.286	0.340	0.384
9	10	0.076	0.122	0.154	0.186	0.226	0.254	0.287	0.321	0.361
9	11	0.076	0.121	0.154	0.185	0.225	0.255	0.281	0.317	0.341
9	12	0.077	0.122	0.154	0.185	0.226	0.254	0.280	0.316	0.340
10	10	0.075	0.123	0.155	0.185	0.225	0.255	0.283	0.317	0.345
10	11	0.076	0.122	0.154	0.186	0.224	0.255	0.279	0.317	0.341
10	12	0.076	0.121	0.153	0.185	0.225	0.255	0.282	0.316	0.341
∞	∞	0.071	0.117	0.152	0.187	0.233	0.268	0.304	0.350	0.385

Source: Batschelet, 1981; adapted from Zar, 1974

Table 37 Maximum likelihood estimate $\hat{k}$ for given $\bar{R}$ in the von Mises case

For the solution $k = A^{-1}(\rho)$, replace $\hat{k}$ by k, $\bar{R}$ by ρ.

$\bar{R}$	$\hat{k}$	$\bar{R}$	$\hat{k}$	$\bar{R}$	$\hat{k}$
0.00	0.00000	0.35	0.74783	0.70	2.01363
0.01	0.02000	0.36	0.77241	0.71	2.07685
0.02	0.04001	0.37	0.79730	0.72	2.14359
0.03	0.06003	0.38	0.82253	0.73	2.21425
0.04	0.08006	0.39	0.84812	0.74	2.28930
0.05	0.10013	0.40	0.87408	0.75	2.36930
0.06	0.12022	0.41	0.90043	0.76	2.45490
0.07	0.14034	0.42	0.92720	0.77	2.54686
0.08	0.16051	0.43	0.95440	0.78	2.64613
0.09	0.18073	0.44	0.98207	0.79	2.75382
0.10	0.20101	0.45	1.01022	0.80	2.87129
0.11	0.22134	0.46	1.03889	0.81	3.00020
0.12	0.24175	0.47	1.06810	0.82	3.14262
0.13	0.26223	0.48	1.09788	0.83	3.30114
0.14	0.28279	0.49	1.12828	0.84	3.47901
0.15	0.30344	0.50	1.15932	0.85	3.68041
0.16	0.32419	0.51	1.19105	0.86	3.91072
0.17	0.34503	0.52	1.22350	0.87	4.17703
0.18	0.36599	0.53	1.25672	0.88	4.48876
0.19	0.38707	0.54	1.29077	0.89	4.85871
0.20	0.40828	0.55	1.32570	0.90	5.3047
0.21	0.42962	0.56	1.36156	0.91	5.8522
0.22	0.45110	0.57	1.39842	0.92	6.5394
0.23	0.47273	0.58	1.43635	0.93	7.4257
0.24	0.49453	0.59	1.47543	0.94	8.6104
0.25	0.51649	0.60	1.51574	0.95	10.2716
0.26	0.53863	0.61	1.55738	0.96	12.7661
0.27	0.56097	0.62	1.60044	0.97	16.9266
0.28	0.58350	0.63	1.64506	0.98	25.2522
0.29	0.60625	0.64	1.69134	0.99	50.2421
0.30	0.62922	0.65	1.73945	1.00	∞
0.31	0.65242	0.66	1.78953		
0.32	0.67587	0.67	1.84177		
0.33	0.69958	0.68	1.89637		
0.34	0.72356	0.69	1.95357		

Source: Mardia, 1972

Table 38　Mardia–Watson–Wheeler test

$n_1 = $ smaller of the two sample sizes n_1, n_2; $n = n_1 + n_2$.

		Level of significance α			
n	n_1	0.001	0.01	0.05	0.10
8	4				6.83
9	3				6.41
	4			8.29	4.88
10	3				6.85
	4			9.47	6.24
	5			10.47	6.85
11	3			7.20	5.23
	4			10.42	7.43
	5		12.34	8.74	6.60
12	3			7.46	5.73
	4		11.20	8.46	7.46
	5		13.93	10.46	7.46
	6		14.93	11.20	7.46
13	3			7.68	6.15
	4		11.83	9.35	7.03
	5		15.26	10.15	7.39
	6		17.31	10.42	8.04
14	3			7.85	6.49
	4		12.34	9.30	7.60
	5		16.39	10.30	7.85
	6	19.20	15.59	12.21	7.94
	7	20.20	16.39	11.65	8.85
15	3			7.99	6.78
	4		12.78	8.74	7.91
	5	17.35	14.52	10.36	7.91
	6	20.92	17.48	11.61	9.12
	7	22.88	16.14	11.57	9.06
16	3			8.11	5.83
	4		13.14	9.44	7.38
	5	18.16	15.55	10.44	9.03
	6	22.43	16.98	11.54	9.11
	7	25.27	18.16	12.66	9.78
17	3		8.21	7.23	6.14
	4	13.44	11.76	9.74	7.64
	5	18.86	16.44	11.03	8.76
	6	23.73	17.76	12.21	9.41
	7	27.40	17.98	12.63	10.11
	8	29.37	19.11	13.36	10.15

Source: Mardia, 1972

REFERENCES

Anderson, R.L. (1942) 'Distribution of the serial correlation coefficient', *Annals of Mathematical Statistics*, 13: 1–13.

Batschelet, E. (1972) 'Recent statistical methods for orientation data', in S.R. Galler *et al.* (eds), *Symposium on Animal Orientation and Navigation*. Washington, DC: US Government Printing Office.

Batschelet, E. (1981) *Circular Statistics in Biology*. London: Academic Press.

Bennett, C. and Franklin, N.L. (1961) *Statistical Analysis in Chemistry and the Chemical Industry*. New York: Wiley.

De Jonge, H. (1963–4) *Inleiding tot de Medrische Statistick*. Vol. 1: *Fundamentele Begrippen en Technieken: Verdelingsvrije Methoden*, Vol. II: *Klassieke Methoden*. 3rd edn. Leiden: TNO Health Research.

Dixon, W.J. and Massey, F.J. Jr (1957) *Introduction to Statistical Analysis*. New York: McGraw-Hill.

Durbin, J. and Watson, G.S. (1951) 'Testing for serial correlation in least squares regression II', *Biometrika*, 38: 159–78.

Fisher, R.A. (1958) *Statistical Methods for Research Workers*. Edinburgh: Oliver and Boyd.

Fisher, R.A. and Yates, F. (1974) *Statistical Tables for Biological, Agricultural and Medical Research*. 6th edn. Edinburgh: Oliver and Boyd.

Geary, R.E. and Pearson, E.S. (n.d.) 'Tests of normality', *Biometrika* Office, University College, London.

Hart, B.I. (1942) 'Significance levels for the ratio of the mean square successive difference to the variance', *Annals of Mathematical Statistics*, 13: 445–7.

Mardia, K.V. (1972) *Statistics of Directional Data*. London: Academic Press.

Massey, F.J. Jr (1951) 'The Kolmogorov–Smirnov test for goodness of fit', *Journal of the American Statistical Association*, 4(6): 1990.

Merrington, M. and Thompson, C.M. (1946) 'Tables for testing the homogeneity of a set of estimated variances', *Biometrika*, 33: 296–304.

Natrella, M.G. (1963) *Experimental Statistics*. National Bureau of Standards Handbook 91. Washington, DC: US Government Printing Office.

Neave, H.R. (1976a) 'The teaching of hypothesis testing', *Bulletin in Applied Statistics*, 3(1): 55–63.

Neave, H.R. (1976b) 'Non-parametric testing – why and how', *Bulletin in Applied Statistics*, 3(2): 49–58.

Neave, H.R. (1978) *Statistical Tables*. London: George Allen & Unwin.

Pearson, E.S. and Hartley, H.O. (1970) *Biometrika Tables for Statisticians*, Vol. 1. Cambridge: Cambridge University Press.

Pearson, E.S. and Hartley, H.O. (1976) *Biometrika Tables for Statisticians*, Vol. 2. London: Charles Griffin.

Sachs, L. (1970) *Statistische Methoden: ein Soforthelfer*. Berlin: Springer-Verlag.

Sachs, L. (1972) *Statistische Auswertungsmethoden*. 3rd edn. Berlin: Springer-Verlag.

Stephens, M.A. (1964) 'The distribution of the goodness of fit statistic U_n^2 II', *Biometrika*, 51: 393–7.

Walpole, R.E. and Myers, R.H. (1989) *Probability and Statistics for Engineers and Scientists*. 4th edn. New York: Macmillan.

Wijvekate, M.L. (1962) *Verklarende Statistiek*. Utrecht: Aula.

Zar, J.H. (1974) *Biostatistical Analysis*. Englewood Cliffs, NJ: Prentice Hall.

INDEX